RISKS

Books

Alone in Community:
Journeys into Monastic Life Around the World

Another World: A Retreat in the Ozarks

Journey Man: A World Calling

Play

Quiet Gardens

RISKS

a memoir

William Claassen

Cornel & Williams
Columbia, Missouri

RISKS: a memoir

Publishers Cataloging-in-Publication Data

Claassen, William, 1948-
 RISKS: a memoir / William Claassen
 p. cm.
 ISBN 978-0-692-87044-0
1. Claassen, William, 1948-. 2. Spiritual retreats. 3. Volunteers in Service to America. 4. Civil rights workers--Biography. 5. Civil rights movements--United States. 6. Kibbutzim--Biography. 7. United States—Description and travel. 8. Canada--Description and travel. 9. United States—Social conditions--1960-1990. 10. Hoedads, Inc. 11. Pendle Hill School, Wallingford, PA. 12. Actors--Biography. 13. Peace Corps (US)--Biography. 14. Latin America--Description and travel. 15. Americans--Foreign countries--Biography. 16. Sanctuary Movement. 17. Gay men--Biography. l. Title.

BL628.8 .C53 2017
230.51-dc23   2017938709

Cornel & Williams Publishing
PO Box 1921
Columbia, Missouri 65205-1921
(573)449-8764
CornelWilliams48@yahoo.com

First printing: July 2017
Printed in the United States of America

Design: Ric Wilson
Photograph: Tom Brown

To
Amy Goodman and Glen Greenwald,
Chelsea Manning, Laura Poitras, and Jeremy Scahill,
Bernie Sanders, Edward Snowden, Elizabeth Warren,
and *Yes! Magazine.*

Contents

Acknowledgments   ix

Foreword   xi

Preface   xiii

Part One

Chapter 1   Haves, Have Nots, Have a Little   3

Chapter 2   Walking Backward   25

Chapter 3   Dear John Letter   31

Chapter 4   Hitchhiker's Sinkhole   59

Chapter 5   Wise Men Fish Here   83

Chapter 6   Swimming in Sand   97

Part Two

Chapter 7   Call Me a Madman   109

Chapter 8   Bare Ass Naked   117

Chapter 9   Sleeping with the Dead   131

Chapter 10   Rural Free Delivery   151

Chapter 11   Desert Spirit   157

Chapter 12   Red Star Recruit   171

Chapter 13   Elephants, Giraffes, Hyenas, Oh My   181

Part Three

Chapter 14   Don't Think, Do It   207

Chapter 15   Blue Plate Special   215

Chapter 16   Weighty Friends, Silent Meetings   239

Chapter 17   Three Sisters' Hotel   257

Chapter 18   Sitting on the Fault Line   273

Chapter 19   Meyers, Briggs, and Carl Jung   285

Endnotes   297

About the Author   307

Acknowledgments

My heartfelt thanks to the acquaintances, activists, actors, adversaries, artists, authors, clergy, dancers, family, friends, gurus, journalists, lawyers, lovers, monks, musicians, organizers, photographers, playwrights, poets, police officers, teachers, and workmates whom I included in the memoir. Your life stories became a part of mine.

And to you: Elle Anthony, Lucy Banks, Ingrid Beach, Robert Claassen, Lillian Clayman, Beth Downs, Marcia Garcia Rodman, Tom Gillooly, Judith Greentree, Bob Gribble, Dennis Hearn, Jim and Pat Herrewig, Zen Judith, Bill Kauth, Rocket Kirchner, Lisa Lapp, Ann Lehman, Mike and Terry Malone, Mankind Project, James O'Barr, Steve Podry, Patty Purvis, Joel and Laura Rosenblit, Tony and Sue Smolenski, Marsha and David Speener, John Summer, Barbara Sussman, Denise Taylor, Charlotte Thorpe, Dyck Vermilye, and Lucy West.

Thank you to the staff at the Hugh Stephens Library and the Ashland Branch of the Columbia Public Library.

And to Daria Barretta, Jeff Belden, Brian Page, Robin Perso, Steve Weinberg, Marlene Lee, and Pippa Letsky.

Special thanks to my editor Lisa Jerry.

Foreword

"No man is an island entire of himself," wrote the seventeenth-century English poet John Donne. "Every man is a piece of a continent, a part of the main." Although the particulars of our separate lives may vary greatly, we share a common humanity. I could not have written this memoir without including the personal stories of dozens of other men and women who have played a significant role in creating mine. Our stories are interwoven.

My memoir takes the reader across the United States, Canada, and into a half-dozen other countries, on four continents, over a span of twenty years. The book begins at an intense civil rights training program sponsored by a small, little-known, Kentucky college. It concludes at a successfully disruptive demonstration on the grounds of the Pentagon.

The reader will delve into unfamiliar communities, widely diverse cultures, and challenging political territory from the 1960s through the 1980s. Over those two decades, my political, sexual, and spiritual identities evolved in unpredictable ways. During that time, I worked as a civil rights organizer in the South and a laborer on an Israeli kibbutz. I took to the road as a long distance hitchhiker and walked onto the New York stage as an actor. I joined an Oregon tree-planting cooperative, served in Kenya with the Peace Corps, and then became a resident of a Quaker community. Later, I traveled to Latin America and worked as a peace activist.

Memoir chapters are in three parts. David Fontana, in his

Secret Language of Symbols, reminded me that in humanity's vast range of religious and spiritual traditions the number three has always been symbolic of unity in diversity.

Every chapter is in chronological order. Each experience builds on the ones preceding it.

My resources included detailed journal notes, personal correspondence, newsletters, magazine and newspaper quotes, excerpts from books and plays, phone conversations, photographs, and memory. I tried to reproduce as accurately as possible both the statements and the manner of speaking of my hosts.

For the sake of clarity, I italicized my personal correspondence and journal entries. I have changed some first names out of respect for privacy. I usually included last names when referring to a person deceased, an author, faculty member, administrator, artist, journalist, political activist, historical and religious figures, or an individual mentioned previously in a newspaper or magazine article.

Preface

Another sweltering August day in Kentucky's Derby City. It felt like the air conditioning had been turned-off. Squeezed into a small, windowless administrative office, we had been sitting on the industrial carpeted floor for most of the day. Hoarse from chanting demands and singing protest songs, we were hungry, sweaty, and tired.

In the doorway stood the solemn-looking, Louisville, police chief. In a clearly contained low voice, the partially bald man began to read the arrest warrant held tightly in his right hand. As he spoke, the chief's wire rimmed glasses slipped midway down the bridge of his nose. The officer paused for a moment, pushed them up with his middle finger, and continued to read. For the third time in as many hours, he told us that we could still get up and leave the building without an arrest. For the third time, we locked arms and refused to vacate the office.

"Louisville police last night arrested 22 persons representing the Louisville Welfare Rights Organization on disorderly conduct charges after they had occupied the office of a state public assistance administrator for almost eight hours," disclosed newspaper reporter Bill Peterson. "Police Chief C. J. Hyde made the arrests at 7 p.m. with state police standing by after city and state officials had debated for three hours over the correctness of an arrest warrant."[1]

Peterson's article did not explain that the city officials had conferred in earnest how best to carry out the arrests. At all costs, they wanted to prevent riots from breaking out in the half-dozen public housing projects scattered throughout the city. Most of the demonstrators lived in those projects. City and state officials had good reason to be concerned. A mere two years before, in late May, Louisville had erupted into street fires and looting, as did many cities throughout the country after the assassination of Martin Luther King, Jr. Hundreds of Kentucky National Guardsman had poured into the city to quell the disturbances.

Included in the arrest list, Donna Johnson and I were Volunteers in Service to America, a domestic Peace Corps. The arrest felt liberating. I had embraced my guaranteed right to participate in nonviolent disobedience. It would be my first of many such arrests in the decades to come. "Protest beyond the law is not a departure from democracy: it is absolutely essential to it," proclaimed American historian and social activist Howard Zinn. "It's disruptive and troublesome, but it is a necessary disruption, healthy troublesomeness."[2]

Throughout 1970, Donna and I had worked as community organizers in the city's housing projects. We helped create an advocacy organization that addressed issues faced by men, women, and children on public assistance. The culmination of our efforts had been the demonstration at the welfare office. Months later, police officers arrested Donna and me again for refusing to vacate a dilapidated rental home in the dead of winter; we stood in solidarity with a destitute family scheduled for eviction by their slumlord. That was only the beginning.

Risk — gamble, hazard, venture, run the risk, do at one's own peril, hang by a thread, play with fire, go out of one's depth, go beyond one's depth, bell the cat, make an investment, take the liberty, lay oneself open to, pour money into, go through fire and water, leave the luck, leap before one looks, fish in troubled waters, skate on thin ice, defy danger, live in a glass house.

Charlton Laird
Webster's A-Z New Roget's Thesaurus

Part One

CHAPTER ONE

~

Haves, Have Nots, Have a Little

With anticipation, I ripped open the thick manila envelope and pulled out an acceptance letter from Volunteers in Service to America, better known as VISTA. Along with the letter, I found a collection of articles on inadequate health care in America and Black Lung Disease that slowly suffocated Appalachian coal miners. There were write-ups on the mistreatment of migrant farm workers and a booklet that exposed lead poisoning of children across the country. There were charts, diagrams, and graphic black-and-white photographs. Michael Harrington, founding member of the Democratic Socialists of America, called it *The Other America*.

By the time the manila envelope arrived, I had just completed a challenging sophomore year at Kansas State University. I had pledged a fraternity, become close friends with Mike, Terry, and Paul in the house, and begun a relationship with Judy, a bright and soft-spoken sorority member from Dodge City. I had completed a semester of Reserve Officers' Training Corps and become an active member of the College Republicans. I had campaigned for the Republican gubernatorial candidate and supported Richard Nixon for president.

At one of our campus-wide meetings I recall witnessing the dour guest speaker, Senator Bob Dole, berate a small gathering of antiwar demonstrators. The tall, dark-haired man peered down at them from an expansive second-story window inside the student union. With a scowl, he called them anti-American. In my gut, I knew he was wrong but I did not speak out.

That year I felt a spiritual emptiness and sought relief through religious ritual at St. Paul's Episcopal Church in Manhattan, the university's hometown. After attending months of catechism classes, the bishop confirmed me. In retrospect, that confirmation initiated my spiritual odyssey just as the VISTA experience would launch my political journey.

Midway through that school year, I experienced disconcerting grand mal seizures. After each episode, I would wake up in the university health center with no memory of the disruption I had caused in the fraternity or the ambulance rides. Following medical examinations, the doctor prescribed Dilantin used to treat epilepsy. As a result, my local draft board gave me a medical deferment: 4F Classification.

"Son," the physician said to me, "think of your seizures as a cloud with a silver lining."

My mom had a different take on things. "They may be clouds with silver linings as far as the draft board is concerned," she granted, "but that's not how potential employers will view them." Mom encouraged me to keep that medical information to myself, which I did.

Outside fraternity life, I became friends with Tom, an enlisted Army private and a rock 'n' roll musician vehemently opposed to the Vietnam War. He eventually went "absent without official leave" (AWOL) from the Fort Riley Army Base. Unbeknown to my fraternity brothers, I accompanied Tom to music gigs in funky, strobe-lit nightclubs near the army base. We were the only white faces in the house. Tom played in the band while I gyrated on the crowded dance floors.

I had also befriended a lanky, olive-skinned woman named Alice. She had temporarily settled in Manhattan, Kansas. A strikingly attractive college dropout, Alice grew up in Madison, Wisconsin, where her father taught at the university. She intrigued me. Unlike any woman I had ever known, Alice dressed in long colorful skirts and draping cotton blouses, outfits worthy of fashion designer Eileen Fisher. Alice never wore makeup and always smelled of patchouli. Moving through space with an easy gait, she frequently walked barefooted, swinging her long arms back and forth, as I trailed alongside her whenever possible. I did not have a love interest in Alice. I just wanted to walk into the mystery of that woman.

Alice talked about current events, poets, and authors unfamiliar to me. She invited me to my first Zen Buddhist gathering. Following an extended silent meditation that night, participants discussed Alan Watts's *The Book: On the Taboo against Knowing Who You Are*. At the time, I did not know Buddhism from Hinduism or Sikhism for that matter.

By the end of the school year, my grades were mediocre and my academic curiosity had withered. The relationship with Judy had come to an end. I had lost interest in fraternity life and no longer identified with Republican politics. I did have, however, a lot of big stuff stirring up inside of me. I had an urge to break out of that university and into the streets. VISTA became my ticket.

Two political activists from Louisville and a Philadelphia psychologist facilitated the first few weeks of the program's in-house training at Kentucky's Georgetown College, a small, four-year, liberal arts school. It coincided with the Apollo 11 crew landing on the moon. With a cluster of other volunteers, I watched that phenomenal event progress on a black-and-white television. During those intense and challenging two weeks of introductory training I, too, felt like I had landed on the moon.

Our orientation as community organizers focused on issues of welfare and tenants' rights, civil rights and civil liberties. We learned through lectures and simulation games in addition to reading assignments and intense small group discussions. Donna Johnson remembered that the Philadelphia psychologist encouraged us to "bare our souls" and reveal our "innermost secrets." Day to day, he evaluated our strengths and weaknesses.

The trainers advocated major economic and political reforms. Our group orientation would be the last session that emphasized community organizing for significant social reform. VISTA trainers and volunteers around the country were raising hell and challenging federal government programs and policies. Collectively, we advocated an end to the Vietnam War. As a result, the Nixon administration made a concerted effort to cut the cord and close the training centers.

Professional organizers from all over the county arrived by plane, bus, and car at Georgetown College. The intense and dedicated crew were recruited specifically for our training–likely their last hurrah. Mostly men, they were trained by Chicago's Saul Alinsky, the guru of community organizing, who divided the world into the Haves, Have Nots, Have-a-Little-Want-More.

The organizers came to proselytize the word according to Alinsky. His books, *Reveille for Radicals*, and later *Rules for Radicals*, would soon become my Good Books. "Machiavelli told the Haves how to maintain themselves in power," stated a blurb on the hardback cover of *Rules for Radicals*. "Saul Alinsky, in this book, tells the Have-Nots how to take this power away. His hard-headed tactical advice provides an alternative not only to the powerlessness that threatens our democracy but to the random violence and bitter alienation by which so much radical energy is wasted."[1] Alinsky advocated change by pressure tactics not violence. He frequently incorporated a wonderfully cryptic sense of humor into his organizing efforts. A *Playboy* magazine interview highlighted that aspect of the organizer as he described a successful pressure tactic from the past. He had many from which to choose.

Alinsky explained that in 1964, an election year, Chicago's Mayor Daley had begun to back out of commitments made to the Woodlawn Organization, a neighborhood group shaped by the guru. The mayor believed the group had lost its political-clout. What could the organization do to prove the mayor wrong?

"The most effective way to do this wasn't to publicly denounce or picket him but to create a situation in which he would become a figure of nationwide ridicule," pointed out Alinsky. The organizer's target became the O'Hare Airport, Daley's pride and joy. Alinsky planned to have the nations' first "shit-in" at the busiest air terminal in the world. "Some of our people went out to the airport and made a comprehensive intelligence study of how many sit down pay toilets and stand-up urinals there were in the O'Hare complex and how many men and women we'd need for the country's first 'shit-in,'" revealed Alinsky. The Woodlawn Organization determined that a successful action would require twenty-five hundred people that they could provide. "For the sit down toilets, our people would just put in their dimes and prepare to wait it out. We arranged for them to bring box lunches and reading material to pass the time. What were desperate airline passengers going to do – knock the cubicle doors down and demand evidence of legitimate occupancy?" All of the women's lavatories would be occupied and Alinsky planned to use the same tactic with the men's toilets "and then have floating groups moving from one urinal to another, positioning themselves four or five deep and standing there for five minutes before being relieved by a co-conspirator, at which time they would pass on to another restroom. O'Hare would become a shambles! You can imagine the national and international ridicule and laughter the story would create. And who would be more mortified than Mayor Daley?"[2] When the organization leaked the plan to an insider in Daley's administration, the reactions were immediate. Mayor Daley fulfilled his commitments and the Woodlawn Organization canceled the event.

By the conclusion of our in-house training, I had banded together with four other volunteers. We wanted to work together on an organizing project in Louisville. A motley assortment, we were all in our early twenties.

Stocky and curly haired Tony had grown up in Baltimore, recently completed his undergraduate degree, and planned to attend graduate school after VISTA. A lovable and eccentric fellow, Tony could have easily been a character in one of Anne Tyler's Baltimore-based novels. Donna, a native of Philadelphia, would have passed for a finishing school graduate with her simple but classic wardrobe. She made jeans, a blouse, and loafers look stylish. Intelligent and insightful, Donna frequently shared her deliciously acerbic comments and observations. She appeared prim and proper. Underneath that façade, however, Donna revealed a street-smart woman. Yvonne, an Italian American from La Crosse, Wisconsin, possessed a quiet intensity. The least political of our group, she preferred to listen rather than talk. Her keen observations of people and events were insightful. Frequently frustrated, Yvonne often felt out of her element.

A fifth member of our determined coterie, Jennifer, grew up the daughter of a Presbyterian minister in Rockland, Illinois. Jennifer reminded me of a back room politician. Trainers recognized her as bright, challenging, and manipulative. VISTA coordinators deselected her by the end of our in-house training due to conflicts with staff and other volunteers. Despite her elimination from the program, tough-minded Jenny moved to Louisville and ultimately participated in some of our organizing efforts.

The final four weeks of on-site training in Louisville became a baptism by fire. Temporarily housed in a two-story, red brick home with a revolving door, located in the predominately black West End of Louisville, I never knew who I would meet in the bathroom, the hallway or the kitchen, morning, noon or night. "Local members of the Black Panther Party were always coming in and out of that place for strategy meetings," Yvonne commented when recalling our first month in the city. We heard frequent talk of revolution inside the house and observed constant police surveillance outside the house.

When we discovered that each person's salary would be $180 a month, our foursome decided to live together and pool our income. In the span of four weeks, we signed a lease for a ramshackle, roach-infested, shotgun house on Rowan Street where layers of aged linoleum covered the floors; we split the rent four ways. All the houses, up and down the street, were shotguns. When opening our front and back doors, we could see all the way through. The four-room abode, in the one-time German Irish neighborhood called Portland, became our home for the next twelve months.

In a matter of days, we had furnished the shotgun with discarded items from the streets and used furniture from the Volunteers of America warehouse, Louisville's equivalent of the Salvation Army and Goodwill. We picked up four bedsprings with mattresses and divided them between the middle rooms. Tony and I settled into the bedroom with the faded blue paint. The women moved into the other one with pink wallpaper peeling from the walls. In our training at Georgetown College, we understood a clear directive that discouraged sexual relationships among the four of us. They could negatively affect our work. The directive, however, did not apply to persons outside the household.

We soon rescued a wired-haired mutt from the city pound, an Airedale Terrier mix. He became our dependable burglar alarm. Collectively, we named him Mafis–an acronym for mother, apple pie, and the flag impede socialism. One of three dogs to join our household, Mafis survived the other two, despite being picked-up by the city dogcatcher. Lucky for the mutt, the ever-vigilant Donna Johnson rescued him just in time from the clutches of euthanasia at the pound.

In the remaining weeks of field training, we scrambled to begin building a network of contacts, potential allies in the religious, social service, and civil liberties communities. First, we introduced ourselves to the Louisville Legal Aid Society staff, our soon-to-be sponsor. Then, with assistance from locals, we diagrammed the city's progressive leaders and organizations like an English teacher would diagram a sentence.

Our foursome visited the Louisville Quaker Meeting House, attended services at the Unitarian Universalist Fellowship, and introduced ourselves to the clergy of other progressive religious denominations. A group of activist Roman Catholic sisters and brothers, many of whom had worked in the city housing projects, hosted a meal for us in their collective household and gave us an update on local political and social issues.

Donna and I sought out an invitation to the headquarters of the decade's old Southern Conference Educational Fund (SCEF), whose mission had always been to build the civil rights movement in the South with black and white together. Our initial introduction there became a history lesson about the McCarthy Era when, between 1950 and 1956, Senator Joseph McCarthy of Wisconsin spearheaded congressional investigations in an attempt to uncover Communists who, he claimed, had infiltrated the federal government although he never provided any of their names. The senator played on the public's fears about the spread of Communism.

At SCEF's headquarters, we met the directors Anne Braden and her husband, Carl. Onetime newspaper reporters for the *Louisville Times,* they later became infamous political figures in the city. Thin and drawn looking, with cigarette in hand, Anne seemed cordial but made it clear that she had a limited amount of time to talk with us. Stern-looking, white-haired Carl clearly could not be bothered. He grunted "Hello," without a handshake, and quickly disappeared into a back room of the two-story onetime family residence. Carl and Ann considered us dilettantes, not yet committed or seasoned political activists. They were right; we had much to do to earn their notice.

In the mid-1950s, with Senator McCarthy's Communist witch-hunting in full swing and the repercussions from the Supreme Court's landmark decision <u>Brown v. Board of Education</u> that declared state laws upholding segregation in the public schools to be unconstitutional, Carl and Anne purchased a house in an all-white neighborhood in the Louisville suburb of Shively. Then, they promptly sold it to a black couple, which had always been their intention. They were singlehandedly attempting to desegregate Louisville. Soon after the black family moved in, the Ku Klux Klan burned a cross on their front lawn and threw bricks through their windows. Eventually, the group firebombed the home. Anne detailed the experience in *The Wall Between*.

Along with five other white activists, authorities labeled Carl and Ann Braden as Communists and charged them with sedition under a Kentucky law. Authorities claimed that the Braden couple, and their co-conspirators, had bombed the house themselves in order to raise hell. Considered the ringleader of the group, the state convicted Carl of sedition and sentenced him to fifteen years in prison; he served eight months. Like so many other progressives during that era, Carl and Anne were black-listed and lost their newspaper jobs. Undeterred, they continued their civil rights work and took jobs as field organizers for the Southern Conference Educational Fund. Ultimately, Carl and Ann became indispensable resources during our stay in the city.

At the conclusion of our on-site training, the VISTA psychologist from Philadelphia paid a visit to our home. After meeting with each of us separately and posing myriad questions, he determined that we were mentally intact and physically fit for a year of volunteerism.

In August 1969, we loaded our overnight bags into Yvonne's car and drove to Detroit. Two months into our service, we had the opportunity to participate in the National Welfare Rights Convention held at Wayne State University. It would be my first experience in the company of nationally known progressive female political activists from all over the country. The "NWRO convention in Detroit estimated roughly 20,000 dues paying members of the organization and thus roughly 75,000 family members total were affected by the movement."[3]

The plenary session, led by a panel of outspoken women in the fields of civil rights, welfare rights, and the women's rights movements, crackled with fireworks. Gloria Steinem, co-founder of *Ms. Magazine*, sat on the panel. Despite her surprisingly quiet, low-key, demure personality, she played an important role.

Decades later, when I read Steinem's autobiography, *My Life on the Road,* her subdued behavior became clear. "I was terrified of public speaking. I'd so often canceled at the last minute when magazines booked me on television to publicize this or that article – as writers were often expected to do – that some shows had blacklisted me." She explained that at a certain point her African American friend, Dorothy Pitman Hughes, a fearless pioneer in the field of multiracial childcare had suggested that they speak to audiences as a duet. "Then we could each talk about our different but parallel experiences, and she could take over if I froze or flagged. We started in school basements with a few people on folding chairs, and progressed to community centers, union halls, suburban theaters, welfare rights' groups, high school gyms, YWCA's and even a football stadium or two."[4]

Next to Steinem sat Florynce Kennedy, a civil rights lawyer and a charismatic speaker. Dressed in her customary cowgirl outfit with leather vest and Texas-sized ten-gallon hat, Kennedy held the attention of the audience with her booming voice and noted sense of humor. Fannie Lou Hamer sat on the panel, too. A onetime cotton picker in the South, Hamer was a nationally known voting rights activist and a leader in the Mississippi Freedom Democratic Party at the 1964 Democratic National Convention. Of course, the two major National Welfare Rights Organization's leaders, Beulah Sanders from New York City and Los Angeles native Johnnie Tillman, brought East and West together for a successful convention.

I participated in an inspiring organizing workshop led by Richard A. Cloward and Francis Fox Piven, nationally recognized sociologists, political activists, and members of the Democratic Socialists of America. When teaching at the Columbia University School of Social Work, Cloward and Piven developed the organizing strategy for the National Welfare Rights Organization: "The ultimate objective of this strategy–to wipe out poverty by establishing a guaranteed annual income,"[5] The two sociologists advocated a major redistribution of income in the United States. Their book, *Regulating the Poor: The Functions of Public Welfare*, provided a thorough critique of the function of public assistance in a capitalist economy.

Cloward and Piven, an attractive and charismatic duo, held my attention. Piven spoke with a smoky, sultry, voice that reminded me of actor Lauren Bacall. Cloward looked like Superman's Clark Kent. At the conclusion of their workshop, I remained in the classroom to speak with them one on one. I had numerous questions about organizing techniques.

As the year progressed, Donna and I became the primary organizers for the Louisville Welfare Rights Organization. Strong-willed and determined to build the movement, we knocked on doors in the housing projects scattered around the city, participated in endless meetings with potential members, and became involved in the city's progressive politics. Gradually, Tony took a backseat in the process, but he remained a volunteer until the end of the year. Yvonne, clearly not interested in street politics and community organizing, struck out on her own.

The Wisconsin native raised a ruckus in the local school district. She valiantly challenged the common practice of corporal punishment in the elementary school just a few blocks away from where we lived. Unfortunately, on numerous occasions, Yvonne confronted the school principal without the support of community members. At her final confrontation, a school counselor threw Yvonne up against the student lockers, dragged her to the principal's office, and kept her there until the police arrived and hauled her downtown to the city jail. Yvonne's solo campaign became a losing battle.

I developed a daily routine of my own, an attempt to grasp what felt like the appropriate life for a community organizer. Picture a Mormon missionary. Rather than proselytizing the *Book of Mormon*, I preached the community-organizing gospel according to Alinsky, Cloward, and Piven. Instead of wearing black pants, white shirt with tie, and a name-tag, my missionary attire became faded blue jeans, a T-shirt, and desert boots. I alternated between a mustache and a beard, long hair and a crew cut. Daily, I knocked on doors and passed out leaflets preaching the word. I had an unwavering mind-set as to the right and wrong way to organize. At times, that compulsion became difficult for my fellow volunteers to tolerate.

Frequently, I began the day walking to the nearby St. Anthony's Roman Catholic Church on Market Street. Built in the Gothic Revival style, the impressive red brick structure incorporated a belfry and a vaulted ceiling. Sunlight streamed into the sanctuary through its expansive stained-glass windows. The church seemed out of place, as if it belonged in a neighborhood of the Haves rather than the Have-Nots. I would sit in silence, watch the votive candles flicker, and ponder. The alone time at St. Anthony's helped collect my thoughts. Although challenging and exciting, my new geographical and political environment could be anxiety provoking, too much new information to digest all at once. Day by day, I gained new insights on a range of issues from welfare policy, bank practices, and economic class structure to the corporate press, capitalism, and organized labor. I had left my conservative politics behind and embraced change. "Question authority" became my mantra.

VISTA transformed my world-view. I had the privilege of working with former coal miners fighting for their Black Lung health benefits and empowered mothers on public assistance organizing to improve the daily lives of their children. I received support from community lawyers with ethical standards, clergy who practiced what they preached, and political activists with visions for a better world. As an organizer, I lived our country's labor and progressive political history, the history omitted from my high school and college textbooks. I began to read about the lives of such important historical figures as labor organizer Elizabeth Gurley Flynn, women's rights advocate Sojourner Truth, Democratic Socialists Eugene Debs and Norman Thomas, actor activist Paul Robeson, and anarchist Emma Goldman. "If I can't dance, I don't want to be part of your revolution!" Goldman proclaimed according to rumor. I had not heard anything that lively in the university classroom.

The *Appalachian People's History Book,* Emma Goldman's *Living My Life,* Abbie Hofmann's *Steal This Book,* and *Soul on Ice,* by Eldridge Cleaver, along with Alinsky's two organizing guides and Cloward and Piven's *Regulating the Poor* were just a few of the books that filled my shelves. Local organizing workshops added material to my resource collection: *The Care and Feeding of Power Structures, So You Think You Have a Free Press, Common Group Problems, How to Put Out Community News,* and a *Tenant's Rights Handbook.*

I became acquainted with progressive political analysts

Howard Zinn and Noam Chomsky. I began to pay attention to the lyrics of songs written by folk singers Woody Guthrie and Pete Seeger, Odetta and Barbara Dane, Phil Ochs and Richie Havens. Guthrie's "This Land Is Your Land" became my national anthem. It still is. My political education mushroomed when a full-time organizer with the Vietnam Antiwar Movement, Steve Goldsmith, invited the four of us to volunteer as monitors at an antiwar coffeehouse. Located in Muldraugh, Kentucky, near Fort Knox, the coffeehouse had been fire bombed recently. He also asked if we would help distribute the antiwar newspaper in downtown Louisville on Saturday nights. Although officially called *Fun, Travel and Adventure*, activists more often referred to the bi-weekly paper as *Free* or *Fuck the Army*. The four of us agreed to do so.

A hyper-energetic activist, Goldsmith helped establish the coffeehouse that opened in August 1969. It became one of dozens of antiwar activity centers, opened near military bases across the country, as the Vietnam War dragged on. Outside the white, two-story, wood frame building, next to the upstairs window, hung a simple sign printed in black capital letters–COFFEEHOUSE. Inside, covering an entire wall, activists had painted an American flag upside down. In the flag's star quadrant hung a covered toilet seat. When opened, a picture of Lyndon Baines Johnson became visible.

"Soldiers were mostly the driving force," Goldsmith explained in David Zeiger's gripping documentary *Sir! No Sir* released in 2005, "and we were there to support them."[6] Focused on the antiwar coffeehouse and alternative newspaper movements, the documentary contained black-and-white footage never before seen by a national audience.

Goldsmith revealed that local authorities tried to shut down the coffeehouse. "They indicted six people for two offenses," he commented on screen. "One [offense] was maintaining a place visited by idle and evil-disposed people." Indicted with five others, Goldsmith talked briefly about his experience "I spent thirteen days in this little jail. It still had a trap door from when they did lynchings from before the Civil War. There was a hook up on the wall," he said. "They were tryin' to drive us out of town. But we weren't goin' away."[7]

Saturday nights, the four of us began to pass out copies of *Fun, Travel and Adventure* in downtown Louisville to enlisted men and women taking rest and relaxation (R&R). Although not official VISTA business, the paper's distribution became an important part of our own political agenda. One of hundreds of papers affiliated with the underground press, local activists typed and mimeographed the alternative biweekly. It covered a range of topics from antiwar demonstrations, rebellions in army bases, and personal testimonies to lists of sympathetic lawyers, local support groups, notices of coffeehouse speakers, and dates and times for film showings.

One night when passing out papers, I encountered a neighbor who lived a few blocks down from us on Rowan Street. A police officer six days a week but a preacher on Sundays, he invited me to attend the next morning's service at his storefront church. Holy roller, the common name for his congregation, offered an appropriate description of their religious services.

My upbringing, in a caring small-town Presbyterian Church in south central Kansas, had not prepared me for the experience on that day. A baby's cry was the most emotional outburst I ever remembered hearing during those Presbyterian services. That Sunday morning in Louisville, I spent more time standing and clapping, singing and shouting "Hallelujah" and "Amen" than I did sitting in the pew but when the preacher encouraged individuals to come down front and "speak to Jesus," my Presbyterian upbringing kicked in big time and I held back. However, without missing a beat, a big, handsome, proud-looking woman yelled, "Amen, I'm a comin'!" She proceeded to march down that aisle. Each heavy step of the way confirmed her determination. Once near the pulpit, she began to whisper, then to talk, and finally to shout out her confession to Jesus. The woman startled me when she began to sway and sweat, and dance and jump as if shaking off the devil. I quickly joined a group of church members who moved up front to form a support circle in case she passed out, which she did briefly. She came to, got herself back up, and finished what she had set out to accomplish. "Amen!" By the time she calmed down, I felt gratefully exhausted. At the end of the service, I hugged that radiant woman and thanked her. She had awakened something inside of me.

At that Holy Roller celebration, it became clear that I–and no one else–would be responsible for creating my own spiritual journey, a gift of a lifetime. "Hallelujah!" In gratitude, I dropped a meager donation in the collection plate before leaving the church.

Even when we pooled our money to meet our costs, $720 a month did not always cover the basics. I kept that in mind when I imagined how a family of four, a mother and three children on public assistance, could get by on $400 a month, which is what the state of Kentucky required.

"Remember that time we went to the Plasma Bank and the attendant couldn't find your vein?" Donna asked during a telephone conversation when we reminisced about our Louisville experience. The Plasma Bank became a fall-back for money when things got tighter than tight. "That woman just kept poking and poking and poking that needle into your arm," said Donna. I made so many trips to the Plasma Bank that I could not remember that particular event. "Wow, how can you not remember that one!" she exclaimed with laughter.

"No, don't remember that incident," I told her. "But I do remember the night I got mugged." Donna vaguely recalled the incident. "It was a late, muggy, summer night, you know. I'd decided to walk around a few blocks just to cool off," I told her. "Don't know what I was thinking. I was shirtless and barefooted." As I replayed the scene in my mind, I could feel my gut tighten up. "As I rounded a corner and headed back to Rowan Street, I noticed three shadowy figures about a half block away. Didn't think much about it. Just kept on walking." I paused then continued. "Soon, I felt a hard object bash against the back of my head, saw a bright flash of light, and crumpled down to the ground being cursed and kicked. They got my wallet, but not the spare change or the house key in my front pockets." The three men disappeared as quickly as they had jumped me. "Never saw their faces," I told Donna. I pulled myself up and dragged my aching body home, where I called the police and made a report. The knot on the back of my head and the bruised ribs would heal. I never recovered the wallet.

That first winter in Louisville, when the temperature fell below zero, the four of us pulled two of our mattresses out into the front room and snuggled up in a pile next to the space heater. We would close off the two middle rooms, where the walls iced up, and used the kitchen in the morning where we turned on the small, four-burner stove for heat. Once a week we went out for dinner to Masterson's Steak House, near the University of Louisville, and ordered chef's salad with extra turkey, ham, and cheese. During the meal, we would review the past week's activities and discuss plans for the week to come.

One morning, much to cold to be knocking on doors, two unexpected visitors showed up, FBI agents. They only identified themselves as such once they were in the house. I cannot explain why we let them in. Although we did discuss it afterwards. Sitting in our front room, they inquired about our community organizing efforts. Surprisingly, we began to share our activities. By about the fourth question, it occurred to the four of us that we had the right to refuse to answer and boot them out of the house. We did. They never returned.

In late spring, feeling frustrated and out of place, Yvonne left and returned to Wisconsin. Tony departed in June after completing his commitment. Donna and I decided to sign up for an additional year and agreed to remain apartment mates. Encouraged by the Louisville Legal Aid Society director, we moved into a rent-free apartment above their newly opened branch office on 18th and Broadway in one of the city's worst neighborhoods known for its heavy drug traffic. Mafis made the move with us, but after two break-ins below us, within a span of four weeks, we returned to our old neighborhood and rented an upstairs apartment on Main Street. Donna and I continued our work with Louisville Welfare Rights Organization and assisted local activists in pulling together the Louisville Tenants' Rights Movement. That second winter, we managed to drive to Ann Arbor, with a Legal Aid lawyer, and attend the National Tenants' Rights Conference at the University of Michigan, a hotbed of political activism. The conference provided the opportunity to reconnect and receive political updates from activists we had met at Wayne State University the year before.

Once again, Richard Cloward and Francis Fox Piven facilitated an organizing workshop on tenant's unions. In conjunction with their welfare rights work, the two sociologists had also developed a strategy to build the nationwide Tenants' Rights Movement. "The key to a disruptive rent strike is for tenants to pocket the rent, not place it in escrow," explained the two sociologists. "Widespread action of this kind would throw the slum housing economy into chaos, for many landlords would have to abandon their property, leaving thousands of buildings without services or even minimal maintenance. As health hazards multiplied and the breakdown of landlord-tenant relations threatened to spread, the clamor would mount for governmental action to solve the crisis."[8]

Donna and I returned to Louisville recharged and promptly became involved in tenants' rights issues as they applied to welfare recipients. Soon the police arrested us a second time for refusing to vacate a shotgun house where a low-income family were to be evicted in the middle of winter.

Given our strong wills and stubborn natures, Donna and I found tensions arising more quickly between us, without two other housemates to diffuse emotions. There wasn't anyone else there to mediate when we disagreed about organizing strategies.

Outside of our political work, Donna had created a social network. She understood the importance of having a support system. When tensions built up between us, Donna would simply leave for a few days and spend time with friends in another part of the city. I remained focused on the organizing work six or seven days a week. I did not realize the importance of creating a social life outside my organizational efforts.

Seldom do I remember going out just for relaxation aside from our weekly chef's salad at Masterson's Steakhouse. Relaxing meant that I had not been taking my work seriously. If I did do something socially, Donna usually arranged it through her network of friends. A few times, acquaintances gave us free tickets to go to see a play at Louisville's Actors Theatre. Only once do I recall going to a commercial film during my two years in the city. Ken Russell directed that sensual, erotic, and visually stunning film *Women in Love*, an adaptation of D. H. Lawrence's book by the same title. It became memorable for reasons I would truly appreciate years later.

I had read and reread *Lady Chatterley's Lover*, late at night by flashlight, during my junior high days. A friend let me borrow his parent's copy unbeknown to them. In college, I remembered reading Lawrence's *Fathers and Sons*, but I had not been aware of *Women in Love*. A week after viewing the film, I bought the book. It became one of the few works of fiction, perhaps the only one, on my bookshelf.

The relationship between the two male characters, Birkin and Gerald, and their nude wrestling scene made me take notice. I had never seen anything like that on the screen. The men's struggles with their sexualities and the women in their lives challenged my traditional way of thinking about male and female relationships. I admired their friendship. I felt as though I would like to have that kind of open and intimate bond with another man someday.

At the time, I did not consciously think about being bisexual or gay or even feel the desire to have a sexual relationship with another man but I sensed that I would like to have the kind of intimate male friendship Lawrence revealed through his writing and Ken Russell portrayed on film. If I did not, I would be missing a part of myself. "Let us hesitate no longer to announce that the sensual passions and mysteries are equally sacred with the spiritual mysteries and passions," Lawrence wrote. "Let man only approach his own self with a deep respect even reverence for all that the creative soul, the God mystery within us, puts forth. Then we shall all be sound and free. Nothing that comes from the deep, passionate soul is bad, or can be bad so there is no apology to tender, unless to the soul itself, if it should have been belied. Any man of real individuality tries to know and to understand what is happening, even in himself, as he goes along."[9]

In late spring, soon after Donna and I had recruited a New York couple to replace us as Louisville organizers, friends of hers invited us on a picnic. Larry and Missy were a married couple and both academics. They drove us out of town to a rural, hilly landscape in the Bluegrass Country close to the Abbey of Gethsemani, a Trappist monastery not far from Bardstown. We could see the monastery from where we ate our lunch, spread out on a blanket, but we did not visit the community.

While eating our sandwiches and sharing bottles of wine, Larry mentioned that he made a silent retreat at the abbey every year. He talked at length about his spiritual life. I had never heard a man talk so intimately, sincerely, and openly about the subject. He mentioned the Trappist monk Thomas Merton, a onetime member of that monastery. Larry informed us that Merton had died an accidental death three years before while attending a conference in Thailand. He recommended Merton's autobiography, *The Seven Storey Mountain*, which I read months later. The book provided my first glimpse into monastic life. It fascinated me. Merton wrote from the perspective of a young religious zealot. His theology did not strike a chord with me. It felt oppressive. However, the monk's unwavering commitment to his beliefs, his willingness to leave the material life behind and live in a collective community, captured my attention.

CHAPTER TWO

~

Walking Backward

Inside Louisville's crowded and noisy bus depot, I waited eagerly for my ride. An hour later, I sat between two Trappist monks in the cab of an old Ford pickup. We were on our way to the Abbey of Gethsemani. The monastery's guest master had granted me permission to make a Christmas retreat during my two-week break from Livingston College at Rutgers University. I had transferred there after completing VISTA.

The new acquaintances soon made me feel at ease. We shared thoughtful conversation and laughter during that bumpy truck ride. I recall the heater did not work properly, and heavy snowfall from the night before crunched underneath the tires as we drove slowly over the country roads. Bouncing along, I thought back to my introduction to the abbey two years earlier at a picnic with friends. They mentioned Thomas Merton, a Trappist monk, profilic writer, and former resident of the religious community.

Merton's spiritual journey intrigued me, particularly his resolute commitment to life in the cloistered monastery. What called him into the religious life? Why did he choose that particular order of monks? How did he structure his days? Who were the other men that lived behind the walls? Did his example have some bearing on my life? Those were but a few of the questions that came to mind. Merton's *The Seven Storey Mountain* had sparked the desire to arrange that holiday visit.

I can still visualize scenes that were an integral part of that experience. Above the metal entrance gate, leading into the cloistered area where the monks resided, were three Latin words: Fuge, Tace, et Quiesce. They declared a life of Solitude, Silence, and Inner Peace. Each night, I fell asleep in a sparsely furnished room with a cold bare floor, firm bed, and crucifix on the wall. On the desk, next to the lamp, set a worn *Jerusalem Bible,* and a daily schedule of community worship referred to as the Divine Office or Liturgy of the Hours. Beginning with Vigil at 3:30 a.m. and ending with Compline at 7:40 p.m., the daily routine remained consistent from one Trappist monastery to another.

The monks' medieval prayer schedule became a reality soon after I settled into my room. A bell in the church steeple rang out across the Bluegrass Country announcing Compline. The bell's toll kept time and marked their rhythm of life. The sanctuary, with a formidable vaulted ceiling, walls painted stark white, and simple elongated, stained-glass windows was divided into two sections. On one side, the monks sat in the choir facing one another. Visitors occupied the other side. I sat in a front pew where my eyes gradually adjusted to the darkness. Candles flickered behind the altar, with air sweetened by the smell of incense. In their nine-hundred-year tradition, the monks chanted praises to their God.

During the Christmas Eve service, rituals of the Mass unfolded amid the haze of censer smoke and candlelight. Antiphonal sounds of Gregorian chant emanated from the hooded figures in the sanctuary.

Solo walks in the dense Kentucky woods and visits to the onetime hermitage of Thomas Merton remain in my memory. That simple, concrete-block abode became my daily pilgrimage site. Not once during my time at the monastery did I feel awkward or out of place. I knew after a few days that monastic retreats would become a part of my life, a refuge of sorts. I had discovered a community that understood and supported my longing for periods of solitude, a community that would strive for cooperation rather than competition.

When reading in the Gethsemani library, I discovered that a sixth-century contemplative named St. Benedict had written *The Rule* that continued to govern most aspects of the community. Their rigorous routine maintained a daily discipline of prayer, study, and manual labor. According to Trappist tradition, hospitality extended to people of all faiths or no faith at all. I learned that some retreatants chose to participate in the Liturgy of the Hours with the monks and seek out spiritual counseling. Others would schedule their time around hikes, reading, and meditation. I tended to fall into the latter group. We were free to plan our own agendas, depending on our particular needs, provided we respected the ground rules of the community.

The men at the Abbey of Gethsemani, some ordained priests and others lay brothers, quickly dispelled the image of monks as withdrawn and always silent. Contrary to popular belief, a vow of silence had never been a requirement of the Trappists. "You could always talk to two people: the abbot and the novice master," explained one of the monks. "But we had complete silence from 8 p.m. to 6 a.m." Prior to Vatican II, 1962 to 1965, when Pope John XXIII initiated progressive changes in the church, the Trappists did follow a strict rule of silence. In fact, they used sign language to communicate to anyone in the monastery other than the abbot and their novice master.

On my third day of retreat, I discovered Merton's book *The Asian Journal,* a compilation of the monk's entries made as he traveled throughout Asia in 1968. Merton died an accidental death in Thailand where he had participated in a Christian Buddhist monastic dialogue near Bangkok. In *The Asian Journal,* Merton expressed thoughts about his chosen way of life. "In speaking for monks I am really speaking for a strange kind of person, a marginal person, because the monk in the modern world is no longer an established person with an established place in society. He is a marginal person who withdraws deliberately to the margin of society with a deepening fundamental human experience."[1] The book made it clear that Merton had evolved from a narrow-minded young Catholic zealot, the author of *The Seven Storey Mountain*, into a mature citizen of the world who acknowledged and honored the range of religious and spiritual practices around the globe. "Merton sought the fullness of man's inheritance; the inclusive view made it impossible for him to deny any authentic scripture of any man of faith," commented Amiya Chakravarty in his preface to *The Asian Journal.*[2]

Theologian and academic Henri J. M. Nouwen wrote an account of his extended stay at a Trappist monastery in upstate New York titled *A Genesee Diary*. In that book, he captured the essence of Merton. Nouwen explained that the monk never tried to be systematic and did not worry about being consistent. "He articulated skillfully and artfully the different stages of his own thoughts and experiences and moved on to new discoveries without worrying about what people made of his old ones."[3] That is what I would come to admire most about Thomas Merton.

A day before my departure from Kentucky, I went for a hike along a narrow country road. On my return to the abbey, I decided to walk backward.

"Whataya doin?" A retired factory worker on retreat, also out for a walk, had spotted me and approached.

"Walking backward," I replied.

"Why ya walkin' backward?"

I paused a moment. "Wanted to see if I observed things differently," I told him.

"I understand," he said. "Sometimes I tie my shoes starting with my left foot just to see how I do it differently than the right one."

There wasn't any yammer about resumes or political philosophies, just simple talk about how to look at things differently. The factory worker planned to leave for home after lunch.

"Think you'll make another retreat in the future?" I asked out of curiosity.

"Don't rightly know," he answered. "But this retreat sure has helped me out in many ways." After we said our good-byes and shook hands, I headed toward the abbey walking backward. "Ya know what I appreciated the most?" yelled the man waving at me from a distance. "Everyone treated me like a brother."

CHAPTER THREE

~

Dear John Letter

Dressed in green fatigues and black berets, the German armed guards stood alert at the El Al Airlines departure desk in Frankfurt's International Airport. They watched every move I made. An airline employee gruffly ordered me to unload my book bag onto the conveyor belt then empty my pockets, remove my watch, belt, and shoes, and place everything into the plastic container. "Walk slowly through the two security gates in front of you," he commanded.

Once all passengers were on board and doors sealed, we waited indefinitely on the tarmac. "Engine problems," reported the captain tersely over the intercom. He assured us that there was no reason to be worried. "I heard there was a bomb scare," whispered the dark-haired Israeli woman sitting behind me. I wished she had kept that information to herself. Since I had flown out of Kennedy International Airport, engine problems had delayed three of my flights.

As we departed, I white knuckled the seat handles. Plane take-offs had always been difficult for me. Once in the air, I loosened the handles and began to chat with the woman sitting to my right. She introduced herself as Sharon. Born in Brooklyn where her parents still lived, she worked as an accountant, had two children, and lived on the outskirts of Tel Aviv. Sharon said that her husband, born and raised in Israel, was an architect. A few weeks before, he had begun to fulfill his annual military duty in the army, a requirement for most Israeli citizens, male and female.

"Is this your first time abroad?" she asked.

"Uh, no, I've been out of the States one other time," I told her, "back in '68." I explained that I had joined my college choir that made a three-week singing tour in England, Scotland, and France. I sang baritone. "It was an incredible trip. We sang in huge cathedrals in the cities and more intimate churches in smaller communities." I told Sharon that between scheduled performances the choir had managed to tour Stonehenge, attend a production of Shakespeare's *Richard the Second* at Stratford-upon-Avon, stand in the spot at the Canterbury Cathedral where King Henry's soldiers murdered Archbishop Thomas à Becket, and walk the halls of Cambridge University. I kept babbling on, very unlike me. "When we got to Paris, I toured the Louvre with my girlfriend and we had dinner in the restaurant half way up the Eifel Tower." I remembered that she and I had eaten slices of cheese and a loaf of French bread, along with a bottle of wine, in a city park where we had to pay to sit on a bench.

"And you?" I asked. "Do much traveling?"

"Only back and forth between the States and Israel," Sharon replied, then she got quiet.

I was talking too much, probably put her off. Sharon pulled a paperback out of her handbag and began to read.

Too wired to read, I started a conversation with the woman on my left. From Flatbush in Brooklyn, Anita told me she had arranged to work on Kibbutz Revivim and planned to participate in their Ulpan Program, work half a day and study Hebrew the other half. To my surprise, Anita gave me the name, address, and phone number of her aunt and uncle in Tel Aviv where she would be staying for a few days.

When the plane landed, we shuffled past columns of armed guards on the tarmac and inside the terminal. It felt like we were under siege. I joined the time-consuming passport inspection line and then proceeded to the baggage pick-up area and the money exchange office.

To compensate passengers for the flight delay from Frankfurt, El Al offered to pay for a two-night stay at the Hotel Monopol just a few blocks from the beach. By 11 p.m., I arrived at the hotel, checked in, and found my room at the end of a poorly lit hallway. Too tired to unpack, I peeled off my wrinkled clothes and fell into bed.

Awakened refreshed the next morning, I took a shower, dug clean clothes out of my backpack, dressed, and walked downstairs for breakfast. Near the hotel's front desk, while finishing my morning coffee, I dropped unfamiliar coins into the pay telephone and dialed the number of a former girlfriend scribbled in my journal. After five rings, I wondered if I had the right number. Six rings, then seven; I fumbled to check the journal again. Eight rings, bingo!

"Boker-tov, Kibbutz Bet Kama," The woman on the other line wished me good morning in Hebrew. Kibbutz Bet Kama was a collective agricultural community located in Israel's Negev Desert.

"Boker-tov," I replied. "Excuse me but do you speak English?" My question resulted in a pregnant pause on the other end of the line.

"Of course I speak English," she responded curtly. "Why are you calling?"

"I'd like to talk with Lauren Feingold." Lauren was participating in Rutgers University's year abroad program. She had studied at Hebrew University and then began to work on the kibbutz. Her father, a leader in their Jewish community in Rhode Island, had encouraged her to study in Israel.

Lauren and I met more than a year before in a political science class at Livingston College, taught by Carey McWilliams Jr., my mentor. McWilliams, son of the highly respected and longtime editor of *The Nation* magazine, chaired the department. Livingston College had been a godsend for me. With

small classes, a progressive faculty, and an activist and multiracial student body, I felt right at home.

Lauren first caught my attention when she spoke out in class
on a controversial topic. An ardent feminist, the native Rhode
Islander had an opinion on every issue and never hesitated to
express it. We constantly argued politics. Our bantering could
be exhausting but usually enlightening. Lauren and I began
an intimate, but rocky, relationship. She taught me the importance, or rather the necessity, for private space in a sexual
relationship.

Originally, I had planned to live and work with Lauren on
Kibbutz Bet Kama but months after she left for Israel, I received a Dear John letter. Lauren informed me that she had
fallen in love with Yaakov, a member of her kibbutz. Despite
the end of our relationship, we continued to communicate.
I could tell by her letters that she had gone through major
changes. Lauren had begun to identify as an Israeli, which
overshadowed other political issues paramount to her in the
past.

"Who do you want to speak with?" the woman asked gruffly.

"Lauren Feingold," I repeated, "a long-term volunteer."

"Oh, you mean Lauri," her tone softened a little. "Who's
calling?"

"Bill, my name's Bill," I replied. "She's expecting my call."

"Hold on a minute. I'll check the work board." The woman
clunked down the receiver.

I waited so long that the pay phone began to make an ob-
noxious beeping noise. Clumsily, I pulled more Israeli coins
out of my pocket and dropped them into the slot. The beeping
stopped.

"Hello, hello?" The Bet Kama woman had finally returned
out of breath.

"Yes, yes, hello. I'm here."

"Lauri's working in the kitchen," she told me. "I called her.

She will be here shortly."

"Toda," thank you, I sputtered in Hebrew.

"Ken." Yes, she replied and put down the phone, gently that time.

Another wait. I dropped more coins into the slot. Finally, someone picked up the receiver.

"Hello, Bill?"

"Yea, it's me."

"Welcome to Israel!" she exclaimed cheerfully.

"Toda," it felt good to hear her voice. "I arrived in Tel Aviv late last night. Cause of flight delays, El Al has put me up at the Hotel Monopol for two nights."

"That's great," she replied. "How were your flights?"

"Oy vay," I quipped in Yiddish, "long and crowded."

"Oy is not a word: it is a vocabulary," pointed out Leo Rosten in his delightfully humorous book *Joys of Yiddish*. "It is a lament, a protest, a cry of dismay, a reflex of delight. But however sighed, cried, howled, or moaned, oy! is the most ubiquitous exclamation in Yiddish. Oy is often used as a lead-off for 'oy vay!' which means, literally, 'Oh pain,' but is used as an all-purpose ejaculation to express anything from trivial delight to abysmal woe."[1] Lauren had taught me the Yiddish phrase when we first met.

"So, what are your plans?"

"Monday morning, I'll walk over to the kibbutz volunteer office and arrange an assignment."

"Good for you," she said in a supportive tone. "Remember to tell them you wanna work on a traditional kibbutz like mine."

By traditional, she meant an agricultural collective that continued to practice the original tenets of the pioneer kibbutz movement. In those nonreligious Jewish communities, work assignments rotated among the men and women, members shared meals in a communal dining hall, and adults and children maintained separate living arrangements. The kibbutzim governed themselves by democratic socialist principles and supported an educational system that always focused on group projects.

I switched the telephone receiver to my other ear as Lauren talked on and on about Yaakov, her boyfriend. Funny thing, I felt jealous. I thought I had come to terms with our break-up months ago.

Shoving more coins into the slot, I told her that I had recently been in a relationship with Lillian, a first-generation Polish woman. I purposely began to jabber on myself. I shared that Lillian's father, who spoke his native language at home as did all her other family members, fought in the Polish Underground in World War II. "Her community is an entirely new culture for me to experience," I told Lauren.

"Sounds like you're still searching for a cultural identity." Lauren knew how to push my buttons.

"Oh, yeah, well, maybe you're right," I snapped back. "Actually, I think I'm searching for community." When the phone began to beep again, I told her I had run out of coins, although I had not, and we abruptly ended the conversation.

Biblical records revealed the Jews' earliest successful attempts at communal living. "The names of the Essenes have come down to us through history, reflecting the attempts of small groups to withdraw into the desert away from the turbulence surrounding them and achieve justice and equality, in the isolation of the wilderness."[2] Leo Rosten explained that "Essenism became a monastic sect–perhaps the first organized in the world of Mediterranean cultures."[3] The Jewish, pre-Christian, coed monastic order numbered in the thousands between 538 BCE and CE 70.

Making a historical leap into the early twentieth century, during a period of Russian tsarist oppression and a Jewish national renaissance, two wealthy European businessmen funded an organization called the Jewish Colonization Association. The association's mission was to establish the first Jewish agricultural collectives in Palestine. Populated by young democratic socialists from Eastern Europe, they called their collectives kvutza, the Hebrew word for group. They were the predecessors of the kibbutz movement.

Jewish farmers founded the agricultural movement upon the idea of living collectively and sharing profits: from each according to his ability, to each according to his needs. "There would be no class division between employer and employees;" wrote kibbutz member Dan Leon, "those responsible for running the farm would be democratically elected, but would enjoy no special privileges: all decisions on the economic and social life of the commune would be made by the members themselves."[4] Thus, each individual would share equally in both responsibilities and compensation.

Shortly after hanging up with Lauren, I phoned Anita, who graciously invited me over for dinner that night. I spent the day exploring Tel Aviv and swimming in the Mediterranean Sea, warm like bathwater, three blocks from the hotel.

Anita's aunt and uncle, Polish Jews, welcomed me with open-arms. A longtime hugger myself, I appreciated the physical contact. Dinner started with chicken soup, and then her aunt brought to the table baked fish, some fried meat, a bountiful salad, and a loaf of bread baked that afternoon. The feast concluded with a jigger or two of brandy; I had two and would have accepted a third had it been offered.

Our conversation bounced all over the place. With my talking English and her relatives speaking Yiddish, Anita served as translator. We were communicating in Yinglish! Anita kept up as best she could. I learned that her aunt and uncle had escaped the Jewish ghetto, in Warsaw, just before the Nazis began to block off the streets and restrict the comings and goings. Her relatives immigrated to Palestine, prior to 1948, and had lived on Ben Yahuda Street for more than a decade.

The next day, I stuffed my belongings into the backpack, left the hotel, and schlepped over to an international youth hostel. While waiting to check in, I struck up a conversation with an American from Massachusetts who happened to be sweeping the floor. Tall and thin, Josh sported a full beard and a ponytail. Instead of shaking hands, he gave me a bear hug as if we were longtime friends. Putting aside the broom, Josh sat down next to me, and we began to share life stories before the office attendant showed up. Josh, about my age, had served in Vietnam. Upon his return to the States, he became active in the antiwar movement. Using the GI Bill to pay for college, Josh had recently completed his undergraduate degree at the University of Hawaii and then decided to travel. To help with expenses, the veteran worked at youth hostels wherever he happened to land.

I asked what motivated him to travel. "Needed to work out some things," he replied without getting into specifics. "Thought I'd cleared them up but discovered a few months ago that I hadn't." Josh said that he planned to get a kibbutz assignment in the next month or so.

"Maybe we can work on the same kibbutz," I told him. "I'll let you know where I'm headed before I take off."

Later that afternoon, as I sat in the front room of the hostel writing in my travel journal, in walked Ann, a fellow student from Livingston College. Most recently, we were in a Legal Reasoning class together where Ann always had her hand up and usually gave the right answer. Although not friends at that time, we were acquaintances. Of course, I jumped up and gave her a hug. By the end of our conversation, we had become friends. Ann and I had known about our respective plans to volunteer on a kibbutz, but her original idea was to fly to Europe and then eventually get to Israel. At the last minute, she changed her mind and reversed the travel schedule.

On a Monday morning, in September 1974, I found my way to the Kibbutz Aliya office in Tel Aviv. When I explained that I wanted to work in a traditional community an office staff member promptly assigned me to Kibbutz Maabarot, located midway between Tel Aviv and Haifa, near the Mediterranean Sea, then handed me a fact sheet that I scanned.

Founded in 1932, Maabarot featured an industrial component in addition to its agricultural production. Approximately seven hundred men, women, and children resided in the community. "Four percent of Israelis live on more than two hundred and fifty kibbutzim," she remarked as I kept reading. Before I left the office, the woman gave me a contact name and told me to arrive at the kibbutz on Wednesday afternoon.

Two days later, after giving Ann and Josh my mailing address and insisting that they keep in touch, I boarded a bus. Within hours, I stood beside a highway shelter in front of Kibbutz Maabarot, an expansive oasis with green lawns and leafy trees spreading out in front of me.

"Planned as an architectonic unit, the kibbutz is built up roughly in concentric circles," explained the authors of *The Kibbutz*. "At its center are the public buildings, such as the dining hall, children's houses, and the cultural center. Immediately around these are the living quarters of the members–low houses with red roofs, surrounded by broad lawns, gardens and trees–and on the outer perimeter are the farm structures, the workshops, and the industrial enterprises." [5]

On the other side of the two-lane highway sat a small, dilapidated farm with a simple one-story house and a few sheds, surrounded by a five-foot earthen wall in disrepair. I soon met the Palestinian family who lived there. They had a small candy and soda shop frequented by the volunteers. During the weeks to come, they would sell me quart-sized bottles of hot Coca Cola, the only drink that quenched my thirst after a hot day's work. With each purchase, I felt like an ugly American. My dependence on American soft drinks made me feel uncomfortable, but that did not prevent me from purchasing them.

I approached the largest building on the grounds, entered it, and told a passer-by that I wanted to speak with the volunteer coordinator. I am not sure whom I expected, but the greeting by a white-haired, grandmotherly-looking woman, wearing a navy blue dress with white polka dots and a pair of sandals surprised me. She spoke with a British accent. Rachel extended her hand, welcomed me to Maabarot, invited me into the huge, community, dining hall then poured me a glass of iced tea.

"Why did you decide to work on Kibbutz Maabarot?" she asked as we settled at one of the extended tables.

"I wanted to find out what it's like to live in a democratic socialist community," I told her. I knew that Maabarot maintained the original tenets of the kibbutzim movement. "In the past, I've lived in communal housing arrangements." I shared with Rachel my experience of working as a community organizer in Louisville and living cooperatively with the other three volunteers. I explained that we had pooled our meager monthly incomes to cover rent, food, and transportation costs. Between the time that I left Louisville in 1971 and returned to academia in 1972, I had also lived, briefly, in a communal household in Washington, DC, where a dozen men and women split the rent and food costs. We shared maintenance duties, too. Rachel sat there quietly with hands in lap giving me her full attention. "Last year I made a monastic retreat over the Christmas holiday," I told her. "I was impressed with how the men were able to keep the monastery solvent. They lived and worked collectively like members of the kibbutz."

She nodded knowingly, pulled a small notepad and pen out of her bag sitting on the table, and continued to ask questions. "How long do you expect to be with us?"

"Three or four months," I told her. After leaving the kibbutz, I planned to hitchhike around Israel and then continue my journey on to Greece, Italy, and Western Europe. "Need to be back in the States by the spring," I said, "gotta make money for grad school."

Rachel explained that she tried to accommodate each volunteer's needs and interests as best she could. "Any particular interests that you would like to pursue while you're here?"

"Yea," I replied eagerly, "I want to get to know some of the early settlers." She began to write on her pad, "also interested in Maabarot's politics." Because I planned to write a newspaper article on daily life in a kibbutz, I would be keeping a day-to-day account of my experiences in a journal. "I'd like to attend your community meetings, too, witness the decision-making process."

"You'll always be welcome at our weekly meetings," Rachel assured me with a smile. As we continued our conversation, she mentioned that her son, Mickey, lived on Kibbutz Kerem Shalom. "It's a new community near the Gaza Strip." She paused. "They are the founding members of the Peace Now Movement. You may have heard of it." I had read about the political movement. Rachel confirmed that Peace Now advocated a two-state solution with the Palestinians. "Perhaps I can arrange for you to visit him before you leave the country."

The soft-spoken woman began to talk about the logistics of Maabarot. She was responsible for posting the daily labor assignments for volunteers on the bulletin board. The workday began at 6:00 a.m. and lasted from seven to eight hours with a midmorning break and lunch at noon. Rachel informed me that I needed to attend weekly orientation meetings for the volunteers and showed me the location of the work board and the laundry room then we walked into the kibbutz clubroom where adults gathered for recreation and refreshments in the evening. "There's only one television set in the community," Rachel said. "It's over in the conference room. We only use it for news programs and documentaries."

We continued the tour beyond the main complex and passed by the community bomb shelter. The thick-walled concrete entrance, beside a two-story, stone, wall, led to a descending staircase. "If you ever hear the siren; this is where you should come immediately." There had not been any raids recently, and Rachel did not expect any. Then we sauntered over to the volunteers' living quarters a short distance away from the main campus. On the way, Rachel mentioned that more than a dozen short-term volunteers had come from South Africa, Canada, and England as well as Western Europe.

Living quarters were wood frame structures with concrete floors that looked like basic, unfinished motel units. Every building, divided into four rooms, housed eight volunteers each. Clotheslines, sagging from the weight of drying laundry, hung between the columns that supported the verandas. Communal showers and toilets were behind the living quarters.

The volunteer coordinator directed me to a room in the unit closest to the showers. "You'll be living here with Élan, a Frenchman," she informed me. "He is a quiet and dependable worker. I am sure that the two of you will get along just fine." Before leaving me, Rachel offered a suggestion. "Kibbutz members will really appreciate it if you make an effort to speak some Hebrew." Although most of them spoke English, she encouraged me to learn elementary vocabulary like daily greetings, words that expressed appreciation, in addition to yes and no.

"Dinner's at 6:00 p.m. Remember volunteers are always welcome in the clubroom, after the meal, for a coffee and dessert." Rachel encouraged me to take advantage of that time to socialize with the community. "It's a good place to meet people, read newspapers, play board games."

Later that afternoon, Elan returned to our room after working all day in the fishponds. He smelled like a seafood market. At first glance, Élan reminded me of Detective Jacques Clouseau, actor Peter Sellers's character in *The Pink Panther*. The Frenchman stood tall and thin with a neatly clipped mustache. His English was impeccable. Before leaving for the showers, he told me that he also spoke German and Hebrew.

"Last year I completed my advanced business degree," he informed me upon returning to our room. "Because I wasn't ready to enter the business world, I decided to volunteer on a kibbutz." Élan said that his parents objected to the decision, but he felt working on the kibbutz made a contribution. "I will return to Paris in a month and begin job hunting." Élan had an easy manner about him. Rachel was right; we would be compatible roommates.

I tagged along with him to the communal dining hall for dinner where hundreds of people were sitting together at the long tables and served by their comrades. Élan mentioned that all of the fruits and vegetables came from Maabarot. After dinner, we visited the clubroom for coffee and dessert as Rachel had suggested. The kibbutzniks were welcoming but not overwhelming. I felt at ease.

"Want to play backgammon?" Élan asked.

"Never played it," I told my new roommate. "I'll give it a try." Over the next few months, I became a consummate backgammon player.

My first two weeks on the kibbutz were challenging. I felt like a klutz, especially when I attempted to communicate in Hebrew. A klutz is a "clod; a clumsy, slow-witted, graceless person, an inept blockhead."[6] Leo Rosten's definition captured my character exactly. I repeatedly said no when I meant yes. Sometimes in the morning, I greeted my fellow workers with good evening. When I intended to say thank you, I would blurt out the Hebrew word for please instead.

September 18: It is Rosh Hashanah, the Jewish New Year. To-

day and tomorrow are free days for everyone in the community. I spent time getting better acquainted with Élan and the other volunteers, read, and wrote in my journal. I have so much to learn. I always feel like I am catching up!

Both nights I made a point of going to the Club Room after dinner and introducing myself to more members of the community. I really pushed myself to participate in conversations regardless of the topic. I played backgammon when asked.

September 20: Working in the kitchen, washing dishes, cleaning tables, and mopping floors. The communal dining hall serves three meals a day to all adults on the kibbutz. The children take their meals in their respective houses.

After dinner, Rachel and her husband, Joseph, invited me over to their comfortable apartment. They lived in a duplex with an adequately sized front room, a small kitchenette, one bedroom, and a bathroom. The front lawn, landscaped with colorful flowers and shrubs, reminded me of living arrangements in contemporary co-housing communities in the United States. Their apartment was quite a contrast to the single room, wooden shacks once occupied by Maabarot pioneers. One of those structures remained on the grounds as a historical icon.

Joseph offered to make tea. Like his wife, he came from England. Tanned with thinning white hair and a bit stooped over, he dressed in the typical kibbutz attire for men, short-sleeved cotton shirt, cotton shorts, and leather sandals. Reserved and thoughtful, the man appeared more comfortable listening than talking. I appreciated that quality about him. Wearing another polka dot dress with sandals, Rachel sat in a straight-backed chair rather than the couch. The woman had a prim and proper quality about her that was becoming but somehow seemed out of place on the kibbutz.

"I worked with British Intelligence for five years," she revealed during our conversation, "then taught school here for more than two decades." I imagined she typified a conscientious pedagogue. Joseph did not offer any information about his life before the kibbutz and I did not ask. I wanted to listen rather than talk until I became better acquainted with the older folks. He did mention they were active in a left-wing political party.

September 24: This morning I unloaded kitchen supplies and cleaned the floor drains. My afternoon assignment was to work in the cotton fields.

Rachel made a concerted effort to connect me with older kibbutzniks, the pioneers. During dinner, she introduced me to Zahava and Dov, who then invited me over to their place for the evening. Their living room was orderly, filled with books on politics and art and a classical music collection. On one wall hung prints of pastel watercolors, painted by the Israeli artist Mshuel Katz, which they proudly pointed out to me. Katz frequently painted subject matter from Jerusalem's Old City.

In their apartment, olive-skinned Zahava removed her sandals, curled up on one end of the couch, and tucked her pleated, cotton skirt underneath her knees. She had pulled her long brown hair into a pony-tail. I guessed her age to be in the early fifties. Born in Manhattan's Lower East Side, she came to Israel in her late twenties. Zahava did not share anything about her life in New York or family members she may have left behind.

Looking like an academic with thick-lensed, black-framed glasses and bushy white hair, and probably a decade older than his wife, Dov told me that Germany was his birthplace. As we talked, he removed a classical recording from its sleeve and carefully placed it on their small phonograph. Dov held that record like an antique dealer might grasp a rare piece of porcelain. He handled it delicately. As music filled the room, we moved in and out of silence. I felt at home with them. The couple did not mention having any children, and I did not see any family photographs on the walls or the bookshelves.

They were both politically active. "In the sixties, our party formed an alliance with the more centrist Labor Party," Zahava mentioned. "It was necessary to combat the rising influence of the right wing here in Israel." Because of the alliance, she said many people had dropped out of the party, including Rachel and Joseph.

Dov admitted that decades ago their political party had supported the Soviet Union as a model socialist state. When they discovered the country had become a police state and that Stalin had ordered the deaths of untold numbers of former comrades in his infamous Purge Trials, beginning in the late 1930s, they withdrew their support. "That issue caused a lot of disillusionment with many younger kibbutzniks," Dov said. "It killed their initiative to participate in politics." Zahava informed me that she worked a few days a week at the party headquarters in Tel Aviv and offered to take me to the office before my departure from the Maabarot. "It'll be a good introduction to Israeli politics."

September 27: Another day in the cotton fields. A few of us stand in the back of the truck and stomp down the cotton as it spews out from the combine chute. Even though the work is hot and sweaty, I am glad to be out of the kitchen.

Rachel and Zahava remained diligent and shared reading material that furthered my understanding of kibbutz life. They gave me introductory pamphlets on the governing structures in the community. Every year members elected a secretary to oversee the work of eight governing committees. Clearly, the secretary's position was one of the most demanding jobs on the kibbutz.

Since my arrival at Maabarot, I felt like I had more in common with the kibbutzniks than with the other volunteers except for an Australian long-termer named Philip. Most volunteers seemed uninterested in the kibbutz dynamics or Israeli politics and hung out around our living quarters rather than mix with the natives.

September 28: The community has a day off. It is Shabbat (Saturday); the one day of the week that the men and women do not work.

In the evening, I attended the weekly community meeting where all major decisions were determined by a simple majority vote. The old and young, male and female, debated the issues with conviction. The decisions they made weekly directly affected their lives. It was democracy at its best! That is what I had come to witness.

September 30: Today is the holiday of Succoth. The kibbutzniks call it the celebration of the harvest. In the more traditional and religious Jewish world, Succoth honors the biblical story of the forty years that the Jews wandered in the desert. I did heavy yard work in preparation for the evening's celebration, which will take place in the central plaza.

At Maabarot, holidays were not restricted to traditional religious interpretations but rather broadened to include their original pagan and agricultural significance. The evening began and ended with Israeli folk songs and dances. I enthusiastically joined with others in clasping hands, forming circles, and dancing the Hora, the most popular folk dance on the kibbutz.

October 5: Finally meet a volunteer who is a political activist. Her name is Lisa. She and her family immigrated to Israel from Chile. Her long blonde hair and blue eyes make her look more European than Latin American. I am attracted to her.

Lisa revealed that her father was a civil servant under President Salvador Allende's short-lived administration. She spoke about the US involvement in the military overthrow of the democratically elected Allende government. The activist talked at length about the thousands of Chileans who had disappeared under General Augusto Pinochet's brutal military dictatorship. The former Chilean said that she would volunteer on the kibbutz for a month then return to Jerusalem to begin her required military service.

October 10: I am back in the cotton fields.

That evening Rachel had invited a kibbutz pioneer, Bumi, to speak about Maabarot's history to our group of volunteers. I looked forward to his talk. Bumi, a short, weathered-looking senior, wore a faded baseball cap and rocked back and forth on his bowed legs as he spoke to us.

"Maabarot was born in 1927," he began. "At that time, we had two dozen people. Three were women. And all of us did the same work." Bumi continued, "Most of us were from the Balkan countries. Later, there was a large contingent from Germany and Chile." They were "black workers", unskilled laborers. "Until we received land in 1932, most of us worked construction on the highway between Tel Aviv and Haifa in order to survive," said Bumi, "and that was damn hard work. The hardest physical labor I'd ever done." Rocking back and forth, Bumi continued to share their history. "Shortly after we moved onto this land, a nearby Bedouin tribe attacked us. They were afraid we were going to eliminate them." The pioneer told us that the kibbutzniks finally reached a peace agreement with their tribal leaders and began to pay them for transporting materials to and from the acreage. "In 1936, when there were major attacks against Jewish settlements, the Bedouins helped defend Maabarot." In turn, Bumi told us that in 1948, members of the kibbutz protected the Bedouin tribe against attacking Jewish troops.

Following the question-and-answer session, I headed to the clubroom. On my way, the long-term Australian volunteer, Philip, asked me join him for a game of backgammon. His invitation surprised and pleased me. We had never had much of a conversation before that night. The handsome, darkly tanned Aussie was usually by himself when I would see him in the community. I had heard his name mentioned many times. Rachel and Joseph, as well as Zahava and Dov, considered him a role model for the rest of us volunteers. Philip had worked there for almost a year and lived by himself in a single room within the kibbutz community. The Aussie reminded me of a high school acquaintance of mine, a championship wrestler with taut muscles and boundless energy. I had seen Philip work in the fields doing the labor of two men.

After playing a few games, he began to open up a bit. Philip revealed that he planned to leave Maabarot soon. "Been accepted at the Bezalel Academy of Art and Design in Jerusalem," he informed me. Later, I discovered that Bezalel, Israel's premier art school, had an international reputation.

When I asked if I could see some of his work, Philip turned me down. He said he did not feel comfortable showing his art to people in the community. I respected his feelings and never mentioned it again.

October 13: Zahava and Dov invite me over for the evening. They want to talk politics.

Sitting in their living room, Zahava and Dov revealed that they were very concerned about the crisis in Israeli politics. To me, there seemed to be so many unresolvable political issues in Israel. "Right-wing factions are trying to establish settlements in the occupied territories," Zahava explained. "It's causing serious problems within our government and the population in general." Dov completed her thought. "The settlements threaten potential peace agreements with the Palestinians as well as the bordering Arab countries. The right wingers are always creating a crisis."

October 16: My work supervisor shows me how to operate the tractor, and I spend the day turning over the soil in the cotton fields. It is ironic. Although I grew up surrounded by corn and wheat fields in south central Kansas, I had to come all the way to Israel to learn how to drive a tractor!

October 23: I have been curled-up in bed with serious cramps for the past few days. I am running at both ends and burning up with a fever. Luckily, my dutiful French roommate brings me toast, chicken broth and tea several times a day. He is a good man.

No one seemed to be worried about my condition except me. Élan and others called it the Devil's Grip, a common malady in the volunteer community. I felt like a dybbuk had discovered its way into my body. Pronounced dib-book, the demonic character "is the closest thing in Jewish folklore to a ghoul, vampire, incubus—a migrating spirit who had to find a living body to inhabit," revealed Rosten. "It is an evil spirit—usually the soul of a dead person that enters a living person on whom the dead has some claim."[7] The walking dead was exactly how I felt.

October 25: Élan left today for France. I will miss him and his quirky sense of humor. I could not have asked for a kinder, more considerate roommate. It's hard to imagine Élan in the corporate world. He is much too sensitive, compassionate, and empathetic. Rachel informs me that I will have a new roommate in a few days.

October 26: Rachel makes plans for volunteers to visit children's houses. They are located in a different section of the community than the adult duplexes.

We began the tour in the Kindergarten House, which had a kitchen, a large classroom with a lot of natural light, a playroom, and bedrooms then we moved on to the living quarters for children ages six through ten. The houses were all-inclusive units for living and learning. The separation of the two communities made so much sense to me. The arrangement allowed for parent and child to have their own living space and maintain their family relationship.

"Until their early teens, the boys and girls sleep in the same room [four to a room] and shower together," Rachel explained. "They grow up like sisters and brothers." For that very reason, I had read that kibbutz youth tended to marry partners from other kibbutzim. She concluded the tour in the babies' house, during naptime, where cribs filled two bedrooms. Staff members were cleaning the kitchen and the front room and making repairs outside in the play yard. "Children are truly the privileged class on the kibbutz," Rachel remarked.

"For the first six weeks of a baby's life the mother is released from her work duties on the kibbutz and devotes herself exclusively to feeding and looking after the child." [8] Following that span of time, the mother returned to work four hours a day until the baby stopped breast-feeding. Throughout that transition period, the mother continued to nurse her child and maintain frequent contact. When she was not available, a trained nurse attended to the needs of the young one.

"I'm kibbutz born, and I grew up in a children's house," commented Israeli citizen Rina Shir in a booklet she authored. "On opening my eyes first thing in the morning, the first person I saw was not my mother, but the nurse. She got me up, fed me, bathed me, took me for walks and played with me. Every afternoon they [parents] would come and fetch me to their room, where we would spend a few hours. My most wonderful childhood memories are those hours. Are there many mothers in the world who can devote a few hours a day totally to their children, fully rested and relaxed, free from household cares and financial worries?" [9]

October 27: I discover my new roommate when I come home from work. It is Josh, the man from the Tel Aviv youth hostel. What a hoot! He gives me a bear hug then a big kiss on the cheek. Josh has cut his hair and trimmed his beard. He looks better.

Now it would be my responsibility to orient Josh to kibbutz life. He accompanied me to dinner and then to the Club Room. The war veteran seemed at home from the beginning. The Massachusetts native had no trouble socializing with community members.

October 28: Rachel invites us to visit the classrooms of different age groups. Of course, education is of upmost importance to her.

One teacher reiterated that every house was also a classroom with an emphasis on cooperation rather than competition. Children learned at a very early age to work together as a group. Kibbutz Maabarot had adopted the project method of learning, focused on specific themes. For example, if the classroom decided to study the subject of cotton, then the students created their math problems, geography and history lessons, as well as their science projects around the theme of cotton. I noticed that classrooms contained no separate desks. The students clustered around tables and solved problems as a group.

November 3: Josh had another difficult night, more serious than a few nights ago. He tells me that he is struggling with flashbacks from his service in Vietnam. Josh said that he had not had any problems with it for awhile but the nightmares started coming back a couple of months ago.

I woke in the middle of night to Josh murmuring to himself then he started to scream. I grabbed the flashlight from the night table and flicked it on. The Vietnam vet was tangled-up in his sheets, eyes wide open and trembling. Josh looked wasted. I jumped up, went to his bed, and sat down.

"Everything okay over there?" shouted a volunteer from next door.

"Yeah, it's okay," I yelled back. I did not know if everything was okay or not. "How can I help," I asked Josh. "What can I do?"

"Hold me," Josh whispered, "just hold me." I lay beside my roommate and held him close for the rest of the night.

November 5: For the past two days, I have been working in the pharmaceutical factory, packing boxes with sealed pill bottles, stacking them, and loading them onto the conveyor belt. It is fast moving and makes me think of an "I Love Lucy" comedy sketch. Lucy is working on a conveyor belt packing donuts into boxes and she starts falling behind. All hell breaks loose. It was funny on TV.

It would not be funny here.

An older kibbutznik, Benjamin, works beside me in the factory. He looks a bit like Joseph, Rachel's husband. Both have thinning white hair and sun-toughened skin. At the end of the workday, he invites me to his apartment after dinner for coffee.

Ben and I spread out on the couch and talked while his wife, a high school science teacher, sat quietly in the chair next to their bookshelf. Self-conscious about her English-speaking ability, she preferred to listen rather than talk. During our conversation, my workmate brought up the controversial issue of hired labor on the kibbutz. "Since we've introduced industrial production into the Maabarot economy, we have had to hire outside labor," he said. That clearly troubled him. "Seems to me that hiring outside labor contradicts the foundation of kibbutz life," Ben told me, "but not everybody agrees with me." I had not thought much about the complexity of the issue until that moment, even though Rachel had given me a booklet that expressed a clear opinion on the issue. "A kibbutz that accepts, justifies, and benefits from paid labor slips, willy-nilly, to the other side of the barricade: from the camp of labor to that of the employer. The laborer will see the kibbutz as his employer; exploiting his work." [10]

Ben informed me that the issue of hired labor in the agricultural and industrial sectors of the community caused concern for the kibbutz movement. "If we don't find a workable solution about hiring outside labor, that issue will ultimately destroy us."

November 8: The last few days I have been working with the Aussie in the orchards. I like spending time with him. We work well together and move efficiently from tree to tree. I am glad to be out of the pill factory. When Philip and I leave the orchard at the end of the workday, we agree to meet in the clubroom following dinner.

"Still interested in seeing my art work?" Philip asked after winning our third backgammon game. What a surprise. We had not talked art since the long-term volunteer made it clear he did not want to show his work in the community.

"You bet," I responded.

"It's over at my place," he said. "Let's go over there now?"

Located in an older section of the kibbutz, he lived in a complex set aside for long-termers and family visitors. Furnished for only one person, his tidy room held a single bed, a desk with a straight-backed chair, and a floor lamp beside a lounge chair. In one corner, near the window, was an easel.

Philip pulled out a large, black vinyl portfolio from under the bed. With care, he placed it near the pillow and unzipped it. The artist removed the pencil and charcoal drawings and slowly passed them over to me one by one briefly commenting on each. He had sketched them on large pieces of thick textured paper. His work, mechanical and architectural looking, integrated small, compact geometric figures into various formations. Their dark and enigmatic web-like connections reminded me of the mind-twisting woodcuts and lithographs created by M. C. Escher. Like Escher, his art explored perspective, physical space, and mirrored images.

"I was willing to show you my work because I'll be leaving in a couple of days," Philip told me, "and I've gotten to know you better." After I handed back the last drawing, it felt like the appropriate time to return to my room. When I got up to leave, he asked if I would stay longer. Philip wanted to schmooz.

"There's nothing better, to get something off your chest, than a schmooz with a friend," Rosten explained. The word is both a verb and a noun. "Schmooz means a friendly, gossipy, prolonged, heart-to-heart talk . . ."[11]

We moved onto the veranda and sat on the concrete steps in the dark. Following a comfortable silence, Philip shared thoughts about living on the kibbutz and his personal life.

"I love the people here at Maabarot," said the artist, "but it's difficult for a single male or female to live here." He paused. "The kibbutz way of life is designed for couples and families."

"That why you spend so much time by yourself?" I asked.

"Of course," he replied. "I am part of the community because I've been here so long but I do not feel like it 'cause I'm an older, single male. It's a weird situation to be in."

I shared my experiences as a short-term volunteer. I mentioned how meaningful my relationships with the old-timers had become, how supported I felt working in a community that encouraged cooperation above competition. I mentioned the educational system, too. "I wish I'd had the opportunity to grow up in that kind a classroom, that kind of approach to learning. But most of all," I added, "I'm bowled over by the love and respect between parents and their kids." The experience had opened up a completely new perspective for me on parent and child relationships.

As we continued to schmooz, Philip revealed compelling aspects of his family life, a version of a story I had heard many times during my stay in Israel. He told me that both of his parents were concentration camp survivors. "They fled Germany in 1948 and immigrated to Australia."

"Why Australia?"

Philip shrugged, "Because it was as far away from Germany as they could get." He stretched his legs out in front of him, swinging one foot over the other, and wrapped his arms around himself tightly as if trying to hold something in. The long-termer remained quiet for a time. Perhaps he felt conflicted about going on with his personal story. Finally, he broke the silence. "Those camp experiences scarred them for life. They would always talk about it when I was growing up. It was an obsession with them." Another pause, "As an only child, I could not escape their chronic sadness and pain."

After completing his engineering degree, Philip realized

he needed to put distance between himself and his parents. To accomplish that, he decided to live in West Germany for a time. He needed to experience the country of his parents' births and nightmares. "Just wanted to mix with the people," Philip told me. "You know, listen to their conversations, walk their neighborhoods," he paused, "reclaim my family's history." Philip fell silent again, let out a sigh, released his arms, and relaxed. His ultimate destination had always been Israel. Philip knew he wanted to experience kibbutz life and study at the Bezalel Academy of Art and Design. As I listened to the Aussie liberate his story, I thought about the sketches I had just seen. Clearly, they expressed the man's childhood and his training as an engineer.

I needed to get to bed. After I told Philip how much I had appreciated our time together, we got up off the steps, stood for a time looking out into the night without speaking, then hugged.

November 13: Left the kibbutz early this morning to backpack around the country. Plan to return in a couple of weeks.

The previous night a few volunteers had arranged to meet with Rachel to express our appreciation for her kindness. She talked, at length, about her life, her views about the kibbutz, and the future of the movement. Rachel sounded optimistic but concerned about the right-wing political factions, religious fanatics, and their plans to expand settlements in occupied territory.

November 15: I am at Kibbutz Kerem Shalom. Rachel arranged for my visit. The dry, barren countryside is a stark contrast to the green of Maabarot. There are few trees here. It looks like the community just dropped into the middle of nowhere. It is in a precarious location, close to the borders of both Egypt and the Gaza Strip. Original plans were to meet Mickey, her son, and spend time with him for a couple of days but Mickey is in Tel Aviv and will not return until after my departure.

Mickey's former wife, Michelle, greeted me when I first arrived. The woman seemed distant. Rachel had not told me they were divorced, and Michelle had not expected to be my tour guide.

As we wandered around the small community and shared a few stories about our lives, she became more welcoming. "We have about sixty members in the community mostly between the ages of nineteen and twenty-seven," Michelle told me. "All of us grew up on kibbutzim and then formed a golan when we got to be army age." She explained that a golan was an arrangement by which a selective group of men and women went through basic training in the army, served six months then worked at developing land for a new kibbutz. They only reported to the military periodically. Michelle said that in three years, they had successfully grown three crops, raised turkeys for the market, and opened up a repair garage.

I stayed in Mickey's one-bedroom duplex, met his very young son, and became acquainted with other members of the community. My second night there, when looking through his book collection, I discovered a photo album filled with nude color photographs of Michelle. They were extraordinary shots taken through the progression of her pregnancy. With each photograph, her breasts became fuller and her belly grew larger. The color shots were stunning, intimate, and sacred.

Early the next day, I left for Jerusalem. Two weeks later, I flew to Athens with my classmate, Ann. Then we hitchhiked across Greece, boarded a ferry for Italy, and continued our trek into Western Europe. By the end of March, I had returned to the States and moved to New York City.

CHAPTER FOUR

~

Hitchhiker's Sinkhole

At one end of my block sat a Puerto Rican bodega stocked with Spanish canned goods and a selection of liquor. Open cardboard boxes, overflowing with fruits and vegetables, lined both sides of the narrow center aisle. Every time I shopped there, I knocked something over. Across the street, an African American family owned the funeral parlor where the bright pink façade screamed for attention. Above the awning, flashing black letters advertised their services for the departed. My Upper West Side Manhattan neighborhood, a bubbling melting pot, offered a microcosm of America's cultural and ethnic diversity.

The upscale flower shop at the other end of the block catered to the well-to-do residing on nearby Riverside Avenue. The florist's colorful and exotic flower arrangements in her display windows always brightened my day. Across the street from the florist, a two-for-the-price-of-one cinema occupied the corner where the enticing smell of buttered popcorn wafted from under its double doors day and night. I went out of my way to walk past the theater just to catch a whiff of that seductive aroma. In the middle of the block was a century-old, red brick Roman Catholic Church. Latinos, Haitians, a smattering of African Americans, and Asians squeezed into its crowded pews at Sunday Mass. The church's basement provided space for a senior citizen center and AA meetings in addition to a soup kitchen and an active youth group.

I had recently moved into a nine-story building on West

107th, between Broadway and Amsterdam, with my girl-friend, Lillian. We shared the apartment with three other people and a neurotic cat. Our sparsely furnished bedroom looked onto the brick façade of the building next door. At night, we could hear a mix of Salsa and Motown, police sirens, and family quarrels.

Lillian had a summer job with Brooklyn Congresswoman Elizabeth Holtzman. In September, she planned to begin a women's history graduate program in upstate New York. I had completed my first semester of graduate night classes at New York University. My day job with the Vera Institute of Justice, a criminal justice research organization, had ended by the middle of June. Although selected to participate in the UN Student Internship Program, with dozens of others from around the world, my assignment with their Press Office would not begin until the first week of August. I had July free.

With limited funds, a thirty-day window, and an appetite for adventure, I decided to hitchhike to Alaska and back to celebrate the Bicentennial. The trek would cover more than eight thousand five hundred miles.

In preparation, I acquired detailed Canadian and Alaskan road maps, plotted my route, and pored over scads of travel literature. I patched up my weathered backpack, blue pup tent, and an old ground cover. I washed my sleeping bag, purchased a set of lightweight cooking utensils along with a durable rain poncho and a cloth-covered canteen then replaced the worn soles on my weather-beaten hiking boots. In my first aid kit, I made sure to include mosquito repellent and a month-long supply of mega-vitamins.

My final purchase, a St. Christopher's medal, invoked the patron saint of travelers. Defined as objects that protect a person from danger, I had discovered the psychological importance of carrying amulets on the open road. My collection included an agate given to me by a friend, a piece of turquoise found on a Navajo Reservation, a silver scarab purchased at a music festival, a smooth, black stone picked up on the Jersey shore, and a string of red worry beads that I haggled over at a shop in Jerusalem's Old City. My amulets, reminders of spiritual guides, friendships, and experiences, helped ground me. They kept me company.

The night before departure, I stuffed two changes of cotton clothing, a pair of shorts, and a wool sweater into my backpack, along with a jacket, a pair of long underwear, and a baseball cap. My first aid kit, ace bandages, two lengths of rope, and a hand-sized Hohner harmonica fit into one of the side compartments of the pack; flip-flops, a flashlight, and a deck of cards filled the other one. I arranged the maps and a small box of matches along with a copy of the *International Youth Hostel Booklet* and my Swiss Army Knife in the front compartment. A blank journal, Norman Spring's *Alaska: The Complete Travel Book* wrapped in a clear plastic bag, and my shaving kit fit snugly on top of the packed clothes just underneath my rain poncho and small bath towel.

As spiritual preparation, I set aside solo time for a visualization exercise and conjured up the images of three outstanding American road warriors. Dust Bowl minstrel and political activist, Woody Guthrie, provided an expansive vision and a sense of self-confidence. The spirit of author John McPhee reminded me to maintain a keen eye for details and respect for cultural differences. Charles Kuralt, television commentator and *On the Road* narrator, encouraged me to be a compassionate listener to the life stories of everyday heroes I would encounter on the road.

Just before take-off, I spent a few days with former Livingston College friends, Tony and Sue, who lived in Buffalo. Late June, they drove me across the Canadian border and dropped me on the side of the highway just outside a village north of Niagara Falls. I planted myself on the shoulder of the blacktop, displayed my cardboard sign printed in big, black letters–STUDENT: ALASKA OR BUST, extended my arm, and raised my thumb.

In less than thirty minutes, a yellow green Volkswagen Van pulled off the highway. An arm appeared out a window, and the hand motioned for me to come forward. Hoisting my pack and clutching my sign, I shuffled up to the front passenger side where a young woman with frizzy blonde hair braided into pigtails stuck her head out the window.

"Goin' to Alaska, eh?" she asked with a wide grin.

"That's my plan," I replied. "How far are you folks going?" I could see three adults, same number of kids, and luggage piled up in the very back of the van. There would be just enough room for one more person and a backpack.

"We're headed for Vancouver," she said, "we're gonna drive day and night." I leaned in closer to hear. "We'll only stop for bathroom breaks and food."

"Sounds good to me," I told her.

A pony-tailed man, on the driver's side, hopped out and raised the back door where I loaded my pack and sign. After one of the kids slid the side door open and scooched over, I jumped in. The intoxicating scent of patchouli permeated the interior of the van. I could hear the smoldering voice of Canadian Joni Mitchell singing "Help Me" on the cassette player that hung just beneath the dash. Within a short time, we introduced ourselves and began to talk like old friends. Tom and Rebecca, in their mid-twenties, were sitting in the front seat. They were the parents of the two young kids, a boy and a girl, who sat with me in the back seat. The other little girl, curled up like a kitten with the luggage and taking a nap, belonged to Linda, a single mother in her late twenties sitting by the window on the opposite side of the kids.

The adults were graduate students and residents of Canada's New Brunswick Province where they lived in a commune. For part of their summer break, they had decided to visit friends in Vancouver. "We stopped in Niagara Falls for the kids," Tom explained. Within a few hours, we were on the Trans-Canada Highway heading north and west around the expansive Georgian Bay and up to Sudbury, Ontario.

We drove continuously, swapping stories, listening to mellow music, and playing car games with the kids. They were bright and enjoyable travel partners. The highway hugged the waterfront through Sault Sainte Marie and around Lake Superior then began a slow climb into the lake country of Ontario. No time for photographs. Images were just imprints on my mind. Day turned to night turned to day as we alternated drivers and slept in between shifts. Weaving its way westward through Winnipeg, Manitoba, the Trans-Canada carried us into the plains of Saskatchewan and around its capital city, Regina. Later, it crossed the border into Alberta Province and eventually skirted past Calgary. In the early evening, my cross-country ride ended at Lake Louise, a village in Banff National Park, where the highway split in two.

My Canadian friends continued to drive south all the way to Vancouver. The next day, however, I would head north on Highway 93.

Near the center of town, I spotted the youth hostel, checked in, and threw my pack on a lower bunk beside an open window. I knew that fresh air would be a blessing when sleeping in the same room with a half-dozen other backpackers. After a welcomed hot shower, I heated a can of soup in the communal kitchen, ate by myself, and spent the rest of the evening writing in my journal.

Early the following morning, I cooked hot cereal with toast and black coffee before making my way back onto Highway 93 with sign in hand. Soon, an old green Ford pickup pulled over just ahead of me, and the passenger door swung open. A young man with a moustache and long sideburns sat behind the steering wheel with a Cleveland Indians baseball cap angled atop his head. A cute, short-legged, long haired, mutt sat beside him.

"Toss yer stuff in the back and hop in," said the baseball fan. I threw my pack into the truck bed but carried the sign into the cab where the three of us shared a lumpy, imitation leather seat.

"Name's Marty," he said and extended his arm for a handshake. Marty had a strong grip. "Hairy little critter is Toby." When I put out my hand, Toby sniffed it and offered me his right paw.

Driving north through the park, Marty introduced himself as a student at New Hampshire's Franconia College but originally from Cleveland, where his folks still lived. "Actually, I'm on my way to Vancouver," he said, "but decided to take a detour through the park. I've heard so much about it." Marty, a skilled potter, eventually planned to open a ceramics shop in that West Coast city.

When the conversation leaned into politics and human rights, I mentioned my stint with VISTA and work with a local Amnesty International chapter on the Upper West Side of Manhattan. "My dad's a heavy contributor to Amnesty," Marty told me, "has been for years."

Banff National Park, comprised of a half-dozen individual recreational areas, swelled with dramatic mountainscapes and dense forests. They bordered the provinces of Alberta and British Columbia. Near a trail-head, Marty pulled over and stopped. Opening up the glove compartment, he pulled out a small plastic bag of weed and papers. "You smoke?" Marty asked as he began to roll a joint.

"Once in a while," I replied. The last time I smoked a joint I was visiting former house-mates living in a dilapidated, three-story, Victorian in Washington, DC. We lit up and passed it around the table after a big dinner in the communal kitchen. I got so stoned that I talked endlessly in at least a half-dozen accents. They could not shut me up. I walked out of the house and all the way down to the Lincoln Monument where I had a lengthy conversation with Honest Abe, about what I cannot recall. I do remember that Jim and Pat, my closest friends in the house, came looking for me after my extended absence. They finally tracked me down on Vermont Avenue, near Thomas Circle, casually making my way back to the house. When Marty handed me the joint, I took a hit and passed it back. It did not take much marijuana for me to begin acting silly. When Marty passed the joint back to me, I took another hit and called it quits.

We walked for a stretch along the trail while Toby explored up ahead. By the time we turned around and headed back, I could fully appreciate the intensity of nature's myriad colors and the movement of the giant trees. Every other word out of my mouth happened to be "Wow!"

When we reached a fork in the road, near Tete Jaune Cache, British Columbia, Marty and I parted ways. The Cleveland Indians fan planned to drive south to Vancouver on the Yellowhead Highway, but I continued to venture northward. I offered Marty gas money, but he refused to take it.

"Keep it," he said. "You'll need it to get all the way back to New York. It was great havin' you along for the ride," remarked the potter.

A few brief, uneventful rides with native British Columbians got me as far as Prince George where my ride let me off at the intersection of Yellowhead and Highway 97. In no time at all an Assemblies of God minister, on his way to a religious conference in Dawson Creek, picked me up. Pastor Larry, a frumpy man in dark suit pants, wore an open-collared, white shirt that pulled tightly at the buttons over his belly. He had combed his thinning brown hair over an obvious bald spot. Pastor Larry had covered the back seat of his dated, dark blue, sedan with religious literature that he intended to distribute at the conference.

"Whataya think of Jimmy Swaggart?" I asked the pastor. We had already introduced ourselves and shared some small talk. In the news lately, I knew that Swaggart had an affiliation with the Assemblies of God denomination.

"Yer askin' about the televangelist?" He glanced at me peering over the top of his black-framed glasses.

"Yea, the man from Louisiana," I answered. "He's an Assemblies of God minister, right?"

"Yea, he is," replied the pastor. "In answer to yer question, I don't care much for his preachin'. He's in it fer the money."

"I think so, too." A long period of silence ensued. Then Larry asked me the question that I was anticipating.

"You accepted Jesus as yer Lord and Savior?" he inquired. I think he asked out of genuine interest.

"Well, I can tell ya this," I talked slowly, thinking about each word coming out of my mouth. "I accept Jesus as an extraordinary role model for his time and for ours." That is all I said about the Savior.

The pastor appeared to be satisfied with my answer, and we did not talk about Jesus or religion anymore. Instead, Larry spoke about his wife and two sons. I could tell he had wanted to talk about them all along. The family man told me that his younger son had frequent run-ins with the law and Larry clearly blamed himself for his son's problems. He questioned if he had been a good father. The pastor unloaded his concerns, and I listened with interest.

Drivers frequently opened up to me about their personal problems and shared intimate details of their lives, as I did with them. We would never see each other again. I listened to Larry's stories and sometimes gave feedback in appreciation for my ride. The remainder of our time together, Pastor Larry mentioned his wife's medical problems and said that he thanked the good Lord for Canada's universal medical coverage. "I'd be in the poor house now without that coverage." He also shared stories about his flawless older son who was doing well in college. Just north of Dawson Creek, he pulled into a truck stop off Highway 97, known as the Alaska Highway, and bought me a sandwich and a cup of coffee.

Shortly after Larry drove back into town, I caught a ride with a local trucker just as he pulled away from the gas pump. When we reached his turn-off, some miles past Fort Saint John, the driver let me out at a basic rest area. Although dark, I spotted a few picnic tables, a garbage barrel, and an outhouse. With no traffic on the road and an overcast sky threatening, it occurred to me that I only had a Swiss Army Knife to protect me from wild critters. In a flash, I felt an anxiety rush. It grabbed my chest then quickly spread into my arms and legs. My heart began to thump hard against my ribcage and I started to shiver from head to foot. When a wave of nausea hit me, I sank down to the ground and stayed there for a spell. As my mind began to clear and the nausea dissipated, I got up, gave myself a pep talk out-loud, and started to jump around. I needed that physical release.

"It's about havin' faith, brother!" I shouted like a Holy Roller preacher man. "It's about havin' faith in myself! Havin' faith in others! Havin' faith in God!" I prayed aloud, too. Pastor Larry would have been pleased. By the time I wrapped up my pep talk and finished the prayer, something had changed. I felt at peace. Then I went about the business of setting up a camping spot near one of the picnic tables, lay the ground cover, and pitched my tent. Just as it began to sprinkle, I crawled inside with backpack and cardboard in hand.

At 3:45 a.m., I woke up with a start. I checked my watch with the flashlight. The rain had stopped, but I could feel wet at the bottom of my sleeping bag. My feet were damp. I shined the flashlight on a puddle of water in the bottom quarter of the tent. I curled up around the backpack and waited for daylight to break.

The following day brought good luck. As soon as I reached the Alaska Highway, a trucker stopped for me. Chuck, the driver, was hauling construction materials from Dawson Creek all the way north to Whitehorse in the Yukon Territory. A bushy red beard and wild hair framed the man's cherubic face. His green flannel shirt, faded blue jeans, and tanned leather boots gave the appearance of a cowboy, perhaps his intention. Probably in his early forties, Chuck said that he had hauled goods between the two towns for almost a decade.

When he stopped in Fort Nelson for unexpected repairs on his rig, the trucker asked me to join him for lunch. Chowing down on eggs, bacon, hash browns, and toast, he shared some his personal story.

"I'm a loner," Chuck revealed. "Both my folks are dead, but I have a sister who lives in Prince George [New Brunswick]." He paused a second and took a sip of coffee. "But we hardly ever communicate." Because Chuck liked to hunt and fish, he had built a cabin on Lake Williston, west of Dawson Creek, a few years back. The truck driver spent a lot of his free time there. "I play the acoustic guitar," he said proudly as the waitress cleared the dishes and refilled our coffee cups. "Used to play in a Country Western band before I took up truck drivin'." He explained the obvious; with a truck driver's schedule, he could not maintain regular rehearsals or a performance routine. "I miss the band, the gigs, the guys," he added. "They were my family, ya know?" Our layover in Fort Nelson took longer than expected. We didn't get back on the road until later that afternoon.

Chuck, an easy man to ride with, had a mellow personality. We slipped in and out of casual conversation while listening to Merle Haggard, Willie Nelson, and Dolly Parton on cassette tapes. Crossing the provincial border into the Yukon Territory, just on the other side of Watson Lake, we drove head on into a wall of rain that would not let up. Chuck slowed the diesel truck to a crawl. "We may have to stop somewhere soon," he warned, leaning over the out-sized steering wheel and gripping it tightly, "hard to maintain control of the rig in this kind of downpour." The heavy cloud cover made it black outside. Eventually, he steered into an isolated two-pump gas station with a small café and a boxy, wood frame house next door. A single light shone in the front window behind closed curtains. Chuck said he knew the couple who owned the place.

After pulling on his rain poncho, the trucker climbed down from the cab and clomped through puddles to the house, walked up the front porch steps, and knocked on the door. The outside light flicked on and a woman, wrapped up in a long, pink, terrycloth robe with curlers in her hair, opened the door. She stood there halfway in and halfway out. The woman appeared to be happy to see Chuck by the way she positioned her body up against the doorframe. As they talked, she lit a cigarette, took a few puffs then walked back inside the house. In a flash, she returned wearing a long raincoat and a pair of galoshes.

When Chuck motioned for me to get out of the truck, I pulled on my poncho, lowered myself down into the muck, and followed them around to a makeshift bedroom behind the gas station. Once inside, he introduced me to Stella. A bedside table, with a kerosene lamp, stood between two cots piled high with blankets. A porcelain pitcher of water sat on top of the dresser and a back door led to the outhouse. It did not take long for the two of us to sort things out, claim our respective cots, and crash. Eventually Chuck's snoring became white noise, and I fell asleep.

Stella treated us to bowls of hot oatmeal with butter, brown sugar, and raisins and cups of strong black coffee early the next morning. Chuck called the food "trucker's fuel." While we ate, they bantered affectionately as close friends, or occasional lovers, tend to do. I never did meet her husband.

When we reached Whitehorse, the trucker kindly drove me to the other side of town where the Alaska Highway continued to Haines Junction. I didn't expect to have problems catching a ride but that one hundred-mile stretch, between Whitehorse and Haines Junction, became a hitchhiker's sinkhole. I stood there so long that I became part of the scenery, made me think of Gertrude Stein's pithy comment about Oakland, California. "There is no there, there!" Finally, I tagged a lift.

On July 4, 1976, I stood tall and proud in Tok Junction, Alaska, the Land of the Midnight Sun. I had successfully reached my destination. Happy Birthday, USA! Tok Junction, along with Fairbanks and Anchorage, were three major points that constituted what natives called the Alaska Triangle. If I continued north, I could reach Fairbanks by that afternoon. If I headed south, I would have probably made Anchorage by the end of the day. I pondered then turned over my cardboard sign, pulled out my black magic marker, and printed–STUDENT TO FAIRBANKS. Soon, I joined two middle-aged men named Carl and Sammy, in their beat-up station wagon weighted down by a metal ladder tied to the roof and paint supplies piled high in the back. The car's interior smelled like turpentine. I had not thought to ask what they were doing in Tok Junction but suspected they were picking up supplies.

Carl, the driver, and his sidekick, Sammy, proved to be big talkers, hard drinkers, and accomplished tale-spinners. Along the way, we made two beer stops at funky roadside bars where Sammy and Carl were well acquainted with the bartenders. They drank beer like water. I accepted their offer of one draft but turned down a second one. "More'n one beer and I'll have to stop on the side of the road every fifteen minutes to take a whiz," I admitted to the painters. Besides, someone in the car had to stay sober. When we left the second bar, I volunteered to drive and Carl handed me the keys.

"Where do ya wanna get out?" Sammy asked when we finally reached the outskirts of Fairbanks.

"At the university," I replied.

"We know it," Carl told me. "We'll drop ya off at one of the dormitories"

They directed me onto the university grounds and over to a complex of four dormitories where I parked the car. "Here's our address in Anchorage in case ya run into any trouble," Sammy handed me a card. "We share the apartment with a two other painters. There's usually someone there."

"Yeah and once in a while we hire a couple of women to come over and show us a good time," declared Carl with a snicker. "Yer welcome to bed down there if you need to."

After they pulled away, I wandered around the dormitories in search of an unlocked door. At Lathrop Hall, I discovered a side door propped open with an empty soda can. Walking inside as if I belonged there, I discovered a living room with a kitchenette on the first floor. Showers and toilets were just down the hall. The place was deserted. Students must have been gone for the long holiday weekend. After storing my pack and sign in a corner of the living room, just behind the couch, I headed for the showers with my towel and shaving kit in hand. After drying off and changing into clean clothes, I hiked into town, tracked down a Laundromat, left my dirty clothes in a washer, and walked the nearly empty streets. The town appeared to be shutdown except for a lonesome grocery store and the gas station. The attendants told me that the natives did not celebrate with fireworks because it never got completely dark that time of the year. After returning to the dorm with a pack full of clean clothes, a bag of groceries, and a bottle of beer, I heated a can of beans, made a ham sandwich, downed the brew, and collapsed onto my sleeping bag stretched out close to an open window. I fell asleep to the familiar sounds of a polka band playing in the distance.

When I woke up in the morning, I could barely move. I ached all over, and I felt like puking, must have picked up some kind of bug along the way. I stayed flat on my back most of the day except for shuffles back and forth to the bathroom.

By mid-afternoon, a day later, I had arrived in Denali National Park, home of Mount McKinley. It is the highest peak in North America, measuring more than twenty thousand feet. The park and the preserve, spanning nine thousand five hundred miles, were just off Highway 3 between Fairbanks and Anchorage, where grizzlies and caribou, lynx and moose, Dall sheep and wolves, existed in a natural balance. I checked into the park's youth hostel and stored my pack in one of the lockers. Having recovered from my malady, I spent the remainder of the day exploring the rugged acreage within doable hiking range of the park's visitor center.

I boarded a bus, the following day, that transported me deep into the park's interior and made frequent stops to let the moose and caribou amble their way across the two-lane road. Sixty-five miles into the interior, I got out at the Eielson Center from where I could see clearly the outline of the massive Alaskan Range and the Muldrow Glacier field. "A place so vast and unpeopled that if anyone could figure out how to steal Italy, Alaska would be a place to hide it," noted author John McPhee in *Coming into the Country*. Returning to the hostel late that day, I joined a group of fellow backpackers in preparing a community spaghetti dinner as we swapped road stories.

Parents of a New York friend, who worked with the Amnesty International office in Manhattan, met me in downtown Anchorage the following day. They kindly put me up in a spare bedroom with the luxury of an adjacent bathroom. Tom worked as a bush pilot, and Helen taught in the public school system. Before my departure, the pilot cooked a freshly caught salmon on his backyard grill that melted in my mouth. The next day my Anchorage hosts drove me out to Highway 1, where I climbed out of their van with a new cardboard sign– STUDENT TO TOK JUNCTION. By noon, I had reached Tok and turned over my sign–HAINES OR BUST!

To reach Haines Ferry, I had to hitchhike out of mainland Alaska, back into Canada's Yukon Territory, then travel south until I reached the Alaskan Islands. No land route existed between Anchorage and the Haines ferry dock. Having stood by the side of that road in Tok for hours, I became increasingly anxious. Before leaving New York, I figured out where I needed to be, at a particular time along the travel route, in order to be back in New York in time to begin my UN Student Internship Program. I had fallen behind a couple of days and drivers just continued to zip by me without even a glance. I felt invisible. Not far from where I had begun to feel rooted stood a convenience store. Maybe I could cadge a ride with a customer. Just as that thought popped into my head, I noticed a man drive up in a battered Volkswagen Van and park in front of the store. Although curtains covered the van's windows and hung down just behind the front seat, there did not appear to be anyone with him.

The long-haired driver, lanky, barefoot, and dressed in denim overalls, stepped out and stretched for a moment. From a distance, I followed him as he sauntered into the market and back to the dairy section. That is when I approached the man.

"Scuse me," I blurted out. The man swung around and faced me with a vacant look in his deep-set dark eyes. Thinner than I had thought, close up that man looked emaciated. "You headed towards Haines?" I did not even give him time to answer. "I need to catch the ferry in Haines." I paused for just a second. "My name's Bill," I said and stuck my hand out for a shake but he did not reciprocate. I dropped my hand but kept on blabbering. "If yer headin' in that direction, I can help you with gas money and the driving. Only luggage I have is my pack." I stopped to catch my breath and wait for his reply. He stood silent for the longest time, staring, as if he were looking right through me. I felt uncomfortable but determined to get the hell out of Tok.

Finally, the man responded in a listless monotone. "I think that'll be okay," he told me. "I'm drivin' over to Whitehorse. I can getcha to Haines Junction."

I let out a sigh of relief. "What's your name?" I asked but kept my hand down at my side.

"Jake," he told me.

When I hoisted my pack into the rear of the van, I noticed a pile of dirty camping equipment beside a narrow, blanket-covered, foam mattress and a good-sized covered washtub. After Jake loaded his bag of groceries next to my pack and sign, he retrieved packages of Hostess Cupcakes and Twinkies along with a plastic bottle of water, which he carried with him to the driver's seat. I tried to get a conversation going with the man but Jake stayed quiet. He seemed burned out, perhaps by drugs.

"I'm on my way back to New York," I told him.

No response. Jake continued to look straight ahead. He wolfed down a cream-filled cupcake, took a couple of swallows of water then finished off the other cupcake in no time at all.

"Where you from?"

He finally responded, "Lower forty-eight."

"How long you been in Alaska?"

"A year."

"What've you been doing?"

He did not answer my question directly, but said he had lost his job a few months ago and not been able to find any work since then. Jake did not look at me when he answered my questions. He clearly had no interest in asking me anything. The driver opened the package of Twinkies and began to consume them. His diet must have been sugar on top of more sugar. I gave up on conversation and tried to enjoy the scenery. Jake appeared to be a competent driver and certainly awake after having wolfed down four cream-filled treats by then.

After crossing into the Yukon Territory and passing through a small logging town, Jake slowed, pulled over, and asked me to drive. "I'm gonna get in the back," he told me. Jake crawled into the back and I slid over to the driver's seat. "Okay, you can start drivin' now," he said in his flat tone of voice. He spoke from behind the curtain not bothering to shift it aside. "Take it easy goin' around the curves."

I pulled back onto the Alaska Highway and began to drive. The quiet in the back triggered my macabre imagination that kicked into high gear. Jake could be a slasher. Any second, I thought, he might reach out from behind the curtain and slit my throat. Good Lord, maybe he'll pull a wire around my neck, choke me to death then dump my body in the woods. I finally realized that if Jake killed me, while I sat behind the steering wheel, we would both die. That helped calm me down.

Finally, I heard movement in the back, the sound of a wash-tub cover being removed then water sloshing about, and I smelled the pleasant scent of soap. "Are you kidding me?" I mouthed the words to myself. "Jake's taking a bath?" What a relief. A short time later, I heard him get out of the water, the whoosh of the towel as he dried himself, the clunk of the lid going back on the tub, and the rub of the fabric as he pulled on his overalls. In a few moments, Jake opened the curtain and climbed over into the passenger's seat. He had another package of cream-filled cupcakes in his hand.

"Feel better?" I inquired. He sure looked it.

"Yeah," he replied, tearing open the package.

We did not converse after that. Maybe Jake had always been a man of few words. When we reached Haines Junction, I gave him enough money to cover the gas and a little extra and waved goodbye. I do not think he even noticed. It began to rain. The Junction did not look like much, a single main street with shops that had canvas awnings reaching out over the sidewalks. I sought a dry spot, made a peanut butter and jelly sandwich, and ate it along with the apple picked up in Tok. I doubled over my ground cloth, laid it on the sidewalk butt-up against a building, unrolled my sleeping bag, and slid inside.

The sound of traffic woke me early. When I peered out from my bag, I saw a steady stream of cars and trucks, just a wide sidewalk away. Two kids were staring and pointing at me from inside their passing car. I must have looked like a wild man. Their parents kept looking straight ahead. At one of the Main Street cafes, I bought breakfast and hung around for two refills on the coffee. No need to make another sign, the only road led directly to Haines where travelers boarded the ferries and sailed through the Alaskan Inside Passage down to Seattle.

A couple, with an infant, surprised me when they gave me a lift. Once we reached Haines, they dropped me near the Alaska Marine Ferry office where I purchased an inexpensive deck ticket for foot passengers. Scheduled to depart at 11 p.m., it would dock at Juneau's Auke Bay the next morning.

At the office, I befriended a fellow backpacker named Eric from Detroit. He looked like my hitchhiking twin. We both carried exterior frame packs, pup tents, and sleeping bags attached with bungee cords. We were wearing the same colored baseball caps along with our dirty white T-shirts, droopy khaki pants, and muddy hiking boots. Only one obvious difference, Eric pulled his hair back into a ponytail. I wore a crew cut.

We spent part of the remaining day exploring the small town founded by Presbyterian missionaries in the 1880s. Lumber mills, fishing boats, canneries, and ferry traffic kept that backwater alive. Eric and I discovered a quiet bar, where we lingered over beers, slipped in and out of conversation, read some, and scribbled in our journals. By 10 p.m., the ferry authorities allowed us to board. Accommodations were clean and more than adequate but not fancy. By midnight, we had settled into our sleeping bags spread out on stationary reclining lounge chairs on the deck. In the morning, the ferry docked briefly at Auke Bay, on the outskirts of Juneau, where I disembarked. I planned to spend the day and night there then board another ferry the following day. Eric stayed on-board. He, too, had a self-imposed timetable and needed to get back to Detroit as soon as possible.

"Juneau, bright at night from across the channel, is dense and galactic under the dark shapes of the mountains," described author John McPhee. "From the same perspective in the day—with its ships at wharf side, its small-craft anchorage, its buildings all crowded before an uprising wilderness—it's a pocket city in a setting as wondrous as the setting of a city could ever be."[1]

As I wandered through the quaint streets of Juneau, I thought of New England. The small, wood frame homes, tidy yards, and narrow streets reminded me of Brandon, Vermont, the small village where I had worked with an American Friends Service Committee summer project as a high school student. At a bakery, I bought a warm loaf of sourdough. Later, I thumbed a ride out to the Mendenhall Glacier field and witnessed humongous chunks of the icy mass break off then crash noisily into the sparkling blue water below. Returning to Auke Bay, I pitched my tent on the deserted beach, stripped down, and slipped into the bag. Eventually the sound of water, lapping up against the shore, lulled me to sleep.

"Whoosh, whoosh, whoosh," those enigmatic sounds awakened me. My eyes remained closed but I could feel the warmth of the morning sun filtering through the nylon tent. "Whoosh, whoosh, whoosh," I heard them again. Opening my eyes, I peered out from between the tent flaps. The sounds were coming from the bay. I pulled on my underwear, crawled out of the tent, and walked barefoot to the water's edge. The sunlight sparkled off the greenish blue water.

Not far from where I stood, an immense whirling motion began to form in the bay. The water churned faster and faster and faster. Suddenly, an enormous, glistening, black and white humpback whale broke through the water's surface, lifted itself up into the air, arched gracefully, and plunged back into the depths. Immediately, a companion imitated the movements. They looked choreographed. The waters quieted briefly then began to churn. I heard the now familiar whooshing sounds and, again, the whales playfully leaped out of the water. To my delight, they repeated their dance over and again just for me. I broke out in goose bumps.

Feeling inches tall in comparison to their immense size, I waded into the icy water just to share something in common with those magnificent creatures. Standing there, I had an "Ah-ha!" moment. I owed my entire existence to the natural world that surrounded me, so obvious and yet so easy to forget. By midmorning, I boarded a ferry that weaved its way through the Alaskan Islands. Natural walls of stone, blanketed in myriad shades of shimmering green and blue lichen, rose up repeatedly on either side of the boat.

We docked for a few hours in Sitka, once called the Paris of the Pacific then in Saint Petersburg, referred to as Little Norway. Ketchikan, our final stop before sailing out of the Inside Passage had a reputation for its finely crafted totem poles.

Before arriving in Seattle, I met a middle-aged couple who offered to take me into Portland. In fact, they delivered me to Ann's front doorstep in the wee hours of the morning.

Ann, my Livingston College classmate whom I had encountered two years before in the Tel Aviv Youth Hostel, sleepily greeted me at the door. Upon completing our volunteer stints on the kibbutzim, we had flown to Athens together then backpacked through Greece and Italy. Ann had just completed her first year at Lewis and Clark School of Law. After our brief visit of a few days, she drove me to the outskirts of the city and let me off at a truck stop on Interstate 84. From there, I began the final cross-country stretch of my adventure. I had one week to get back to the East Coast, STUDENT–NEW YORK CITY OR BUST!

My luck held. When a trucker startled me with one long pull of his horn, just as he turned onto the interstate, I scrambled into his cab. After lifting my pack and cardboard sign over the passenger's seat onto a bed made up in the back, I introduced myself.

"Good to meet ya, Bill." The trucker had big hands. "I'm George." He had to reach Omaha, Nebraska, in a few days. That meant I would make it halfway across the States with my first ride. I settled into the comfortable seat with cushioned armrests.

By nightfall, we made a second gas and food stop. The thirty-something trucker started chattering when we got back on the road. Soon, he began to whistle, then broke into song. "Oh Lord, won't ya buy me a Mercedes Benz? My friends all drive Porsches I must make amends. . ."

I could tell he had popped some Speed. That did not surprise me. Over the years, I had hitchhiked with at least a half-dozen truckers who used the pharmaceutical to stay awake on long hauls. Given his pumped up state of mind, I thought it appropriate that he began to belt out one of my Janis Joplin favorites. I joined in and sang verse two. "Oh Lord, won't ya buy me a color TV? Dialing for Dollars is trying to find me. . ." Then we joined voices on verse three. "Oh Lord, won't you buy me a night on the town. I'm counting on you Lord please don't let me down. . ."

George continued to sing, whistle, talk, and chew gum, around the clock, as he barreled through Boise, Idaho, and into Ogden, Utah. After turning onto Interstate 80, he sped easterly through Cheyenne, Wyoming, crossed into Nebraska and kept it floored as he whizzed by North Platte, then Grand Island, and circled around Lincoln. When we reached Omaha, George drove me to a gas station on the east side of the city where my momentum slowed considerably.

Hours later, I sat hunched over in the back of a pick-up with two Mexican migrant farm workers and a full-grown, German Shepherd on our way through Iowa. The dog belonged to the other two gents sitting in the cab. With an overcast sky, the temperature dropped. The three of us huddled together for warmth, shoulder to shoulder, covered with my unzipped sleeping bag. The affectionate Shepherd curled up beside me and laid his furry head in my lap then fell asleep.

Late in the evening, the sky had cleared and the temperature had warmed a bit. Our driver turned into a deserted rest stop where awning covered picnic tables dotted the grounds. Each of us claimed one, stretched out, and fell asleep. Hours after settling down, however, highway patrolmen with high-powered flashlights awakened our crew.

"Git up!" A deep voice made the demand from behind a blinding light. At first, I felt disoriented. "I said git up!" he repeated.

I heard the dog growl then bark. I unzipped my bag and sat up rubbing the sleep from my eyes. Two uniformed officers stood on either side of me.

After rounding up the other men, then illegally searching the cab of the truck, the patrolmen informed us there would be no arrests but told us to move on–pronto! We gathered our stuff, splashed cold water on our faces in the bathroom, hopped into the truck, and sped away. They followed us for awhile then turned off at an exit. A few miles beyond that, our driver stopped at a 24-hour café where we knocked back cups of coffee before continuing the journey.

Hours later, I found myself standing on an entrance ramp, midway through Ohio, late in the afternoon. By dusk, I assumed that I would be camping for the night. That was when Saul, a Jewish Unitarian Universalist minister from Jacksonville, Florida, gave me a lift. "I've been visiting relatives," he told me. The minister planned to stay on the interstate until crossing the border into Pennsylvania. Saul wore an open-collared plaid shirt with khaki shorts and Birkenstocks. The minister's salt and pepper stubble complimented his handsome chiseled face and green eyes. Despite being ten years my senior, we had a lot in common.

Both of us had grown up in small Midwestern towns. We were active in civil rights work in the South during the 1960s and 1970s and demonstrated against the Vietnam War. Saul had also volunteered at an antiwar coffeehouse, Coffeehouse Oleo, outside Fort Hood, Texas, and spent time in jail for nonviolent civil disobedience. Saul and I were comrades. I enthusiastically told him about conjuring up the spirits of Woody Guthrie, John McPhee, and Charles Kuralt, before departing for Alaska. "Couldn't have selected three more capable men for inspiration," he assured me. When he turned south heading for Florida, I continued eastward on that ribbon of highway.

By the end of July, one month after my friends in Buffalo had driven me across the border, and into Canada, I had made it back to New York. Standing near the George Washington Bridge, I folded my cardboard sign, descended the subway stairs, and boarded the train for my ride home.

CHAPTER FIVE

~

Wise Men Fish Here

"There is a strong current of nostalgia for the '70s and early '80s in New York, even among those who never lived through it," explained Edmund White in *T Magazine*, "the era when the city was edgy and dangerous, when women carried Mace in their purses, when even men asked the taxi driver to wait until they'd crossed the 15 feet to the front door of their building, when a blackout plunged whole neighborhoods into frantic looting, when subway cars were covered with graffiti, when Balanchine was at the height of his powers and the New York State Theater was New York's intellectual salon, when John Lennon was murdered by a Salinger-reading born again, . . .

This was the last period in American culture when the distinction between highbrow and lowbrow still pertained, when writers and painters and theater people still wanted to be (or were willing to be) 'martyrs to art.' This was the last moment when a novelist or poet might withdraw a book that had already been accepted for publication and continue to fiddle with it for the next two or three years. . . .

Those were the years when rents were low, when would-be-writers, singers, dancers could afford to live in Manhattan's (East, if not West) Village, before everyone marginal was further marginalized by being squeezed out to Bushwick or Hoboken." White's article "Why Can't We Stop Talking About New York in the Late 1970s?" described the city I remembered.

Graduate school prompted my move to New York but when awarded a Ford Foundation Human Rights Grant, I took a six-month leave from academia to work with the Amnesty International team at the UN following my summer internship. Simultaneously, I began a weekend acting course at the American Academy of Dramatic Arts. The all-day class, taught by Dr. MacDougal, met every Saturday. MacDougal selected Edgar Lee Master's *Spoon River Anthology*, epitaphs spoken by small town residents, as our final production. Each actor played multiple roles. An ideal choice, Master's *Anthology* offered me the opportunity to try on numerous personalities.

Although I had played the lead in high school theater productions and, later, participated in political street theater in Louisville, the American Academy of Dramatic Arts weekend program provided an introduction to study acting as a serious art form. Upon completing the program, I felt a compelled to pursue an acting career.

Upon the suggestion of a workmate, a theater professional, I auditioned for a scene study class taught by the stage and television actor, Rae Allen, at the 78th Street Theatre Lab and she accepted me. Mark and Dana Zeller were directors of the newly opened actor-training studio. On their first floor stood a small theater, acting classes and rehearsal space took place on the second, and Mark, Dana, and their infant son lived on the third. Prior to opening the Lab, Mark had performed primarily on stage and taught voice and Shakespeare at the Herbert Berghof Studios in Greenwich Village. Dana's focus had always been the stage. Both Rae and Dana had studied for years with Uta Hagen at the Berghof Studios. A highly respected stage actor, Ms. Hagen played the leading Broadway role as Martha in Edward Albee's *Whose Afraid of Virginia Wolf.* Hagen's acting technique greatly influenced the Zeller's program.

For the following two years, 1976 to 1978, I studied full-time at the 78th Street Theatre Lab where Mark and Dana had brought together a dozen men and women, most of us in our mid-twenties, to work with one another. Intense, instructive, and supportive, I could not have found a better training program. The small, tight-knit group of actors became my extended family. Mark would eventually cast and direct me in two, one-act plays: *Margaret's Bed* by William Inge and Peter Schaffer's *The Private Ear*.

At the conclusion of my first day in Rae Allen's acting class, she asked me to begin working on a demanding monologue from Edward Albee's *Zoo Story*, a two-character, one-act play set in Central Park. Jerry, my character, a disheveled and isolated gay man in his late thirties had become unhinged. That became clear in the play as he engaged in an increasingly intense conversation with a stranger named Peter, an unassuming, middle-aged man sitting on a neighboring park bench. A few weeks later, I did the monologue in class. In front of Rae and my fellow actors, I paced back and forth like a mad man flailing my arms and spewing out my words. I merely repeated the memorized script. I knew that I had not discovered the Jerry in Bill Claassen. At that point, I didn't even have a technique to help me do so. At the close of the monologue, I collapsed onto the park bench, set on stage, and waited for Rae's critique. I can still visualize the surprised, perhaps shocked, expression on her face. Despite my amateur performance, lack of training, and the fact that all of her other students were professional actors, Rae allowed me to remain in the class.

During my second term with Rae, she introduced me to the physical and creative work of Jerzy Grotowski. The controversial founder and director of the Polish Laboratory Theatre, Grotowski's company had become the vanguard of experimental theater. Rae began to incorporate his physical exercises into the beginning of each class. Grotowski's warm-up exercises were like an actor's Bikram Yoga. They stretched and opened every instrument in a performer's body. His teachings made me see and feel theater as a living, breathing, blood, sweat, and tears art form. Grotowski's "methods of actor training, aimed at the 'holy actor,' draw with unprecedented freedom, range and erudition on the major theatrical traditions of Europe and Asia: mime, Stanislavski, Peking Opera, Japanese No Theatre, Indian Theater." [1] Oftentimes called encounters, his theater company's performances were usually presented in small, intimate settings.

I had an opportunity to attend a gathering with Grotowski. At the Lindesfarne Teaching Center in Manhattan's landmark Episcopal Church on Sixth Avenue and 20th, the Polish director participated in a dialogue with social philosopher and cultural critic, William Irwin Thompson, followed by a lengthy question-and-answer session. I read a quote on Thompson's website that accurately described the Teaching Center and that evening in particular. "Lindisfarne-in-Manhattan was more of an intellectual jazz club, a headier vision of the Village Vanguard, in which Grotowski riffed on theatre." At the conclusion of that stimulating evening, I introduced myself to the Polish director. Richard Schechner, noted theater director and performance studies professor at New York University, captured my experience when he explained, "For many who met Grotowski, encountering him was special. His presence hit like a Zen master's slap in the face. I always approached him carefully, with biblical fear born of respect." [2]

My third scene study assignment in Rae's class came from William Gibson's *Two for the Seesaw*. My character, a soon to be divorced lawyer also named Jerry, had a law office in Nebraska but temporarily practiced in New York. Jerry and his Jewish girlfriend, Gittel, an out-of-work dancer, were in the process of moving into an apartment. In the assigned scene, Gittel slapped Jerry when he refused to move away from the apartment door during an argument. I had never experienced a stage slap in an acting class.

Rae had asked Sally, a talented actor my age, to play Gittel. Sally fit the role perfectly. Over a few weeks, we rehearsed the scene dozens of times. Because of her years of theater experience, Sally knew how to stage slap without injury. We never had problem in rehearsals. One week before we took the scene into class, however, she invited me to spend the night and I accepted. I did not think of that evening as the beginning of a relationship, but Sally thought differently. When she asked me to stay over a few nights later, and I declined her invitation, the woman felt angry and hurt. When Sally and I finally performed the scene in class, she didn't hold back her emotions. The actor smacked me so hard that I fell over a kitchen table on the set. Sally left a hand-print on my face visible for days. Our performance portrayed very real, moment-to-moment, raw emotions and received high praise from Rae. That experience taught me an important lesson. From that point on, I never had a sexual relationship with another actor when cast with them in the same play.

The most challenging studies, at the 78th Street Theatre Lab, were the voice and Shakespeare classes taught by Mark, a stickler for detail. The man had a powerful presence. With a bushy black beard and a commanding voice, Mark looked and sounded like a professional cast member from *Fiddler on the Roof.* In my mind, Mark's insights, observations, and feedback were the gospel truth. "Let your voice come from your groin," he would say repeatedly. Without question, his deep, resonating timbre came from that very place. In my apartment, I would practice his assigned exercises, standing spread-eagled, hanging loose, in search of my voice. Once I found it, I never forgot it.

In his introductory Shakespeare class, Mark assigned me an Angelo monologue from the *Measure for Measure* comedy set in sixteenth-century Vienna. Angelo, a supposedly strict, play-by-the-rules deputy, temporarily ruled the kingdom in his duke's absence. During Angelo's brief rule, he had to deal with a young man named Claudio, imprisoned for impregnating his sweetheart, Madam Juliette, without meeting all the state's legal requirements for a sanctioned marriage. Prior to Angelo's temporary leadership role, legal authorities had found Claudio guilty and sentenced him to a beheading. Claudio's sister, Isabella, a novice Catholic nun, then interceded on her brother's behalf and met with Angelo to plead for her brother's life. Much to Angelo's surprise, he experienced an overwhelming sexual attraction for the nun and offered her a compromise. If she agreed to have sex with him, he would pardon her brother.

Before I began to work on the monologue, Mark instructed me to first buy a used copy of the one-volume *Oxford Universal Dictionary* then look up the meaning of every word in the soliloquy, and he meant every, single word. "Shakespeare is all about the words," Mark would say repeatedly. When in search for that sizable dictionary, I discovered Frances Steloff's Gotham Book Mart on West 47th where I purchased the hefty hardcover. The bookstore, located in Manhattan's Diamond District, featured a shingle above its door that read "Wise Men Fish Here." Known by writers and artists as a literary salon for decades, it would eventually become one of my Manhattan hangouts. Steloff's bookstore specialized in poetry, literature, and publications for the arts. Over the decades, she had acquired a wonderfully colorful reputation. Defying US censors of the 1920s and 1930s and later, she covertly sold banned copies of such books as Henry Miller's *Tropic of Cancer*, D. H. Lawrence's *Lady Chatterley's Lover,* and the erotic works of Anais Nin, all of them labeled obscene.

With my newly purchased used dictionary, I started to work on Angelo's monologue. Mark instructed me to visualize images on each word of the text then string the images together into phrases. He encouraged me to seek out an appropriate physical space in which to rehearse the monologue and to speak it as if talking to myself. "I want you to discover the deputy's sexuality, too," he added.

A mere five blocks from my West 107th Street apartment loomed the magnificent St. John the Divine Cathedral, an Episcopal house of worship. "At St. John's, the length of the nave from the bronze doors to the rear of St. Savior's Chapel behind the high altar is 601 feet, two football fields end to end with room leftover for the football," explained an article in the *Smithsonian* magazine. "There's plenty of room for the Statue of Liberty (sans pedestal) to stand upright under the dome that soars above the crossing. The nave could accommodate a 12-story office building, and a suburban house would pass through the great rose window where the seated Christ, who looks thumb-nail-size from the floor of the cathedral, but is actually 5 foot 7 inches tall." [3] If its construction were to be completed, St. John's would be the largest Gothic cathedral in the world. Whenever I walked into St. John's, I felt transported into centuries past.

I knew the cathedral well. I made brief retreats there when I needed a break from the cacophony of the city. I would visit early in the morning or very late in the afternoon after the tourist buses stopped running. Frequently, I walked the eight-circuit labyrinth superimposed on the stone floor in the nave. Cathedral staff referred to as the pilgrim's walk. On Sundays, I most often worshiped in silence at the Friends (Quaker) Meeting House on Rutherford Place, downtown near Union Square. At the traditional Quaker house of worship, stripped of any religious symbols, attenders spoke only when moved by the Spirit. However, when I longed for ritual, incense, religious theater, and Liturgy of the Eucharist, I participated in High Mass at St. John the Divine, with its gargoyles, flying buttresses, and all.

In August 1976, I had spent the night at St. John's enjoying a Ravi Shankar's dusk 'til dawn concert of traditional Indian music. After we pushed the pews to the side of the sanctuary, I joined thousands of New York Indians dressed in their saris and other traditional attire, sat with them on the stone floor, and shared their dal and chapattis. At some point, I fell asleep on one of the pews and awoke at dawn to the sweet sounds of Shankar's sitar.

Two years later, I attended The Paul Winter Consort's first Winter Solstice Concert that aired on National Public Radio. The musicians were the cathedral's artists-in-residence. The church overflowed with humanity that icy, snowy night. A difficult year for the collective New York psyche, city residents had lived through several high-profile murders, a debilitating summer blackout followed by looting and violence, a prolonged garbage strike, serious subway breakdowns, and violent racial conflicts throughout the boroughs. Hungry for hope and spiritual resurrection, audience members crowded into pews, spilled over onto the floor, and squeezed into the intricately carved wooden choirs stalls near the altar.

We wanted those musicians to lift us up and out of our malaise. Susan Osborne, soloist with the Consort, did just that. Her commanding presence, full-bodied voice, and emotionally satisfying performance raised our spirits up into the vaulting, through the slate roof of St. John's, and into the heavens. Opening the concert, Osborne paraded down the center aisle joyously singing her bluesy number "Oh, Lay down Your Burden." The audience cried, laughed, and embraced her cathartic lyrics. During that unforgettable night, we did lay down our burdens.

So on that chilly weekday afternoon, as I walked up those cathedral steps for my rehearsal of Angelo's monologue, I felt as though I had come home. I wore an outfit pieced together at a midtown thrift shop, stiff leather boots, corduroy pants, and a vest. A heavy dark green poncho, with a hood, covered my head and shoulders and extended near to the ground. In character, and with bowed head, I passed through the cathedral's side doors into the nave and began the pilgrim's walk around the eight-circuit labyrinth. Making my way to the center and back again, I could not think about anyone or anything but that novice Catholic nun, Isabella.

Having completed the labyrinth, I strode down the aisle toward the high altar. In the distance, the sunlight beamed through the immense, elongated, stained glass windows illuminating the substantial metal crucifix that appeared to hang above the altar in midair. Near the front of the sanctuary, I paused, genuflected, made the sign of cross, sidled into a pew, and knelt onto the prayer pad. Clasping my palms and bowing my head, I had every intention of praying but my sexual hunger for Isabella dominated my thoughts. I lowered my hands, peered up at the altar, and began talking to myself.

"From thee, even from thy virtue!
 What's this? What's this? Is this her fault or mine?
 The tempter or the tempted, who sins most?
 Ha, not she. Nor doth she tempt; but it is I
 That, lying by the violet in the sun,
 Do as the carrion does, not as the flow'r,
 Corrupt with virtuous season."

I paused and shook my head in disbelief. Looking around self-consciously, I wondered if any people sitting in the pews nearby were members of the duke's administration. I did not want them to hear me. Again, I tried to pray but lost focus. I continued to speak my thoughts quietly.

"Can it be that modesty may more betray our sense
 Than woman's lightness? Having waste ground enough,
 Shall we desire to raise the sanctuary, and pitch our evils
   there?
 O fie, fie, fie! What dost thou, or what art thou, Angelo?
 Dost thou desire her foully for those things
 That make her good?

O, let her brother live:
Thieves for their robbery have authority
When judges steal themselves. What do I love her,
That I desire to hear her speak again,
And feast upon her eyes? What is't I dream on?
O cunning enemy, that, to catch a saint,
With saints does bait they hook!"

Smirking, I raised my eyes up to the cross and clasped my palms together one last time. I felt lust in my loins. I simply could not pray. Isabella dominated my thoughts. I wanted to bed her.

"Most dangerous is that temptation that doth goad us on
 To sin in loving virtue. Never could the strumpet,
 With all her double vigor, art and nature,
 Once stir my temper; but this virtuous maid
 Subdues me quite. Ever till now
 When men were fond, I smiled and wondered how."[4]

Having completed the monologue but remaining in character, I leaned back against the pew for a moment. I got up, sidled back out, faced the high altar, and knelt down again as I made the sign of the cross. Turning around, I pulled the hood over my head, ambled up the aisle, and out the cathedral doors.

Dodging crowds on the Broadway sidewalk, between West 108th and West 109th, I attempted to maneuver around a tall, broad-shouldered, homeless man with long, stringy, matted hair. Layers of winter coats covered his frame but he walked barefoot. Without warning, the husky fellow swung around and smashed his fist into the middle of my face. In a flash, I was back in the twentieth century. "Goddamnit," he screamed, "followin' too close behind!" Spittle landed on my cheek. The man's eyes were watery and bloodshot. He reeked of alcohol.

Staggering over to the nearby drug store, blood gushing from my nose, I leaned up against the wall to recover. Holding my head back, I folded pieces of Kleenex and tucked them under my lip. As the bleeding slowed, I regained my balance. Moments later, I careened my way home.

One year prior to my work on Angelo's monologue, about the time my prolonged relationship with Lillian had ended, I met a fellow actor at an Off-Off Broadway production of A. R. Gurney's *The Golden Fleece*. The theater, in Chelsea, could only accommodate a small audience squeezed together on three levels of bleachers. I remember sitting down next to the man whom I did not know, saying hello, and making small talk before the house lights went down.

Probably twenty minutes into the show, I felt his leg press up against mine. I moved over a bit to give him some room. Another ten minutes passed, and his leg pressed up against mine a second time. By then, I was not able concentrate on the play. I could only think about that spot of physical contact between the two of us. I moved away a bit more. When it happened a third time, I resisted, and a surge of sexual energy coursed through my body like an adrenaline rush. That had never happened to me, I mean, with another man. By the end of the play, I felt hot, bothered, and freaked-out. I reacted with a sense of confusion, embarrassment, and excitement. When the man lingered in the lobby after the play, I walked over and introduced myself. We were about the same height and build, I suspected around the same age. Handsome with lively brown eyes, dark skin, and an alluring smile, he introduced himself as Manuel. After a brief conversation, we left the theater and walked down the block to a coffee shop where we remained for hours.

Manuel, a first-generation Puerto Rican American, had

grown up in a tough South Bronx neighborhood where his folks owned a grocery store. After graduating from high school, he enlisted in the Marines, completed basic training, and then deployed to Vietnam. When his jeep hit a land mine, Manuel sustained significant injuries. Flown back to the States, he recovered from his wounds and received a medical discharge. The veteran, who had long wanted to be a professional actor, used the GI Bill to pay for his two-year intensive training at the American Academy for Dramatic Arts. Manuel had already been pursuing an acting career for a few years.

With ease, the actor revealed that he had come out of the closet in drama school. I told him that I had never had a gay relationship, that I considered myself straight. When Manuel invited me to spend the night at his nearby apartment, I turned him down; but we made a date to meet for dinner.

That following week, I experienced emotional turmoil. I did not know whether my attraction to Manuel was an isolated incident, a onetime occurrence. Could a straight man have sexual feelings for another man? Did those feelings mean I was bisexual or maybe gay?

On Saturday, we met for dinner. Three dates later, I stayed at his apartment overnight and we began a relationship. Our year together became a wild and unpredictable emotional ride. An intense man with a volatile temper, Manuel could erupt in the moment then get over it promptly. He did not hold onto his anger. Better that way, I thought. I, too, had a temper, but I tended to let tensions build over time then explode. Our tempers ultimately proved a toxic mix.

At times, our disagreements erupted into physical altercations. Late one night, Manuel and I got into a fight in the middle of Bank Street, near his apartment house. Eventually, we tumbled onto the asphalt. I had so much rage inside me that I felt like smashing his head against the pavement. I wanted to kill him. My lethal emotions were a wake-up call, and maybe his, too. We began to pull away from one another.

Soon after Manuel and I ended our relationship, however, I met a woman named Lucy. An accomplished actor, Lucy had studied with Uta Hagen for years and recently joined our group of a dozen students at the 78th Street Theatre Lab. The more time I spent in her company, the more smitten I became. I knew she had feelings for me, too, but we would not, could not, talk about them. Married for three years, Lucy had recently given birth to her son. That personal and emotional conflict, pulling away from Manuel and feeling a strong sexual attraction to Lucy, had made Angelo's monologue come to life. I used my life experience to make Shakespeare's character real for me.

To support myself, I worked a gamut of jobs. I would quit one job when cast in a play then scramble for another at the end of the show. That predicament repeated itself over and again. It came with the territory of life as a struggling actor. I seated customers as a maître d' and waited tables at the popular Buffalo Roadhouse, just off Sheridan Square, down in the West Village. The Roadhouse attracted people from a range of professions. Michael Herr, author of *Dispatches,* would sit quietly at the bar in the late afternoons and engage in casual conversations. His book had been the most intense depiction of the Vietnam War I ever read. "You could be in the most protected space in Vietnam and still know that your safety was provisional, that early death, blindness, loss of legs, arms or balls, major and lasting disfigurement – the whole rotten deal – could come in on the freaky-fluky as easily as in the so-called expected ways," wrote Herr. "You heard so many of these stories it was a wonder anyone was left alive to die in the fire-fights and mortar-rocket attacks."[5]

The Divine Ms. M, Bette Midler, would come late in the evening accompanied by the gravelly-voiced musician, Tom Waits. She would show-up, almost unrecognizable, without make-up while he always wore his signature pork pie hat. They would claim a back booth, inhale cups of black coffee, and talk nonstop into the night. Actors Rip Torn and Geraldine Page, his wife, had organized a small, Off-Off Broadway repertory company around the corner from the Roadhouse. Members of their group popped into the laid-back restaurant during rehearsal breaks and after performances. New York's Mayor Koch, and members of his staff, would frequently drop by for a late lunch or an early dinner. I always made a point of making them wait, like everybody else, unless my boss happened to be on the floor. Parents and their children mixed with film crews and musicians, tourists and graphic artists, actors and New York politicians at the Buffalo Roadhouse.

In Soho (South of Houston), I poured drinks at the small bar in the Spring Street Restaurant. Surrounded by a coterie of young men, Joni Mitchell would show up at the small and intimate place for dinner. On Fifth Avenue, near Central Park, I worked the 11 p.m. to 7 a.m. shift as a doorman. I hailed taxis, carried packages, opened doors, and accessed elevators for the one percent living in the high-rise, luxury apartment building. For a brief time, Mark Zeller hired me as a janitor at the 78th Street Theatre Lab where I swept floors, cleaned bathrooms, made repairs, and kept things in order. At one point, I was a bus-person at an expensive dessert shop in the East 60s. There, on a busy weekend night, I cleared dishes from a table where Candice Bergen and Gloria Steinem were sitting dressed in their blue jeans and fancy cowgirl boots. I had not seen Steinem since we met at the National Welfare Rights Conference at Detroit's Wayne State University in the early 1970s. Seemed like ages ago. I worked high-end small parties and major arts events for a caterer based out of Noho (North of Houston). Catering paid the best money in the shortest time-period with the most flexible hours. Name it; I did it.

CHAPTER SIX

~

Swimming in Sand

I felt like everything nurtured my growth as an actor from dance performances, films, museums, and plays to lovers, personal conflicts, subway riders, and temporary jobs. Many activities were affordable, some even free. I frequented Off-Off Broadway plays, at times two productions in an evening, four over a weekend. Making up for lost time, because theater had not been my academic background, I wanted to become familiar with dozens of playwrights and their range of material. Ticket prices were often only $3.50 and sometimes less. When reviewing my old, dusty, acting journals, notations reminded me that I often attended at least a score of plays in a month if I could find the time.

One Friday night, I went to the Galley Theatre to see the *Dutchman* by Amiri Baraka (LeRoi Jones) and Israel Horvitz's *The Indian Wants the Bronx*. The following evening, I bought a ticket for Peter Schaffer's *Black Comedy* at Soho Rep then walked over to a late night production of Victor Lipton's *Get Lost* at Theatre for the New City. The following weekend, I attended productions of Eugene O'Neill's *Dynamo* at the Impossible Ragtime Theatre, his *Long Day's Journey into Night* at the Manhattan Conservatory Theatre and a Broadway production of *A Moon for the Misbegotten*. I overdosed on O'Neill but eventually recovered.

When I wanted to see a Broadway production, I had perfected a method within my budget. I would show-up at the theater during intermission, when audience members spilled out onto the street, then re-enter with the crowd holding a *Playbill* in hand and claim an empty seat in an upper gallery. Seeing the second act was better than seeing nothing at all. "There was a time when 'second acting' – sneaking into a Broadway theater at intermission before the second act – was as common as the cigarette break in the middle of a musical," revealed reporter Jane H. Furse. "It was a time-honored rite of passage, practiced by generations of starving actors and students of the theater. It required a confident air, a visible copy of *Playbill*, and the belief that somewhere there would be a free seat."[1]

I developed a keen interest in mind-expanding experimental theater that stripped away the oftentimes more predictable relationships and humdrum themes of commercial theater. I kept track of the Wooster Group at the Performance Garage in Soho where I first saw Spalding Gray, a master of the autobiographical monologue. Gray's show, *Sakonnet Point*, introduced me to part one of his *Three Places in Rhode Island*, a trilogy. I watched the show from a galley above, my arms hanging over the metal railings, and my feet dangling above the stage below. Spalding moved through the set wearing a Speedo and interacting with toy-sized objects as essential elements in the play. "*The production was not so much about words but rather movement, a multi-media approach with four characters,*" I had scribbled in my acting journal. Years later, I witnessed the master perform his *Swimming to Cambodia* in Soho at the Kitchen.

In a small performance space at the Joseph Papp Public Theater, on Lafayette Street, I was introduced to the avant-garde work of Mabou Mines with their production of Samuel Beckett's radio play *Cascando*. Philip Glass, their frequent collaborator, composed the musical score.

Meredith Monk's interdisciplinary approach to performance intrigued me. Oftentimes, her work could be seen in a wide-open space, the one-time sanctuary of St. Mark's Church in the Bowery on the Lower East Side. After attending Monk's multi-layered production, *The Plateau Series,* with eight performers integrating experimental music, dance, and theater, I became a lifelong devotee of her creative pursuits. Experiencing that performance transported me into another culture with a different language, sense of rhythm, and musicality. She widened my imagination as to physical, vocal, and theatrical possibilities.

"From the beginning, Monk . . . took an interest in theatricality, persona, transformation, and narrative. Certain preoccupations of the day seemed to strike sparks for Monk; the notion of an objective performing style; the interest in collage as a structure; the use of film; and the exploration of non-proscenium spaces," explained biographer Deborah Jowitt. "Altered and personalized, they have remained integral to her work. Monk decided that she wanted her voice to be as flexible as her body-capable of handling enormously contrasting qualities and pitches (she is gifted with a three-octave range), and the subtle microtonal shadings and occasional nasal timbres that have led music critics to compare her vocal range techniques to those of the Middle East."[2]

When I had an interest in attending a classical music performance at Lincoln Center, I summoned my "second-acting" routine. I would wait outside the theatre until intermission then mix with the audience and return inside with a program in my hand, claim an empty seat, and listen to the remainder of the program but classical music became just the entre to a wider repertoire.

Without definitive expectations, I had the opportunity to observe John Cage perform on the piano, and a range of other instruments, at the Town Hall. Cage's incorporation of electro-acoustic music and his integration of silence as a crucial aspect of the composition took me aback. "John Cage's music taught us to listen," declared my friend and professional musician Rocket Kirchner. "He saw no difference between dissonance and consonance. His chance music invites us to come in, and see, and taste what already **IS** that we are not paying attention to. This paying attention unlocks the creative wellspring in all of us when we hear Cage. Why, because we learn to listen again and be brought back to an original innocence we lost." Sitting in the front row at Town Hall were Cage's fellow collaborators: dancer and lifelong partner Merce Cunningham, assemblage artist Louise Nevelson, and graphic artist Robert Rauschenberg.

My cursory awareness of Cunningham's work as a dancer stemmed from reading Martin Duberman's revelatory monograph *Black Mountain: An Exploration in Community*. Duberman described in great detail the alternative educational program developed by German artists, Josef and Anna Albers, near Asheville, North Carolina, from the early 1930s to the late 1950s. Many of the creative experimental artists, writers, dancers, and musicians of the mid to late twentieth-century rotated through the Black Mountain College program: Bauhaus School founder Walter Gropius, African American painter Jacob Lawrence, writer Paul Goodman, abstract expressionist William de Kooning, musician John Cage, choreographer Merce Cunningham, and poets Allen Ginsberg and Denise Levertov to name just a few.

With access to some of the finest museums in the world, I indulged in considerable exposure to the visual arts. On free admission days and nights, I spent hours at the Museum of Modern Art, The Guggenheim, Whitney Museum of American Art, and the Metropolitan Museum of Art. I became engrossed in exhibits of artists whose works I had only seen in books.

At the Whitney, I discovered a sensuous clay sculpture by Mary Frank. In a small side gallery, the museum had installed her piece, *The Swimmer*, in a sand-filled pedestal. Never had I experienced such a tactile reaction to a piece of art except for Hans Hofmann's Abstract Expressionist paintings. Hofmann painted in rich, deep colors, oranges and yellows, reds and greens, blues and purples, all applied thickly onto the canvas. Mary Frank created works with clay in deep earth tones. In time, I discovered that Frank had studied with Hofmann. I think back to my circling Frank's female clay creation as a kind of ritual trance. I felt as though I was peeling back layers of repressive civilized behavior. Simultaneously magnetic and hypnotic, that clay being, that ancient yet contemporary creature, manifested the human condition. "She pulls the viewer into her sensuality, thereby returning us to our bodies, to earth, to clay," explained author Hayden Herrera. "Her limbs send forth energy as she arches her back to deliver herself to the elements. From her belly and breasts, legs and arms fan out like the sun's rays."[3] *The Swimmer*, assembled in sections, reached almost eight feet long. I wanted to lie up against her: embrace, feel, and smell her. The experience became a welcomed sensual overload.

While in the smallish side gallery, I noticed another museum patron fascinated with Frank's sculpture, too. We struck up a conversation. Cy Nelson, a longtime editor for E. P Dutton Publishers, knew of Frank's work and mentioned that his publisher had recently released a book including works by the artist. We shared, at length, our similar reactions to *The Swimmer*. Before parting ways, Mr. Nelson took down my address. "I'm going send you a copy of the book," he told me, "along with other information that you'll appreciate." He kept his word. A week later, I received a package in the mail with a letter from Nelson enclosed.

Soon after receiving the book, I returned to the Whitney to revisit *The Swimmer*. As I began to wander away from the side gallery in walked the remarkable English actor David Warrilow. Thin and lanky, with sad-looking eyes, and expressive, long-fingered hands, I recognized Warrilow from his work with Mabou Mines at Joseph Papp's Public Theater. He looked vulnerable, almost delicate, whether on stage or in person. Theater patrons knew Warrilow in particular for his performances of Samuel Beckett's plays. We struck up a conversation about the power of Frank's sculpture, reflective of my earlier discussion with Cy Nelson.

"You knew she'd been married to Robert Frank?" he asked.

"The photographer?" I had no idea.

"Yea," replied Warrilow. "Take a look at his black and white photography collection *The Americans*. Last two pages of photographs are Mary and the kids sitting in their car."

I later discovered that Robert Frank had asked *On the Road* author, Jack Kerouac, to write the introduction to that book. "That crazy feeling in America when the sun is hot on the streets and the music comes out of the jukebox or from a nearby funeral," wrote Kerouac. "That's what Robert Frank has captured in tremendous photographs taken as he traveled on the road around practically forty-eight states in an old used car (on a Guggenheim Fellowship) and with the agility, mystery, genius, sadness and strange secrecy of shadow photographed scenes that have never been seen before on film."[4]

Before we parted ways, Warrilow gave me a free ticket to his upcoming one-man show and invited me backstage after the production. Samuel Beckett had written the play, *A Piece of Monologue,* specifically for David at the actor's request.

Frequently, I visited art galleries midtown and downtown. On a weekday afternoon, after my play director canceled a rehearsal, I walked over to the Pace Gallery on East 57th where Lee Krasner's exhibit, *Eleven Ways to Use the Word to See,* had recently opened. Because of my onetime interest in the work of her late husband, Jackson Pollock, I had become aware of Krasner's abstract expressionist paintings.

A *Life* magazine photo spread and essay on Pollock's energetic drip painting technique first lured me into the world of Modern Art, especially Abstract Expressionism. Although my enthusiasm for Pollock's work waned over time, I continued to seek out the paintings by Hans Hofmann, Helen Frankenthaler, Mark Rothko, Joan Mitchell, and Lee Krasner among others. Hofmann remained my favorite.

Until Pollock's death, Krasner had worked in the shadow of his reputation. The Pace Gallery exhibit clearly demonstrated that her art deserved recognition on its own. When I walked into the gallery, there were no other visitors. Krasner's show, a collection of collages applied to large canvasses, was unlike anything I had seen of hers in the past. Arts journalist, Grace Glueck, described the exhibit. "The resulting collage-paintings, in which the energetic forms of the artist's youth – in black, grays, and whites with touches of color – are rhythmically set against the flat canvas surfaces that reflect painting ideas of today, make up a smashing show – also a tough one that seems to recapitulate the artist's turbulent career."[5]

While sitting on the leather-covered bench in the middle of the exhibit space, I heard someone enter into the gallery behind me – Lee Krasner. She wore a plain-looking smock, like the one my Great Aunt Anna used to wear around her house, and a pair of sneakers. Krasner's shoulder length hair looked as if she had cut it herself. The artist smiled, walked over to the bench, said thank you for coming, and joined me. The woman immediately put me at ease. Krasner explained that she made the collages from pieces of oil and charcoal drawings created while studying with Hans Hofmann in the late 1930s. The artist had originally set them aside, after cleaning out her studio, then promptly forgot about them. When Krasner rediscovered the canvasses, she decided to use them for collage. "So, putting a pair of sharp scissors to the drawings – strong abstractions of figures – she cut and sliced them into bold shapes, then juxtaposed them on sized canvas."[6]

One crisp, spring Saturday afternoon, when gallery hopping in Soho, I detoured into the OK Harris Gallery on Main Street. They were exhibiting John De Andrea's life-sized male and female nudes: coupled, seated on pedestals, and standing alone. The figures were phenomenal examples of Hyperrealism. The minute detail of each body fascinated me. De Andrea's figures were created from plastic, polyester, and glass fiber, in polyvinyl casts of actual humans, then poly-chromed in oil in a naturalistic style. From nipples to pubic hair, eyebrows to genitals, the figures were life-like. I could see birthmarks and wrinkles, tiny veins and scars. I felt as though I had entered a confined space with a group of nudists, something I had experienced dozens of times in various clothing-optional outdoor environments, campgrounds, beaches, and hot springs.

A female nude, leaning up against the wall, made me catch my breath. The skin coloring and physical dimensions of John De Andrea's figure were exactly those of Alicia, a woman I had dated; cream-colored complexion, long arms and legs, slightly cupped breasts, with hair pulled into a bun. I touched the nape of the figure's neck when no one was looking. I could not help myself. The devil made me do it. Alicia had come to New York from Sweden to study with a photographer and work as his assistant. More than decade later, when visiting a close friend in Darmstadt, Germany, I encountered that female figure once again. She stood naked and alone in the corner of a second floor gallery at the city's art museum.

At the Metropolitan Museum of Art, I met the engaging Christo and his flaming red-haired wife and collaborator, Jeanne Claude. They were there to introduce two documentaries of their massive art projects, *Wrapped Coast* shot in Australia, and *Valley Curtain* filmed in Colorado. Hundreds of local volunteers had assembled the art works. The documentaries recorded a chronological sequence of events from preparation to construction, including technical data, and the legal wrangles that they had encountered with, sometimes, skeptical local authorities. Christo and Jeanne Claude considered their entire process, from beginning to end, as the work of art.

As I listened to them talk at length about their projects, I thought of my acting coaches, Mark and Dana Zellers. Like Christo and Jean Claude, the Zellers repeatedly emphasized to members of the theatre lab that rehearsal and performance, actor and stage manager, director and producer, set designers and technicians, were all integral aspects of the theater piece as a whole. One person or aspect of the production process had no more importance than another one. Process and performance were one in the same.

Part Two

CHAPTER SEVEN

∼

Call Me a Madman

Having read about the Weston Priory, a Benedictine community in Vermont, I wrote to the guest brother and received permission to spend Thanksgiving with them. I looked forward to hearing the contemporary spiritual music composed by Brother Gregory Norbert whose recordings were a major cottage industry that helped keep the priory solvent.

When my bus drove into Rutland, Vermont, I recognized the layout of the city. I had made weekend trips there as a high school student when working for an American Friends Service Committee summer project in the nearby village of Brandon. After retrieving my backpack from the luggage compartment, I trudged through the snow over to a nearby drugstore, bought a black magic marker, and large piece of white poster paper, then printed a sign–WESTON PRIORY! Three rides later, I arrived there after dark just in time to participate in the Evensong Eucharist.

I joined lay people from surrounding communities in the priory's chapel and sang along with the brothers accompanied by their guitars. The simple, informal service concluded with the breaking of bread and the taking of wine. Participating in the Eucharist felt like an act of solidarity, of being at one with everyone in the chapel, spiritual rather than religious. I had long thought of Communion in that manner. Afterward, we joined hands and started to move in an improvisational liturgical dance. Weaving in and out of different shapes, the brothers led us around the sanctuary in celebratory movement. The Weston Priory monks were recognized, not only for their homegrown music, but, also, for their liturgical dance. In the spring and summer months, they held services in their barn where movement became an integral part of Sunday Mass. At the conclusion of the service, I joined the priory brothers for dinner. Following the meal, I moved into a small room on the second floor of the onetime farmhouse then went outside for a brief walk.

After my tramp through the snow, I found my way into their library and discovered John Howard Griffin's book *A Hidden Wholeness: The Visual World of Thomas Merton.* Griffin's text accompanied a collection of black-and-white photographs taken by the Trappist monk. I recognized Griffin's name. I had read his groundbreaking work, *Black like Me,* in junior high. When working as a newspaper reporter in Dallas, Griffin had darkened his white skin in order to experience a black man's daily life then described it in a first-person narrative. I also perused the most recent issue of the *Catholic Worker* newspaper, September 1978, published by Dorothy Day's activist group by the same name and made a note for myself to visit their living quarters, the Mary House, in the Bowery on East Third between First and Second Avenues. Then the monks' copy of J. D. Salinger's *Franny and Zooey* jumped out from the bookshelf and into my hands. At least that is how it seemed to my weary mind. I took it as a good omen, a nod from another world. "And don't you know," said Zooey to his sister, Franny, in my favorite quote from the book, "listen to me, now – don't you know who that fat lady [in the audience] really is? . . . Ah, buddy. Ah buddy. It's Christ Himself. Christ Himself, buddy." I had recently adapted a two-character scene from Salinger's work, to use as an audition piece. Just a few days before arriving at the priory, I had rehearsed it with my friend Ingrid, one of the dozen students from the 78th Street Theatre Lab. Exiting the library, I noticed a note card taped to the door. Typed on it was a sentence from *The*

Little Prince. "What is essential is invisible to the eye." [1]

Hearing rising bell at 4:45 a.m., I leaped out of bed, showered quickly then quietly descended the staircase into the common room for the candlelit Vigil service. Surprising but appropriate, Vigil began with Neil Diamond's recording "He Ain't Heavy, He's My Brother" playing on a cassette player as I entered the room and sat on the floor. The brothers frequently opened their morning service with contemporary music, followed by scriptural readings, live music, and an extended period of silence. The monks were sitting on black, cotton-filled, zafu cushions in meditative postures, a Christian-Zen centering prayer practice. Looking out the large glass window, onto the forested, snow-covered, landscape, we watched the dawn emerge in silence.

A feeling of holding one another pervaded the intimate setting, a time when men nurtured one another through music, words, and silence. I stumbled upon a quote from my journal written that Thanksgiving Day. I don't remember if the words were mine or written by another. "*Call me a madman but I tell you that I heard the silence. And in doing so came another step closer to the union between myself and the universe.*"

Prior to serving the Thanksgiving feast, the brothers invited retreatants and outside community members into their dining room for a glass of wine and fellowship. At the long, cloth-covered dining table, I sat next a man whom I assumed to be a brother. He happened to be, however, the only other layman on retreat at the time. Miguel, a Yale graduate student, had arrived late the night before. The Cuban-American, who happened to be gay, told me he had grown up in the Miami's Little Havana. We liked each other immediately and took time to become acquainted. That retreat became the foundation of our ever-growing friendship. In the next few years, we would visit one another in both New Haven and New York.

When I returned to Manhattan, I began to feel antsy. I

wanted to perform a play I had recently found at the Drama Bookstore in mid-Manhattan. I knew it would be an excellent showcase for me. Written by Stephen Black, and titled *The Pokey*, the one-act had two characters. After meeting with Mark Zeller, reviewing the play with him, and making my proposal, he gave me permission to perform *The Pokey* at the 78th Street Theatre Lab.

The introspective male character, close to my age and similar in physical build, worked as a small town sheriff in the big state of Texas. Playwright Black had written the female role as an extroverted rock 'n' roll star loosely based on the life of Janis Joplin. Through the progression of the play, less than twenty-four hours, the two characters became acquainted under extremely strained circumstances, fell in love, but soon realized their relationship could never succeed, then sadly, but amicably, parted ways.

I had another reason for performing *The Pokey*. I wanted Lucy to play the female role. To my delight, she agreed. The two characters' emotional lives were similar to our own, unpredictable. Not only did the play offer me the opportunity to work with a skilled and experienced actor, like Lucy, but it also gave us more time to spend together in and out of rehearsals, time to open up emotionally to one another without the pressure of a committed relationship.

My Thanksgiving retreat experience in Vermont had also made me realize the importance of getting out of the city, sometimes for solitude and reflection and other times simply for fun. I discovered an ideal place near Monroe, New York, called Arrow Park Lake and Lodge that fit the bill. An Upper West Side neighbor of mine encouraged me to pay a visit so I did. Arrow Park, a short bus trip from Manhattan, proved to be affordable and appealing.

A onetime private home that resembled an Italian villa, it was located near a waterfall and overlooked a spring-fed lake.

In the late 1940s, the owner sold it to the American Russian Organized Workers, a group of Slavic working-class individuals and families from various New York City and Newark neighborhoods. Over time, the organization added simple, wooden bungalows, with shared bathrooms, for additional accommodations. On weekends and many holidays, the working kitchen would serve both hot and cold borscht, Russian salad with smoked salmon, and pickled herring or maybe Russian dumplings and mini-meat pies. Arrow Park possessed an old world charm, a step back in time.

When visiting, I always expected to find copies of *The Daily World*, the Socialist Worker's Party weekly, *The Nation* magazine, and other progressive publications in the common room. The park had a history of well-attended May Day celebrations when folk singers, the likes of Pete Seeger and Barbara Dane, would show up for an afternoon's entertainment.

On my second trip to the lodge, I invited Zack, a fellow actor whom I had recently started dating. He, too, had studied with Uta Hagen for years. Everywhere I turned, I seemed to encounter Hagen disciples. Tall and sandy-haired Zack, a native of Ohio, was a Renaissance man. He could play a Scott Joplin ragtime tune on the piano, do carpentry work around the house, and write a play, direct it and act in it. He could build the sets, too. Zack could get a business off the ground, cover third base for a softball team, prepare a five-course meal, blow a bluesy number on his harmonica, and write engaging poetry. He fancied himself as a contemporary Walt Whitman without the beard and the belly.

Arriving by bus late on a Friday afternoon, we were carrying light packs and I had my banjo-in-hand. I had recently started taking lessons from Marty Cutler, a professional banjo player with a national reputation. I took the instrument wherever there might be a chance to practice. At the front desk, the attendant gave us the keys to Bungalow 10, Room 2. "Nobody else will be down there tonight," said the friendly lodge keeper, with a disarming smile, as she handed the keys over to Zack. "We'll be serving supper until 7 p.m."

Following a skinny dip in the cool lake then eating a bowl of red borscht with the traditional dollop of sour cream along with a serving of Russian Salad, Zack and I went for a leisurely stroll around the grounds and soon retired to our bungalow. The two unmade single beds, with mattresses atop old metal springs, sat across the room from one another. A shaggy throw rug partially covered the plank floor. Our window looked out onto the lake, with desk and lamp and two comfortable easy chairs on either side. The sheets and the pillowcases, which we grabbed from the shelf behind the door, smelled fresh and sweet. I thought of family. My mom and grandma use to hang the sheets out on the line in warm weather. We made the beds and began to settle in.

Sitting down on my squeaky springs, I took out the banjo then shoved the case underneath with the heel of my bare foot. Zack plopped down on his bed, pulled out a round metal container from his pack, and wedged it open.

"Entertainment kit," the Ohioan told me with a wink and a grin, "just a few things for the night's activities." He pulled out five different colored balloons, then red, blue, and green bandannas, two of each, his trusty Hohner harmonica (I had forgotten mine), a small bag of marijuana, rolling papers, and a pack of matches. After rolling a joint and sharing it, Zack and I began to jam. One of us would set the beat then carry it along until it just naturally took off in another direction. Zack continued to blow on his harmonica while I strummed on the banjo. I loved that man!

Sometimes I used the banjo head like a drum, at other times I moved my fingers up the strings to create a high, twangy, metallic sound before moving in the opposite direction to get more of a dull plunk. I plucked the strings and explored a range of ways to play that instrument. My banjo teacher had encouraged me to do just that. "Open it up," Marty would say. "It can go places you'd never imagined."

Zack and I would stop and talk off and on, altering our two personas with each improvisational conversation. Sometimes we were both male, other times we were females, and a few times one of each. Our improvisations reminded me of Paul Ableman's thought provoking play *Green Julia*. Its two male characters, graduate students, spent almost the entire script improvising different characters. Zack and I wore the bandannas around our foreheads. We also tied them up into balls and threw them back and forth then juggled with them. The colored balloons became pieces of fruit, strange animals, and musical instruments that sounded like nails scratching on a blackboard or long, drawn out farts. We sang Christmas carols, folk songs, then moved on to Janis Joplin favorites. Good thing we were the only residents in the bungalow that night.

In the early morning, while attempting to crawl over Zack to heed nature's call, I fell flat on the floor. Two men, in a single bed, made for a tight squeeze. I do not know why I started to laugh but I promptly stopped when my partner poured a nearby glass of water onto my head.

Sitting by the lake that afternoon, I finished reading Woody Guthrie's autobiography *Bound for Glory* while Zack wrote in his journal. Inside the title page of Guthrie's book, I had written a note to myself earlier in the day. *"Got to hit the road next year. Don't let the city swallow you whole!"*

As we departed the lodge, I noticed a poster on the wall announcing an upcoming concert by folksinger Barbara Dane. Returning a month later, by myself, I heard her perform and re-introduced myself after her show. I hadn't seen Barbara since my organizing days in Louisville. Then, she was travelling around the country performing at antiwar coffeehouses. When Barbara arrived in Kentucky, I had the privilege of picking her up at the Louisville bus depot then driving her to the Coffeehouse in Muldraugh, near Fort Knox, where she entertained service men and women for a couple of nights. Barbara, a onetime blues and jazz singer, had developed into a folksinger's folksinger. In fact, I thought of her as a female Woodie Guthrie. Barbara had been the first musician from the US to tour post-revolutionary Cuba.

CHAPTER EIGHT

~

Bare Ass Naked

"William, what are you doing back there?" called out my acting coach. Kim Stanley, renowned stage and television actor, sat in the middle of the sixth row at the downtown Shelter West Theater yelling at me. The other students, clustered around Kim, hung on to every comment she made.

"Taking a shower," I yelled back from behind the curtain where I stood bare-ass naked.

"I don't believe it," responded Kim.

"I don't either!" I replied

Kim had asked me to do a sense memory exercise from the introductory scene of Tennessee William's *Cat on a Hot Tin Roof*. My character, Brick, a onetime Ole Miss quarterback, had become a professional television sports announcer after graduating from the university. Brick and his wife, Maggie, were temporarily living with his parents in their two-story, white-columned plantation home. The former college athlete had been laid-up, his broken ankle encased in a plaster cast. The couple had a troubled marriage. For months, he had been sleeping on the couch. There was an elephant in their bedroom, Brick's unspoken love for his closest male friend who had recently committed suicide. The sports announcers drinking problem added to the strains in their marriage. As the scene opened, Brick had just started to take a shower, with the bathroom door halfway open, when Maggie walked into the adjacent bedroom ranting about the nasty behavior of his nieces and nephews. "Brick, Brick—one of those no-neck monsters hit me with a hot buttered biscuit, so I have t' change!"[1]

Ms. Stanley had instructed me to take a shower without using water or artificial sound effects. Although I moved through the physical motions, I could not pin down the specific details in my work. I had not discovered the character's emotional and psychological life.

Kim got up from her seat and sauntered to the stage. She climbed the stairs, walked behind the curtain, and moved toward me dragging a folding chair with one hand while holding a cigarette in the other. Kim looked older than her fifty-four years. Alcohol and food binging had taken their toll, but her power had not been diminished. Kim's dark eyes were penetrating and her voice hypnotic.

I did not feel self-conscious about my nakedness, and Kim seemed oblivious. She unfolded the chair, sat down ten feet away from me, and began to ask a string of questions. I remained silent, in character, and listened to her every word. "What color is the shower curtain?" she asked. "What's the temperature of the water?" Kim paused briefly. "What kind of soap and shampoo are you using? What do they smell like?" After taking a drag off her cigarette, Kim continued with her questions. "What do you wash first? What do you wash last?" Another pause, "Are you proud of your body?" Kim fell silent then mumbled something under her breath as if she were talking to herself. "What are you using to keep the plaster cast dry?" She looked up at the ceiling, perhaps searching for more questions. "Were you drinking before you got into the shower? Are you singing or whistling or humming?" Kim inhaled another long drag and released the stream of smoke slowly as she posed her final question. "What's the first thing you plan to do when you step out of that shower?"

She made it clear that those were just a few of the questions that I needed to answer in order to create the reality of the situation. Kim had completed her feedback, thanked me, got up, and returned to her seat. "You can't be good in the theater unless you've immersed yourself in the marvelous detective story of the human spirit," Kim explained in Jon Krampner's *Female Brando: The Legend of Kim Stanley.* "But it's difficult, terribly difficult."[2]

Acclaimed by critics as the greatest stage actor of her generation, Kim Stanley held Broadway audiences spellbound in the 1950s and 1960s. She had mastered her Method Acting skills under the tutelage of Lee Strasberg at the Actor's Studio. Theater critics lauded Kim for creating Broadway's definitive Maggie in Tennessee William's *Cat on the Hot Tin Roof* and Cheri and Millie in William Inge's *Bus Stop* and *Picnic.* Twice nominated for an Oscar, Ms. Stanley had won dozens of awards as a leading actor in live television dramas and on stage. Unbeknown to many, she narrated Horton Foot's film adaptation of Harper Lee's much-loved book, *To Kill a Mocking Bird.*

Having pursued an acting career for the previous four years, I was aware of Kim's reputation and wanted to study with her. I realized the importance of continuing to hone my craft. Prior to working with Ms. Stanley, I studied with Rae Allen, Mark Zeller, and Dana Zeller in the 78th Street Theatre Lab, and with actor Austin Pendleton at the Herbert Berghof Studios. I had performed in numerous Off-Off Broadway productions, acted in a few industrial films, and cast as an extra in a commercial film and a soap opera. I had become a dues-paying member in two of the acting unions: Screen Actors' Guild and American Federation of Television and Radio Artists. Eventually, I joined Actors' Equity.

When I called Ms. Stanley to schedule an audition for her scene study class, she told me not to bring a prepared monologue. Instead, Kim said she planned to give me a set of circumstances and I would improvise a scene. At the audition, I impressed her and she accepted me. That September, during my first night in her scene study class, Kim stressed the importance of character detail by evoking physical environment and drawing from sense memory. A student asked her to demonstrate. In the hot and humid theatre, Kim walked up onto the center of the bare stage and began to narrate. The actor told us that she was walking in Central Park, in the middle of winter, and it had begun to snow. Kim described the coat she wore and the physical sensations she experienced. I could see the snow falling and the color of her coat. I felt the cold, outside air and smelled the evergreen trees in the park. Her virtual reality became mine. "It was like being around white light," commented fellow student Jackson McCarry. "I watched this woman work and it was un-be-lievable."[3]

In my third class with Kim, she asked me to do an improvisational scene with Erica, an intense, red-haired actor from East Germany. Past midnight, Erica and I were exhausted. Kim gave us the framework of the improvisation. We were passionately in love, I had been away from home for two months, and just walked into the apartment without calling ahead. "Whenever you're ready," Kim said.

The scene evolved slowly with very little dialogue. Excited, I entered the improvised apartment and reached out for Erica. Caught by surprise, she became angry because I had not called ahead of time. As we began to resolve the conflict, Erica and I held each other closely feeling the sensuality of one another's bodies. Our kisses were long. Eventually, we moved to the floor and faced one another with her legs straddling mine. I took off my shirt. When Erica began to stroke my chest, I started to unbutton her blouse. "Thank you," said Kim, abruptly, bringing our arousing improvisation to a halt. It felt like coitus-interruptus! "Good work," she told us. Kim had taken us to the very edge before ending the scene.

Kim met with her students twice a week, and we paid by the session. Usually dividing the class into four parts, she began each with an animal improvisation, a warm-up activity.

A sense memory exercise, like my shower scene, followed the animal improvisation. Kim referred to the third phase of the class as need exercises or defining our objectives. The final activity focused on specific scene work that Kim had assigned us.

She would begin at 7 p.m. and often hold the class until midnight or later. Ms. Stanley understood that the longer the session, the more tired and malleable we would become. Prior to leaving class, the night I had worked on the shower scene from *Cat*, Kim called me over. She informed me that we were finished working on the shower scene, we could always return to it later. "In the next two weeks, I want you to find a two-character play that you feel passionately about," Kim told me. "Bring it to class and let me review it."

Immediately, I began to look for a script with two characters in a loving relationship. I searched for a role that would force me to stretch as an actor. I wanted to find a somewhat obscure play. I also sought a script with the intention of producing and performing it Off-Off Broadway. In the coming two weeks, I spent my free time poring over script catalogs at mid-Manhattan's drama bookstores. I read two-character play descriptions in detail, noting the individual's personal and physical makeup as well as their emotional range. I paid close attention to time periods, production requirements, play settings, and previous production dates.

By the end of the first week, I had compiled a list of a few dozen scripts that looked promising. I reviewed almost all of them, considered my potential as the male character, and determined each plays production possibilities. Near the end of my two-week deadline, I had eliminated all the scripts on my list except for the two not on the display shelves. I asked the salesman to check the stockroom. "Sorry," he said upon his return. "I can only find one of 'em. Edward Moore's *The Sea Horse*." The young man handed me the script. "The other one's been on back order for weeks." I plopped down into the soft, leather couch in the display room and began to review it.

The entire two-act play took place in The Sea Horse, a waterfront bar in a northern California coastal town. Harry Bales, the male character, worked as an engine mechanic on a fishing trawler named Sister Katingo. His female counterpart, Gertrude Blum, owned the bar. As I skimmed over the pages, two scenes, in particular, grabbed my attention. They spoke volumes about the characters. I knew I had found the play.

Returning to the beginning of the script, I read every word including the stage directions. Scene by scene, I began to feel an emotional and personal attachment to those two characters. Their conflicts and struggles, when trying to maintain an intimate, long-term, relationship were very familiar. I, myself, had never had much success with one. The playwright provided detailed descriptions of both characters.

Standing six feet tall and weighing one hundred and ninety pounds, Harry Bales looked like an athlete with his broad shoulders, barrel chest, and strong legs. The mechanic, an emotional, compassionate, and romantic kind of fella, had a reputation as a womanizer. The thirty-year-old seaman always had a hard time managing his money so Gerty helped him out with his finances. Harry clearly loved Gerty. He wanted to settle-down, get married, and have a family. Tired of working as an engine mechanic, Harry had tried to start a moving-van business without much success. As the play opened, Harry wanted to buy an old boat and turn it into a rental where customers would pay him to take them out for a day of fishing.

The mechanic's daily work attire included a loose pair of khaki work pants, a sweatshirt worn underneath a lightweight nylon jacket, and a cap that he usually pushed to the back of his head. Harry wore high-topped logger's boots but never laced them up more than halfway. In his seaman's duffel bag he carried rain slickers, along with his other meager possessions.

Playwright Moore described Gertrude Blum as five feet, eight inches tall and weighing one hundred and seventy pounds. Gerty, as her customers called her, was firm, big-boned, and projected a tough exterior although she had a well-hidden sensitive side. The woman usually wore her hair in a ponytail that revealed an attractive, ruddy-cheeked face.

Gerty owned the business and worked as the bartender, the employer, and the employee. She only permitted men to patronize The Sea Horse. Gerty never knew her mother, and her affectionate father, the former bar owner, had died during her childhood. At the age of eighteen, she had married but later divorced because her husband physically abused her. Soon after the divorce, two bar patrons raped her. Those brutal experiences had left her emotionally scarred and wary of intimate relationships with men. In her early thirties, Gerty usually wore dark cotton slacks, a denim work shirt, and a pair of ankle high boots at work but she could dress-up for special occasions and even apply touches of perfume to those very special places. Special outings, however, were few.

When I took a copy of *The Sea Horse* to Ms. Stanley's class, she looked it over and approved the script for a work in progress. She told me to piece together the details of Harry Bale's personal life and his work environment: discover the Harry Bales in William Claassen. Kim always called me William. That night, she also asked me to find a woman in class who would be interested in playing Gertrude Blum.

Peg, who had studied with Kim for more than a year, would be the ideal woman. She had been on my mind since I discovered the play. I gave Peg a copy of *The Sea Horse* to review. A few days later, she phoned me and enthusiastically agreed to play the character. Initially, Peg and I only did one read-through of the script together, a line reading without emotion, interpretation, or much discussion. We agreed to develop our respective characters, alone, for the following few weeks. Then we would meet again and work out a rehearsal schedule.

I knew that when I found the right clothes, I would discover Harry's walk, the way he carried himself, and how he felt about his body. "You are helped in physical reality by the very clothes you choose to wear," pointed out Uta Hagen, in *Respect for Acting.* "Your psychological state of being, your sense of self, as well as the physical manifestation of it, is strongly influenced by what you wear. You must make your clothing particular in likes, dislikes, appearances–and with sensory awareness."⁴ Once I explored Harry's work environment, I could realize his voice, sense of humor, and social life.

The previous year, in 1978, when cast as the male hustler in a workshop of Michael Christopher's *Shadow Box*, I discovered his character when I chose to wear a pair of tight jeans without briefs, high-top military surplus boots, and a sleeveless, skin-tight T-shirt. My character needed to reveal his physical attributes in order to attract business. I wore a ring with a garnet stone inset, my actual birthstone. For the hustler, the ring would be a good conversation starter with potential customers. To gain insight into his work environment, I hung out in pick-up bars and observed the men's interactions. I paid close attention to what they wore and listened intently to their conversations.

Two years later, when selected to play Eric, the finishing carpenter in George Bemberg's *Knitters in the Sun*, I learned the character's physical presence by choosing to wear a plaid flannel shirt with carpenter's pants and rainbow striped suspenders. To complete my attire, I buckled a tool belt around my waist and pulled on a pair of ankle-high, steel-tipped work boots. I got a crew cut and started using rock salt deodorant, which added more detail to my character. I decided that Eric always carried his grandfather's pocket watch hooked to a belt loop on his work pants. The carpenter's grandpa had served as a substitute father during his childhood. Despite the fact that Eric's wife had died of cancer one year ago, I continued to wear the wedding ring. My Eric had not yet to come to terms with her death.

On opening night of *Knitters*, at the Wonder Horse Theater on East Fourth, I received my first Western Union Telegram. "TO OUR FAVORITE KANSANIAN MAITRE D' NAMED BILL. SLAY'EM DEAD, BREAK A LEG, BE SHAMELESS, BE BRILLIANT. LOVE AND BEST WISHES, LIZ, SHEP, JONI and SUMMER" (3/22/80). Weeks later, I read my first write-up in the *New York Daily News*. "William Claassen as a sort of gentleman caller who wants to marry the sister is somewhat overpowered by the pyrotechnics generated by the principal players, but, in a sense, that's how it should be" wrote Don Nelson, the paper's theater critic. "He is a strong, not-so-silent sensible man with a mission he intends to accomplish."[5] When the show moved from Off-Off Broadway to Off-Broadway, I earned my Actor's Equity Association union card. The union membership opened up auditions for Equity shows and gave me legitimacy as a professional actor.

As I began to work on Edward Moore's *The Sea Horse*, I used some of the playwright's ideas for developing Harry Bales and added a few of my own. I made the decision that Harry didn't wear a watch or a ring. They felt too confining to him. Deodorant and after-shave lotions were a waste of his money. Harry liked the way he smelled, natural like. At a thrift store, I bought a pair of loose-fitting, cuffed chinos, an old leather belt, and a washed-out, long-sleeved, cotton work shirt. From my clothes closet, I made use of a green, nylon, windbreaker and a brown, wool, pullover cap. When shopping at the Salvation Army, I came across a pair of logger's boots that I wore laced-up halfway as suggested in the script. On Canal Street, near Chinatown, I found a duffle bag and rain slicks at a used military clothing store.

Dressed as Harry Bales and carrying my duffle bag with rain slicks zipped up inside, I began to make trips downtown. I would lumber onto the Seventh Avenue IRT then exit into the South Street Seaport neighborhood, a working-class area where Fulton Street met the East River. That neighborhood possessed some of the oldest nineteenth-century architecture in Lower Manhattan. I hung out in the fish markets, observed the men, listened to their conversations, and noted their sense of humor. I quickly discovered that Harry knew how to deliver a good joke. He had a healthy sense of humor. It became clear that comfort food appealed to a man who had worked out at sea for a spell. So occasionally, I would eat an inexpensive meal at a simple cafe, frequented by seaman, where butcher paper served as tablecloths. The tables were long and I never knew who would sit down beside me. Those conversations with the fishermen were invaluable.

On one of my treks downtown, I discovered the Meyer's Hotel, a flophouse on the corner of South Street and Peck Slip. Built in the late 1800s, its basic rooms were available for a pittance on the third, fourth, and fifth floors. In my mind, Harry stayed there when Gerty would get pissed-off and throw him out of their apartment temporarily.

The cramped reception area reeked of cigarette and cigar smoke when I walked inside with my duffel bag slung over my shoulder. The desk attendant stood behind the counter where homemade signs, posted on the wall, informed tenants of the house rules and regulations. A wooden cabinet, with open mailboxes, hung on the wall behind him. The disheveled-looking man, bent over reading the *New York Post*, did not pay any attention to me at first. When he finally looked up, I noticed that one of the lenses in his glasses had cracked, he had trimmed his mustache unevenly, and the top button on his open collared, short sleeved, shirt had come off. When the attendant told me there was a vacant room, he more than flattered me. I had passed as Harry! I was reborn! To set things straight, I introduced myself as an actor, described my character in detail, and then briefly summarized the play.

Although the attendant gave the impression that he believed me, the man asked for some form of identification with a photograph. I pulled out my driver's license and Westside YMCA membership card from my wallet and placed them on the counter. When I asked if I could walk upstairs and visit one of the rooms, he removed key #8 from an open mail slot, handed it over then opened the wooden gate leading to the staircase and the rooms above.

Clean but frayed on the edges, a faded red carpet runner partially covered the third floor hallway. The dark varnished wood, underneath, creaked with every step. Room #8, a boxy, high-ceilinged space with one window, looked out at the leaning brick chimneys on the nearby rooftops. The glass panes were in need of a good washing and a single naked light bulb hung from the ceiling. Flower patterned linoleum, covering the floor, curled up slightly in every corner, and the room smelled musty.

I sat and then lay down on the lumpy mattress that sunk in the middle, not helped by the old, coiled bedsprings that supported it. Years of tobacco smoke had left a sepia tint on the wallpaper and the ceiling. The worn upholstered chair reminded me of my parents' 1950s living room furniture, durable but uncomfortable. A framed mirror hung above the scratched-up wooden dresser across from the bed.

The cowboy lamp on a bedside table caught my attention. The western ceramic figure communicated warmth, humor, and personality to the otherwise bleak-looking room. The lamp would be an important object to remember.

Walking down the poorly lit hallway, toward the communal bathroom, I sensed life from behind the closed doors. A radio played jazz in one of the rooms. In another, I heard a man coughing up phlegm. Closer to the bathroom, a tentative meow escaped from under a resident's door. In the lavatory, a single toilet sat next to the sink and a clear plastic curtain circled the ringed bathtub with a shower nozzle hanging above. Before descending the stairway to the reception area, I noticed the pay telephone and a thick, tattered, four-year-old New York City phone directory attached to a chain. A week later, I returned to the flophouse for an overnight stay.

At the end of every South Street Seaport block stood The Sea Horse bar by yet another name. I adopted one conveniently located near the hotel, appropriately called Gerty's. Inside, an uneven plank floor supported the heavy wooden bar and red vinyl-covered stools that spun around with a little push. Salty bartenders served the rowdy crowd that patronized the place day and night.

Nearby ferries, that offered transport to and from Staten Island for a quarter a ride, became my Sister Katingo substitutes, Harry's home out at sea. I casually wandered the boat decks, watched the men at work, and overheard their conversations. I would stand out on the bow, deeply inhale the salty air, and appreciate the wind blowing against my face and through my hair. Those physical sensations suggested adventure and solitude. Hanging out at Gerty's bar, frequenting the fish markets, and jumping the ferries continued to provide rich and useful character material. I picked-up appropriate slang, learned a boatman's vocabulary, and morphed into a distinct physical posturing as the boat mechanic.

After our weeks of solo character work, Peg and I began to meet for rehearsals. We knew *The Sea Horse* would be an ideal showcase for us both. Our enthusiasm and excitement about the plays prospects became a constant. Peg and I were going to bring Harry Bales and Gertrude Blum back to life on a Manhattan stage. Soon, we scheduled an appointment with Edward Moore, the playwright, to secure permission to perform the play. Both of us were confident that it would be a mere formality. Little did we know what was coming.

Late in the afternoon, following a rehearsal, we met with Ed in his West Village apartment. Very welcoming, the playwright invited Peg and me into the front room and offered us coffee and snacks. The man looked like a Harry Bales. They were one in the same. Ed had worked as a boat mechanic. Before the playwright could get a word in, Peg and I began to ramble on about our enthusiasm for *The Sea Horse* and shared stories about our character development work. We let him know that Kim Stanley loved the play and encouraged us to use class time for scene work. Ed appeared as excited as we were about the production possibilities until he asked where Peg and I planned to perform it. "We're gonna rent an Off-Off Broadway space somewhere here downtown," I told Ed. "We'll do it over three consecutive weekends."

Immediately, I could tell by the look on his face there was going to be a problem. Ed glanced down at the floor, shook his head slightly then looked back up. The playwright explained that the movie rights for the play were under consideration. Because of that, he would not give us permission to perform it in Manhattan. Peg and I sat there dumbfounded. "But, I'd consider givin' ya permission to perform it in Jersey," he said as an afterthought.

Peg and I looked at one another. He had to be kidding. The cost and the travel time alone put that possibility out of reach. We also knew that nobody would schlep over to Jersey, from New York, to see the play with the exception of our respective partners, friends, and possible relatives who would feel obligated to do so. We stayed a while longer, trying to get Ed to reconsider his position. Peg and I could not understand how an Off-Off Broadway production would jeopardize negotiations for the movie rights. If anything, we argued, a local production would give the play much needed attention and publicity. Ed would not budge. When we finally got up to leave, the playwright thanked us for liking his script, said how much he admired our hard work, and apologized.

"I'd like to sign your copies of the play," he told us. Our consolation prize, I guess. When we handed them over, Ed grabbed a pen off his desk and scribbled something on the title page of each one. With scripts back in hand, we trudged out of his apartment, down the steps, and onto the busy street. We were at a loss for words. Our conversation with Ed had sucked the energy force right out of us. Nothing left to say. Peg plodded down the sidewalk toward her apartment on Sullivan Street. I dragged myself the opposite direction to catch the subway uptown. On the ride home, I pulled the script out of my shoulder bag, turned to the title page, and read Ed's inscription.

"Dear Bill,
Thank you for caring about my play. You'll
make a great Harry Bales. I hope you have
a chance to play the part.

Ed Moore
Nov 7, 1979"

CHAPTER NINE

~

Sleeping with the Dead

Departing New York City's Port Authority, I settled into an aisle seat and closed my eyes. They popped open again when the citric smell of an orange pierced my nostrils. The woman sitting next to me had unfolded a white napkin in her lap and used her long, dark red, fingernails, to dig into the flesh of the fruit and separate it into single slices.

"Care for a slice?" she asked in an accent that sounded Eastern European.

"Uh, well, yes, thank you," I reached down and picked one off the napkin.

"Take two," the woman insisted, so I did. "My name is Adriana," she told me. Probably in her early sixties, Adriana informed me that she came from Romania but had lived in the US for a decade. Our conversation continued, on and off, until the bus reached Buffalo.

My friend Sue and her brown-eyed, blond-haired son met me at the depot. Four years ago, when I bussed up to Buffalo on my way to Alaska, Sue had just become pregnant. After loading my backpack into her car trunk we drove to Lovejoy, the city's Polish neighborhood, where Sue and her husband, Tony, had recently purchased a house. Tony worked for the Democratic Party in the city while Sue kept busy being a mother and a homemaker.

When Tony and a workmate arrived that evening, we clustered around the kitchen table for hours drinking Ballantine Ale, eating chips and clam dip, while reminiscing about college days. We had become good friends at Rutgers University. Sue and I were Livingston College undergraduates at the time, and Tony had almost completed his master's degree in political science. Before graduation, they were married in the centuries-old chapel on the Rutgers campus and my former girlfriend, Lillian, and I attended the wedding. I remember she wore a simple, but elegant, black dress with a single string of pearls. Lillian looked stunning. Presided over by a Catholic priest for Tony and a rabbi for Sue, the wedding became a high-spirited event. "Mazel tov!" we shouted as Tony and Sue stepped on the napkin wrapped glass.

In the morning, Sue and her son drove me across the Canadian border and let me out on the side of the highway with backpack and cardboard sign printed in big black letters–TORONTO. My Nova Scotia destination would prove to be a leisurely journey compared to the Alaska trek in 1976.

Promptly, a dark red Thunderbird convertible, an older model, pulled over and the driver waved. "I'm going into city center," he yelled. "Hop in." The young man, wearing jeans and a white T-shirt, introduced himself as Elvis. He didn't look like an Elvis, but he could have passed for actor James Franco. During our brief ride into Toronto, as the highway hugged the Lake Ontario coastline, the driver told me that his family had moved to Canada from Italy when he was a child. Once in the city Elvis helped me track down my friend Dolly, at Joe Allen's, a popular bar and restaurant where she waited tables. Elvis knew the place because he had worked at a nearby warehouse a few years before. After Dolly gave me the key to her house on Ellsworth Street, I bought Elvis a beer and we sat down and schmoozed. After finishing the brews, Elvis kindly dropped me off at her house. When Dolly arrived late that night we talked briefly then she gave me a city map, tossed out a few suggestions for activities in the city, said I was welcome to stay for a few days and went to bed.

I had met Dolly and her close friend, Shep, when they came to New York to study with Mark and Dana Zeller. We were in a few classes together. When I expressed an interest in exploring acting possibilities in Canada, they invited me to come to Toronto in the summer and stay at Dolly's house.

On day one, after breakfast, I caught a cable car to the graffiti-free subway that dropped me off on Bloor Street, a main through-way in midtown. I first stopped at Theatre Books on Yonge Street where I hoped to familiarize myself with a few contemporary Canadian playwrights but did not find anything of interest. Later, I dropped by the Canadian Actor's Equity Association, picked up a list of equity theaters scattered across the provinces and inquired about the possibility of working in Canada as an actor from New York. Unless I married a Canadian, the prospects sounded dismal. I discovered the prize of the day when I stumbled upon Theatre Passe Muraille (Theatre without Walls), on Ryerson Avenue. Intrigued by the name, I walked in and met the assistant to Paul Thompson, the company's director. Davis, a slight, partially bald, amicable young man invited me into his office and explained at length the structure and the mission of the company. "Our pieces evolve from in-depth research done by the actors," he told me. Their subject matter always focused on some aspect of Canadian culture or history. Davis said that a good portion of their funding came from the government. "Sometimes we create works out of collected interviews. Other times we live on location, get to know the locals, and create our pieces from that." He informed me that their productions evolved out of improvisational work. The more he described the company, the more interested I became. Before we finished talking, Davis gave me a list of their previous shows and told me I could find the scripts at the main public library.

I spent day two in Toronto's downtown public library pouring over Theatre Passe Muraille scripts. Their approach to theater exited me. The scripts were rich in detail and compelling in content. One production, *I Love you, Baby Blue*, exposed the city's red-light district where the actors did their research and found their characters. Though popular with sold out performances night after night, the local authorities closed the show because they objected to the nudity and lewd content. One of their historical pieces, *Doukhobors*, focused on a group of religious Russian dissenters and radical pacifists who had settled in western Canada in the early 1900s. The Doukhobors lived in communes and rejected personal materialism and public education. The religious sect had a reputation for their use of nude marches and arson as protest techniques. A third script of interest, *The Farm Show*, emerged from company members living and working in rural Canada.

Returning to Dolly's house that night, I found a note on the kitchen table. She had taken off for Nova Scotia, at the last minute, and left me the address of an actor friend, Bill, who lived in Halifax. "Look him up," said the note. "I called him and he said you can stay at his apartment. Bye, Dolly"

Sunday morning, I found my way to the Quaker Meeting House near the University of Toronto. Having arrived just as the silent service began, I quickly found a seat among the more than three dozen people of all ages. After the clerk of the Meeting read a Walt Whitman poem, followed by a biblical scripture, we settled into the quiet but it did not last long. Moved by the Spirit, a surprisingly large number of attenders stood and spoke; something I had encountered in the past. Quakers called it a "Popcorn Meeting", a phrase they used to describe a Silent Meeting that would become as verbal as it was silent. Every five minutes someone would stand-up to share. I found it exhausting, too much information with too little time to process.

An event at the close of Meeting, a time when newcomers introduced themselves, made my attendance worth the effort.

After three of us had stood, given our names, and shared a bit of personal information, the clerk began to make closing comments. Abruptly, up jumped an older woman with rosy red cheeks dressed in a puffy white peasant blouse, long blue skirt, and black wallabies. The woman had pulled back her beautiful, long, silver grey hair into a half bun. With hands folded in front of her, the visitor spoke in a lyrical, high-pitched voice. "My name is Hannah Lawrence, and I'm new here in Toronto," she paused to look around the room. "I am seventy-four years old and looking for a nice, cuddly, woman to spend the rest of my life with." Hannah smiled sheepishly then sat down.

The clerk of the Meeting did not know how to react to the newcomer's forthrightness. She sat there looking stunned, for a moment, before closing the service. I suspect that the delightful Hannah found a taker, or at least a name and a phone number, during the coffee hour that followed.

That night, I received a phone call from Dolly's actor friend, Shep, who had also studied with the Zellers in New York. Shep wanted to perform in New York City and knew that I had an interest in getting a work permit for Canada so we made plans to meet downtown for coffee in the morning before I continued my trip east. At the coffee shop, I thought Shep might just propose to me right then and there. "I've known a number of gays and lesbians who've married to get work permits," she informed me. "It's not that unusual in the theater world." I had never told her that I was bisexual or gay, and she had never revealed that she was a lesbian. Shep informed me that she came from a family of lawyers and was confident that we could make it work legally. According to her, we would have to remain married for at least two years during which time immigration authorities would interview us periodically and make home visits. We had put the possibility of a marriage of convenience on the table for the time being and agreed to talk further once I returned to New York.

I had a heck of a time getting out of Toronto. As instructed by a metro employee, I boarded the subway on Bloor Street and took it to the end of the line at Ishington. When I began to exit the station, the token attendant informed me that the more expedient way would be to take the train to the other end of the line then board a bus to Old Farmer's Road, which I did. Soon after exiting the bus, I found Highway 401 East, pulled off my pack, held up my cardboard sign–NOVA SCOTIA, and stuck out my thumb.

When a blue pick-up stopped, I approached the truck and stuck my head into the passenger's window. "How far are you goin'?" I yelled. "Ottawa," the driver yelled back over the Hard Rock blasting out of the radio. That would be about two-hundred miles according to my quick calculations. My hitchhiker's radar gave the man an okay. After I settled in, he turned off the radio.

Jasper, the driver, did most of the talking. The short, wiry, man, with curly grey hair, and a genial smile, worked as a mechanic for a Chrysler dealership up in Ottawa. The mechanic informed me that he enjoyed camping, described some of his favorite places to pitch a tent, and talked at length about a recent trip he had made to the Utah and Nevada desert. "Boy, you don't see nothin' like that here in Canada," Jasper said shaking his head, "was bone dry and beautiful there, eh?"

Recently diagnosed with breast cancer, he told me that his mother had started chemo treatments. "She always gets sick after one of 'em," commented Jasper in an almost whisper as if talking to himself. "I'm worried about her." There were tears in his eyes then he got quiet for a long stretch and I listened to the hum of the tires on the highway as we continued to drive alongside Lake Ontario. "Know what a car rally is?" he asked abruptly pulling out of his silent slump. I shook my head no. "It's my favorite sport," said the mechanic. "Love it!" Jasper explained that in a rally the driver and navigator followed what he called a blind map. At each stop, the navigator received a new set of directions as opposed to following an already established route from beginning to end. When Jasper made his exit onto Highway 31 heading north, I hopped out.

Making it to Montreal that night, via Interstate 20 East, I arrived at the youth hostel on Mackay Street just as the desk attendant began to close shop. "Yer lucky," he said, "got one bunk left." I showed him my membership card, signed in, and paid. My top bunk was on the third floor in a room with seven other men; some had already gone to sleep, a few were reading by flashlight, and two others had not returned yet. In the communal kitchen, I fixed a peanut butter and jelly sandwich, purchased a small container of milk from the vending machine, and sat down in the living room to write in my journal.

The following day, long-legged, scrunched-up, blue-eyed Norman, a dialysis specialist from Saint Therese, invited me into his green, two-tone Chevrolet on the outskirts of the city. "Heading to Quebec City for business," he told me. Because I had spent a leisurely morning in Montreal, I had not made it back to Highway 20 East until early afternoon. From his size, I knew Norman had to be a basketball player. He confirmed, early in our conversation, that he had played in both high school and college. Before settling down in Quebec, Norman informed me he had backpacked extensively in Central and South America, Europe, and Australia, where he met his wife. He talked at length about Central America, in particular, and the military brutality he had witnessed in Guatemala and El Salvador. Norman had a strong progressive political consciousness and described what he observed in a heartfelt and sensitive manner. I liked being in his company. "My wife and I are gonna sail around the world someday," he told me with resolve just before we stopped for a piss break. When Norman got out of the car, he stood at least 6'4", taller than I had imagined. Just before he took me to the Quebec City Youth

Hostel, I wrote down my name, address, and phone number on a scrap piece of paper and handed it to him. I didn't do that very often, but I felt a connection with Norman. "If you ever get to New York, you gotta a place to stay," I told him.

No empty beds at the hostel. The questionable looking backpacker's motel, down the block, did not have any room either so I decided to get back onto 20 East. Against my better judgment, I accepted a ride with wild and crazy kid. Because the young man had almost collided with a semi when he pulled over to the side of highway, I felt obliged to get into the car. He did not speak English and I didn't speak French. I just wanted to get to the other side of the city, out of the congestion, but that young fellow took a detour and dropped me off a few miles from interstate. I'm still not sure if he did that intentionally. In the dark, I managed to find my way back to 20 East. Exhausted, I stopped at a filling station to bathe in the bathroom sink and buy a cup of coffee. Nearby, I unrolled my sleeping bag on a sixty-degree slab of concrete, underneath an overpass, and fell asleep to the hum of the traffic above.

I woke up to a heavy rain and a bleak-looking day. After folding up my gear and eating a can of mixed fruit, I pulled on my poncho, slipped my sign into a clear plastic bag that I carried for that very purpose, and began hitchhiking. Following the coastline of the St. Lawrence River, I received a string of rides with engaging folks. A woman driver, in her late twenties, told me she had started building a house on her land by day and driving a taxi at night to make ends meet. Two bearded Frenchmen picked me up and in broken English revealed that they were lovers on their way north for two weeks of sailing. A veterinarian, a professor at a Riviere du-Loop College, strongly encouraged me to hike the Cabot Trail once I reached the Cape Breton coast. I eventually took his advice.

By late afternoon, two fellows in a Toyota pick-up gave me a lift. Initially, it felt heaven sent as I spread out in the spacious truck bed, but then they picked up another backpacker a few miles down the road and two more a half hour later; by dusk the driver had added three additional backpackers to the mix. After crossing into New Brunswick, we got out near Hartland, described as the home of the longest covered bridge in the world. I bid my fellow backpackers adieu, discovered a good spot in the woods to set up camp, finished off a tin of mustard sardines on Saltines, and bedded down.

A loud, piercing, and chirping sound, directly above my pup tent, woke me early. When I crawled out of the tent in my underwear and bare feet, then looked up, a bald eagle with an eight-foot wingspan made a claw dive in my direction and I hit the ground flat on my belly. That bird could have torn the flesh right off my back had he been a couple of inches closer. Must have been his warning dive. Before my feathered antagonist made a second attempt, I crawled back inside the tent and got dressed. That darn bird continued his claw diving maneuvers and chirping for another quarter of an hour as I periodically peeked out from between the tent flaps. Thought he might attempt to pick up the tent, with me inside, but he didn't. I must have invaded his territory. Perhaps he had built a nest nearby. After a silent spell, I quickly broke camp, slogged through the thirteen hundred foot covered bridge over the St. John's River and into Hartland where I stopped at a diner for breakfast.

Late in the day, I had reached the Moncton outskirts, walked into town where I bought groceries and grabbed a cup of coffee. By the time I had trekked to the other side of the city, the sun had gone down so I pitched my tent near a cluster of bushes in a cemetery, best place to find peace and quiet. Breaking camp early in the morning, I noticed a fancy green Cadillac drive by slowly on the nearby gravel road. I didn't think anything of it until the Caddy made a U-turn, drove back, and stopped about forty feet from where I had just strapped my bag and tent onto the bottom of my pack with bungee cords. The driver's window buzzed down exposing a bald-headed, ci- gar-smoking man with puffy cheeks "Ya camp here last night?" he yelled. It was obvious but I did not respond. When the man repeated his question, I continued to remain silent. He proceeded to open the car door, pulled himself out of the seat with a grunt, and walked a few yards toward me then stopped. Wearing a tie, a vest, and wingtips, the angry local kept talking at me in a loud voice. "Damn, don't ya have any respect for the dead?" But, he didn't move any closer.

I thought it better to just keep my mouth shut, not antago- nize him; give the local some time to cool down. Eventually he did. Finally, shaking his head and mumbling something under his breath, the man made his way back to the car, wiggled back into the seat, and drove off. I departed that home for the dead in no time at all. I knew that cigar-smoking gent would stop by the police department on his way to work and report a derelict in the cemetery.

Terry, a musician, on his way home to Cape Breton via Highway 2, caught my attention on the other side of Monc- ton. A wool cap partially covered his shoulder-length black hair, and he had trained his mustache to turn up at either end. Terry had a handsome face with a toothy smile. Once settled into his van, Heidi, his affectionate dachshund jumped into my lap and curled up just like a cat. "She almost never does that with someone she knows, let alone a stranger," com- mented Terry. "You've definitely found a friend." He had a gig that night in Cheticamp, Cape Breton Isle. "I'm playin' at the Acadian Pub," said the musician. "Oughta' come by, eh? I sing and play the Bodhran."

"Bodhran?"

"Yeah," he replied, "a Gaelic drum. Heads made of sheep- skin." He also played the acoustic guitar, "Been at it for seven years and make'n a livin'." Born and raised on Cape Breton, his parents had been farmers there for decades.

Entering New Glasgow, we stopped for lunch. Returning to the van, Terry asked me to drive while he took a nap. Green and hilly, the landscape reminded me of the Scottish coastlands that I remembered from past travels.

Near the Canso Canal Bridge, that connected Cape Breton Island with Nova Scotia's mainland, a heavy rain began to fall and it started to blow hard, too. Terry and Heidi were asleep so I didn't bother them at first but by the time I drove across the bridge and onto the causeway, waves were breaking over the stone support walls on either side of us. Midway across, the water started to splash on top of the van. That is when Terry and Heidi woke up. Because slippery seaweed covered the narrow two lanes, I began to drive at a snail's pace white knuckling the steering wheel. "It'll be okay," Terry reassured me patting my shoulder. "Happens all the time, just keep it slow and steady." He did not go back to sleep, and neither did Heidi. Alert, she sat up in his lap looking out the front windshield. "You'll wanna take Highway 19, to yer left, just off the causeway." Highway 19 snaked around the rugged coastline that looked out onto the Gulf of St. Lawrence. Soon, the rain stopped and the sun came out as I continued to drive through the small communities that dotted the island.

I set up tent that night just outside Cheticamp then walked into town after dark to hear Terry perform. What a fantastic musician! Terry introduced me to the rowdy audience as his "hitchhiking buddy from the States."

After breakfast in town the following morning, I wrote a few postcards, mailed them, bought some groceries, and made a new sign–HALIFAX. That was when a senior citizen, named Elsie, spotted me and soon thereafter drove me to the head of the Cabot Trail leading into Cape Breton National Park. She also gave me one of her blueberry muffins, big enough for two, which she had purchased in the town bakery that morning.

The sweet, gray-haired woman told me that I looked like her grandson. That's why she gave me a ride. "I've never stopped for a hitchhiker before," Elsie admitted with a chuckle.

The exhilarating vista on the trail reminded me of Point Reyes National Park in the San Francisco Bay Area, equally spectacular. Not far into the national park, I discovered an inlet, hiked down to it, stripped off my clothes, and plunged into the ice-cold water. With sun and a slight breeze, the weather was ideal. After drying out, stretched spread-eagled on the narrow beach, I made my way back up to the trail with my shorts on, my shirt off, and my arms stretched wide. I felt like Superman. Yes, sir, felt like Superman. I had a revelation, too.

"I'm gonna leave New York!" I yelled out with resolve. "Gonna get out of that city!" I meant it, too. I realized I didn't want to play someone else's characters anymore. I wanted to live my own characters. I did not want to speak somebody else's lines either. I wanted to write and speak my own. I did not want to have to live in New York or Los Angeles for the rest of my life. I wanted to explore the world. That's right. I wanted to go somewhere completely different from New York. I wanted to do something completely different from acting. I did not know where and what, I just knew in that moment I was going to make a change.

Did not pass a soul on the trail the entire day. I hiked until dusk, settled down by a lake, opened a can of beans, and sliced-up one of my apples. For the evening's entertainment, I pulled out my harmonica, and searched for the notes to Bob Dylan's "The Times they are a Changin", a song I had brought along to memorize the lyrics. When the sun went down, it got cold fast. Although still early, I slipped into my bag and drifted off into dreamland.

Come morning, I quickly realized why I had not encountered other backpackers on the trail. As soon as I stepped out of my tent, black flies began to swarm and then attack. It was black fly season. Those vicious critters bit and stung simultaneously. They were unrelenting, determined to take me down. From experience, I knew they were the worst in the morning because of the moist, spongy ground and nearby lake.

Scurrying back into the tent, I ate a small can of pineapple, pulled out my mosquito netting and rain poncho then made me a homemade burqa before breaking camp. As I reached the asphalt road near the trail, swatting at the swarm of wings surrounding me, a mammoth Winnebago pulled over and the driver motioned for me to get aboard. That doggone thing took up nearly two-thirds of the narrow road running through the park. I had not even stuck out my sign yet

Hustling around the monster RV, I climbed the steps into that house on wheels. I almost felt embarrassed, but more relieved. Never before, in all my hitchhiking days, had I ever been picked-up by a Winnebago. Arne, a well-tanned senior citizen introduced himself and his wife. He sat in the driver's seat with his short arms resting on the huge steering wheel. His wife, Lena, who looked like the female version of Arne, sat in the cushioned passenger seat beside him.

I stayed with them through the day and the night. They paid for a spot in a camping area for my benefit, I presumed. Arne even grilled for dinner. What a hoot. As we ate burgers and drank bottles of beer, the couple told me about their lives and family. From Windham, Vermont, Arne had recently retired from the army, and Lena, a full-time homemaker, had finished raising their two girls and two boys.

By noon the next day, I was in a conversation with a Catholic priest from Cheticamp, who also happened to be a fiddler. "I play wakes, weddings, and funerals," announced the man with the white collar. "On my days off I fish." Father Thomas took me all the way to Halifax where he had a gig the next day.

Hungry, I walked into a donut shop for one glazed and a

coffee and initiated a conversation with a Halifax cabbie. We got along so well that he offered to give me a free tour of the city then dropped me at Bill's house, Dolly's actor friend. Bill, with his round, handsome face, short curly brown hair, and compact build, had just returned home from a rehearsal at the Stages Cabaret downtown. We made a spaghetti dinner and spent a good part of the evening kibitzing about acting and survival jobs, travels and books, authors and plays. I told him stories about my most recent acting coach, Kim Stanley, and he shared performance techniques that he had learned from his first acting teacher, Evelyn Garbary, at Acadia University there in Nova Scotia.

"Ever read anything by Joseph Campbell," Bill asked. Earlier, I had mentioned my interest in monastic communities, religion, and spirituality. I did not recognize the name. "Oh, man, you just gotta read his work. He's a mythologist," Bill explained getting all animated and exited. "You'll love the guy." He recommended that I begin with *The Masks of God: Primitive Mythology*. "Campbell's the guy that coined the phrase 'follow your bliss.'"

Campbell, who had spent his life exploring mythological archetypes and comparative religions, would eventually become an important and influential man in my life. His writings, lectures, and interviews greatly enhanced my interest in ritual and comparative religions. Campbell's writings eventually led me into archetypal men's workshops; facilitated by American poet Robert Bly and drummer Michael Meade, participation in men's consciousness raising groups, and intense weekend trainings with a national organization called the Mankind Project.

Bill had already split when I woke up early on the front room couch. The actor planned to rehearse a one-man show he had written about vaudeville performer and singer Al Jolson. Walking into town, I discovered a music store and picked up a harmonica songbook, dropped by the Neptune Theatre, a professional actor's equity venue where Bill planned to perform the next year, and explored the seaport section of the city. Unfortunately, it had lost much of its original historical and cultural character and become a polished tourist site with dripping ice cream cones and schlocky souvenir booths.

I also passed by a tavern, The Sea Horse, and felt compelled to go in and order a beer. Harry and Gerty were nowhere in sight, but I did run into Bill sitting in a back booth and running lines from his one-man show. He invited me to sit and join him.

A day later, I returned to Highway 103, with sign in hand–YARMOUTH! Must have walked three miles to get out of Halifax. Bill would have given me a ride, but his car was in the shop. A British man, Thomas, my first auto companion for the day had recently attended an engineer's conference in Halifax and looked forward to a few days at the shore near the village of Liverpool. Early in our conversation, without any prompting, Thomas informed me that he had joined the Catholic Charismatic Renewal Movement.

"Not familiar with the group," I told him. "Tell me about them."

The engineer mentioned speaking in tongues and the practice of hands on healing as well as a belief in miracles and prophecy. "We believe in a direct encounter with the Holy Spirit," declared the Brit. Awhile down the road, Thomas asked me if I had ever been married and I told him no. He informed me that he had gone through a divorce two years earlier.

"In a relationship?" Thomas inquired. "Sort of," I answered. "What's her name?" he asked.

"She's a he not a she," I replied. "Name is Zack."

"Oh," Thomas replied then cleared his throat. After a pregnant pause, he responded to what I had just told him "I once had an immature relationship. I was in my twenties." I just listened. The Englishman proceeded to inform me that when he got older, he realized that the only right and sensible way for a relationship would be the "female way." Minutes later, when we reached the outskirts of Liverpool, I told Thomas to stop and let me out. That man had to be uncomfortable living in the closet.

If lucky, one more lift would get me into Yarmouth by dusk. Passing a filling station, on the other side of the village, I noticed a senior citizen sitting in an old, battered, black truck with boxes and furniture piled high in the back. He tracked me as I shuffled by. When I waved, he waved back. "Want a ride," he yelled out his truck window. Bert, an octogenarian, admitted that he had passed me a few miles back. "But I wanted to check ya out before offerin' a ride, eh?" The old man and his wife were moving out of their farmhouse and into a trailer in Yarmouth. The wife had remained on the farm packing their belongings. Bert had lived a bigger-than-life life. Our conversation sounded like a Studs Terkel radio interview or something out of the famous Chicagoan's *Division Street America,* an oral history of twentieth-century America. Bert talked about growing up in Cape Breton and told me how he had solved money problems during the Depression.

"Fer three years I worked on a banana plantation in Honduras," he told me, "made $15,000. Was alot of money in those days." Bert paused a moment, checking his side mirror, then continued with his story. On his way back from Central America, Bert stopped in New York City. "Spent $10,000 there in six weeks," he admitted, "never regretted it." While in Manhattan, he saw the uncut version of *Gone with the Wind,* too. "It was completely different than the movie ya see today," he informed me. "Whole scenes and events have been cut out."

As we approached Yarmouth, I offered to help him unload his truck, but Bert had a friend waiting for him who would give him a hand. He left me at the YMCA, the youth hostel in Yarmouth during the summer months, where I paid $2.25 for a mattress on the gym floor and a shower.

Months prior to leaving for Nova Scotia, I had eagerly read Charles A. Fracchia's *Living Together Alone: The New American Monasticism*. His chapter four, titled "The Call to the Desert," described a Roman Catholic, co-ed, spiritual community of the Carmelite Order, called Nova Nada, tucked away in the woods one-and-a-half hours drive north of Yarmouth. Out of curiosity, I had decided to try to contact them and request a three-day retreat in their community. I wanted to discover how men and women lived together alone in community.

"The Carmelites were originally hermits. And, of course, their life was the traditional hermit life known to the east from the earliest centuries of the Church," explained Trappist monk Thomas Merton. "But they were not monks in the western sense. They had no liturgical office in common. They did not live in monasteries or cloisters. They were in fact simple lay-men, living as solitaries in a loosely connected group, in caves and huts, on the side of Mount Carmel." [1]

A YMCA staff member agreed to communicate my request to a Nova Nada contact person. In turn, that individual relayed my message to the community via a two-way radio. I would receive my answer within twenty-four hours. In the morning, the local Apple-a-Day Café served scrambled eggs and hot bran muffins, just out of the oven, with free refills on the coffee and I returned there at noon for their mac 'n' cheese, comfort food. After a hike around the rocky, hilly port town, I sought information about fees and departure times for the ferry to Bar Harbor, Maine. Returning to the Y, I hunkered down with Robert M. Pirsig's *Zen and the Art of Motorcycle Maintenance*. Bill had given me his copy before I left Halifax. "Gotta read it," he insisted. "You'll be glad you did."

Late afternoon, I received the Nova Nada reply–no room at

the inn. Their four, retreat spaces had already been reserved. In the future, they recommended contacting the community in advance to reserve a retreat space. Half-dozen years later, in 1986, I would do exactly that.

After learning the disappointing news, I made my way down to the ferry office and bought a ticket for that night's departure. During the ride to Bar Harbor, I met a fellow from North Carolina who had spent three weeks exploring Newfoundland and planned to drive to Providence, Rhode Island, the next day. The friendly gent offered to take me into Boston, with some other backpackers, where I had made plans to stay with my close friend, Marcia Garcia, for a few days.

Disembarking in Bar Harbor near midnight, the North Carolinian parked his pick-up on a lot nearby where we spent the night. Four of us squeezed together in the truck bed with our camping equipment and three bicycles. The other two snuggled up in the cab. By mid-afternoon, I caught the subway out to Somerville, a Boston suburb, and boarded a bus to Powder House Square as instructed. Soon I found my friend's address on Kenwood Street and waited for her on the porch swing as I continued to read Pirsig's book.

I had known Marcia Garcia, a graphic arts major, since we were students at Livingston College. Employed as the resident advisor of her dormitory, I had received room, board, and a stipend. She and her roommate lived in the room directly above me. Marcia had adopted Garcia as her middle name in deference to Mexican artists Frida Kahlo and Diego Rivera whom she adored. With curly black hair always flying everywhere, tall, long-armed Marcia Garcia had the untamed whirlwind of a tornado on two legs. Spontaneous, emotional, and boundlessly energetic, she frequently wrapped herself into a black cape and applied dark red lipstick just like writer Anais Nin. My first night in Somerville, Marcia Garcia lived up to her reputation. That came as no surprise.

When the artist returned home and discovered me on the porch swing, she wrapped those long arms around me and gave me a big welcome kiss on the cheek. Once I had settled in, Marcia Garcia informed that we were going to attend a birthday party that very night with four of her friends. Now that I had arrived, there would be three men and three women. The event required special evening attire. She told me bare feet and men's suits for the women and evening dresses with bare feet for the men. Marcia Garcia found a tight fitting, slinky, white satin number for me, a tad tight in the chest and a bit saggy around the butt. I had not stepped out in drag since my early grade school years when I played dress-up with the neighborhood kids. Marcia failed to tell me, however, until we arrived at the birthday celebration, that we would be eating with our fingers. The menu–mashed potatoes, with gravy, fried chicken, green peas, salad, and numerous bottles of Chianti. The guests were an unconventional collection of folks. I felt right at home. After dinner, we piled into a van and drove over to Harvard Square in Cambridge where we ate bowls of birthday ice cream with our fingers, of course. For the celebration's grand finale, we drove out to Thoreau's Walden Pond and skinny-dipped under a full moon and a sky splayed with stars.

The following evening, Marcia Garcia and I stayed in and reminisced about our time together in Italy. After leaving Israel in late 1974, I had hitchhiked across Greece with my friend, Ann. We then boarded the Poseidonia, an overnight steamer, to the island of Korfu and a week later sailed to the Italian port of Brindisi. Upon reaching the Italian coast, we purchased train tickets to Perugia where Marcia Garcia had arranged to study art during her junior year abroad. Although it took two days to track her down, Marcia Garcia gave us a grand welcome and invited us to stay in her large, high-ceilinged, pink studio walk-up, near Vannucci Street, that had neither heat nor hot water. They slept in the bed. I got the floor.

Within a few days, Ann left but I remained in Italy for almost a month. Marcia Garcia became my personal docent exploring Italian art. We traveled south to Pompeii and spent a day climbing around the partially unearthed ruins with no one else in sight, the *National Geographic* come to life. In Assisi, she led my individual tour through the Basilica di San Francisco, three churches in one, where we visited the tomb of St. Francis and Marcia Garcia talked me through the extraordinary series of frescoes by Giotto. In Gubbio, known for some of the finest examples of medieval architecture, we explored the Church of St. Augustine and viewed the more than a dozen illustrations of the saint's life painted by Ottaviano Nelli. During our stay in Rome, we wandered through a dozen ruins and just as many cathedrals, got lost in the catacombs, and participated in Christmas midnight Mass at St. Peter's Basilica. Being a Jubilee Year, the entire Roman Catholic hierarchy attended in full regalia and the Pope opened the doors of St. Peters. The Jubilee, celebrated every quarter century, had the spectacle of a Federico Fellini film extravaganza.

Staying with her friends in Florence, we spent days at the Uffizi Gallery and the Academy of Fine Arts where Michelangelo's David stood big, proud, and naked. We crossed the medieval Ponte Vecchio at least a dozen times, visited Dante's home, and toured the Duomo, the city's central cathedral with an intricately designed facade of black and white marble. Marcia Garcia insisted that we stop in Ravenna. She wanted to take me to the Basilica of St. Apollinaire Nuevo, built in the sixth century, to witness the largest mosaics from antiquity, the procession of the Virgins and Martyrs. After celebrating my twenty-fifth birthday in Venice, on December 30, we finally parted ways. Marcia Garcia returned to Perugia for another semester and I boarded a train for Milan.

CHAPTER TEN

~

Rural Free Delivery

Having returned from Canada, I slowly began to prepare for my departure from the city. I needed to leave New York and acting for at least a year or two. Would I ever return? A question I could not answer. I did, however, sign up for Stella Adler's Acting Workshop, a series of lectures she presented at the New School for Social Research in Lower Manhattan. Adler's classes provided an introduction into her much talked about acting technique but required no rehearsal time. I knew that Adler had studied with the famed Russian actor and theater director, Konsantin Stanislavski, in Paris. As a result, she had parted ways with Lee Strasberg and his Method Acting. Adler came to believe that an actor needed to create her character through imagination rather than by memory of personal events and experiences. The actor used Henrik Ibsen's play, *A Doll's House*, throughout the workshop to explain her technique of breaking down a play and developing character.

"You've come here to learn to act, but I want to teach you **not** to act," stated Ms. Adler in *The Art of Acting*. "If somebody tells you they loved the way you acted, I hope you know that means you've failed. Nowadays we don't want artificiality. We want realism, and that's why if the audience thinks you're **acting,** you've failed them. What you have to learn is to perform actions, because if you're performing an action, you're doing something. You're not **indicating**, you're doing."[1]

Although I had stopped auditioning for plays, an acquaintance hired me to perform in a few industrial films and record several advertising voice-overs in the months to come. I also significantly increased my working hours as bartender and waiter for a private caterer. In the past year, I had considered the Peace Corps and finally requested an application, filled it out, and mailed it in.

About that same time, I responded to a letter about a work situation that appeared in the rural, gay, quarterly *RFD*, a creative and unique gay men's publication. Neither slick nor dependent upon advertisers, an ongoing collective of socially and politically conscious men from the gay subculture, Radical Fairies, were responsible for writing, illustrating, and publishing the magazine. Their dedication to rural life, environmental issues, pagan spirituality, and exploration into gay male sexuality had garnered my curiosity and respect.

A gay, Vietnam Vet named Rex, had written the letter to *RFD*. He wanted to recruit men to join a successful tree-planting cooperative, called Hoedads, based in the university town of Eugene, Oregon. The idea strongly appealed to me. I could work outside and live in the woods. I wrote back and expressed my interest. One month later Rex replied. That began our ongoing conversation via the written word.

By early 1981, I received encouraging feedback from the Peace Corps. They were seriously considering my application. As well, I had written a final letter to Rex telling him that I planned to arrive in Oregon in early spring.

Shortly before departing the city, I received a call from Sandy, a political activist. We had become friends six years earlier as participants in the UN Student Internship Program. At that time, I had just completed a graduate semester at New York University and she had recently finished her Sarah Lawrence undergraduate degree. Sandy told me about an upcoming fundraiser for the Plowshares Eight legal defense team led by Father Dan Berrigan, a nationally known Jesuit activist. I knew that Berrigan lived in community with other religious, on West 98th, nine blocks from my apartment building.

In September 1980, Father Berrigan and Sister Ann Montgomery, along with six other anti-nuke activists, had illegally entered General Electric's Nuclear Missile Plant in King of Prussia, Pennsylvania. Once inside, they poured their blood over warhead documents, hammered on two Mark 12A warheads, and remained in the plant to pray for peace and disarmament before their arrests. Drawing from biblical scripture, the two women and six men called themselves the Plowshares Eight. "He shall judge between the nations, and shall decide disputes for many peoples; and they shall beat their swords into plowshares, and their spears into pruning hooks; nation shall not lift up sword against nation, neither shall they know war anymore."[2]

"You should go," Sandy told me. "A day after the fundraiser there's going be an anti-draft action in front of the Army Recruitment Center in Time Square," she paused. "You oughta be there, too," I had not participated in nonviolent civil disobedience since my Louisville days. Before hanging up, Sandy gave me the name and address of the Upper West Side church hosting the fundraiser. Because I had that night off from work, I decided to attend the rally and invited Lucy to accompany me. Much to our delight, additional speakers included Sacred Heart Sister Ann Montgomery, Allen Ginsberg with his trusty harmonium, noted avant-garde poet Denise Levertov, along with Julian Beck and Judith Malina, founders of the anarchist pacifist collective known as The Living Theatre. Hundreds of supporters squeezed into the space to hear the speakers on the raised stage.

Dan Berrigan, a slight man with dark, inset eyes, opened the gathering. The Jesuit looked as though someone had placed a bowl over his head and cut around the edges, a St. Francis haircut. Berrigan and Montgomery, a smallish woman with close-cropped gray hair, spoke passionately about their recent King of Prussia political action and the upcoming trial then introduced poet Denise Levertov.

Levertov wore a colorful Mayan textile over her blouse. She once lived in the Mexican state of Chiapas where Mayan Indians had settled in large numbers. Originally from England, Levertov had become a noted American poet and a leading member of the avant-garde. With Ginsberg's harmonium in the background, Levertov read several of her poems. "Gathered at the River" remained with me. If Lucy and I had not been sitting on the floor, near the stage, we would not have been able to hear the soft-spoken poet.

Partially bald Allen Ginsberg, with his full black beard and familiar bib overalls, followed Levertov. Through dark-framed glasses, he read from his hard-hitting poem "America." Lucy and I rocked back and forth to the cadence of the poet's monotone presentation and the rhythm of his keyboard instrument.

The Living Theatre's Julian Beck and Judith Malina, wrapped in black capes, had made their visually dramatic entrance shortly after Dan Berrigan began to speak. Tall and thin with bushy dark eyebrows, Julian's round, hypnotic eyes never seemed to blink. Judith, short and waif-like, with frizzy black hair, and dark painted eyebrows stood by his side exuding energy and a strong presence. They had recently returned to the States after having moved to Europe, with The Living Theatre, in self-imposed exile for more than a decade. "Over the years since 1947, when The Living Theatre was founded by Malina and Julian Beck, thousands of people have left their seats to find their place onstage in one or another of their spectacles; hundreds have become members of the company," explained Karen Malpede, a longtime friend of the Becks. "If Judith (or Julian, or better, both) were to choose you, they embraced you completely; your work to them was a blessing to be cherished, and although you might argue aesthetics fiercely, they never judged." [3] The couple only spoke briefly that night about their theatrical relationship with anarchism and pacifism. In their opinion, the next day's demonstration would be political theater.

I boarded the subway for mid-Manhattan, early the following morning, inspired by what I witnessed the night before. With three dozen other respectful protesters, I sat down, locked arms, and blocked the entrance into the Army Recruitment Center in Times Square. After my arrest, I had a conversation with an elderly man squeezed up beside me in the crowded paddy wagon. "Been arrested more than sixty-five times for civil disobedience," the lifelong Quaker replied in answer to one of my questions. With arms behind our backs, and plastic handcuffs pulled painfully tight around our wrists, we waited for the officers to transport us to the pokey. During the next few hours, we watched out for one another in the funky holding cell. Then late in the afternoon, the two of us appeared in court, pleaded guilty to the misdemeanor charge of disorderly conduct and paid the imposed fine.

CHAPTER ELEVEN

~

Desert Spirit

It happened just on the other side of Philly. We had not been on the road for more than two hours.

"Pull over," I yelled, "Patrol car is right behind us. Red light's on!"

"Oh shit!" shouted Lucy. Tightening her hands on the steering wheel, she slowed down and pulled over to the shoulder of the interstate.

"I told you to slow down," I huffed and puffed in my self-righteous tone of voice. "You were going 85 mph in a 65 mph zone."

Lucy tried her best to sweet talk that patrol officer but she could not finagle her way out of the sizable fine. I just sat there quietly as the officer wrote out the ticket.

Weeks earlier, I had arranged to transport a drive-away car from New York City to Los Angeles. If I delivered it to the owner's home within ten days after New York departure, I would receive gas money and extra cash for incidentals.

I invited Lucy to join me on the cross-country venture with little hope that she could. Soon after my invitation, I received a letter from her. Why Lucy mailed me a letter when she could have called me on the phone, I never figured out. We both lived in Manhattan. "I haven't made up my mind about coming along for a cross-country car trip," she wrote. "My instincts shout yes and my fears shout no! So I'll keep working on it and you can let me know what the deal is."

At the last minute, she decided to come along. Even though

Lucy had flown to California with her estranged husband, she had never traveled across the country by car. The next ten days proved to be challenging for that big city woman. Still married but separated, Lucy had not been away from her little boy for more than brief periods. My travel partner proved to be as emotionally vulnerable as I was in the days to come. My home for the previous six years, I would be leaving New York and landing in Eugene, Oregon, where I only knew Rex, the tree-planter, but we had only been short-term pen pals.

Before pulling back onto the interstate, after the incident, I rearranged things in the back seat: boxes, a wicker chair with cushion, a small metal table frame and glass top along with my stuffed backpack, banjo, and Lucy's suitcases. She had packed enough clothes to last her for a month. My traveling partner slid over into the passenger's seat, slammed the speeding ticket into the glove compartment along with a string of colorful expletives, and scrunched up against the ice cooler as I settled into the driver's seat. When I picked up the decade-old, faded brown, four-door Chevy, I discovered that the owner had filled the trunk with his belongings so all of our stuff had to fit into the back seat. Until we reached Missouri, where I could unload the boxes and the pieces of furniture with my brother, Bob, there wouldn't be any stretch-out room in the car.

Back on the road, we agreed to continue straight through to Kansas City and share the driving with catnaps in between turns. Arriving in the onetime Jazz Capital of the World, early the next evening, brother Bob and his partner, Roger, welcomed us. Bob had come out of the closet some years before I would. Thus, he bore the brunt of my parent's homophobia during their adjustment period. From what I could tell, Bob handled it very well, as he seemed to do with most everything.

Roger and Bob were renting a spacious, one-bedroom apartment on the top floor of a stately, three-story brick home on Janssen Place in Hyde Park, a historic district of Kansas City.

Lucy and I would spend the night on their carpeted living room floor, a welcome respite from napping while seated in the car.

After a glass of chilled white wine and some catch-up conversation, they took us out for dinner. Following the meal, we drove over to Shawnee Mission, a neighborhood on the Kansas side of the city, for a brief visit with my older sister, Patty, and her two young children. When Patty informed me that our younger sister, Susan, had not been feeling well, I assured her that Lucy and I planned to spend the following night with her in Lawrence, home of the University of Kansas Jayhawks. Everyone in my family, except for Mom and me, were KU graduates. My mom, an Okie from Muskogee, had graduated from the University of Oklahoma.

Very early in the morning, Lucy proceeded to leave the apartment and explore the neighborhood. "When I passed two people on the sidewalk, and they said 'Good morning,' I stopped to look around to see who they were talkin' to," Lucy reported upon her return. "I realized they were talkin' to me," she threw her head back and laughed. "You know, nobody in New York City says good morning to you on the street."

Arriving in Lawrence, we found Susan distraught and alone in the apartment. Her roommates had gone out of town for the weekend and she was experiencing difficulty walking. We took her out for dinner with hopes that might help calm her down. It did not. Back at the apartment, while Lucy took a shower, Susan and I sat down in the living room to talk. My sister began to cry as she told me about recent numbness in her legs. "It comes and goes," Susan said catching her breath between sobs. "Nobody'll believe me," she explained. "Doctor says there's nothing wrong with me. It's all in my head." The former high school gymnast and track star felt confused, frightened, and depressed.

When Susan went to take a shower, Lucy joined me in the

front room. She had heard some of our conversation. "Sounds like ms," Lucy said quietly.

"What's ms?"

"Multiple sclerosis," she replied. Lucy gave me a brief explanation of the disease. "My mother was diagnosed with it a few years ago. Mom's in a wheel chair now."

Before we went to sleep, I called my folks in Newton, Kansas, a few hours away, told them what Lucy had said and suggested that they make a doctor's appointment as soon as possible. "We'll drive her to Newton tomorrow," I told them. Lucy and Susan drove the Chevy to Newton, and I followed behind in Susan's car. We stayed an additional day.

Cornelius Fritz Claassen, my paternal great grandfather, had settled in Newton during the late 1870s after leaving Europe with thousands of other Mennonites. "The reason for migration to this country," wrote my dad in his memoir, "was because Catherine the Great of Russia had granted the Mennonites, who were pacifists, a hundred-year exemption from military service. And the exemption expired in 1880."[1] My great grandfather worked at various jobs, in the onetime Santa Fe Railroad hub, from blackening stoves and selling hardware to helping establish a Mennonite college in North Newton. Eventually, he opened a small town bank with a Ukrainian Mennonite business partner. My grandfather and namesake, Cornelius William Claassen, and later my dad, Walter Cornelius Claassen, continued to grow the business for decades.

My parents welcomed Lucy, whom they had not met before, and bonded within a short time. Walt and Helen listened intently to what Lucy had to say about her mother's experience with Multiple Sclerosis. My folks had already scheduled a doctor's appointment for Susan.

"Your father was somethin' else," Lucy told me years later. "You probably don't remember this, but that afternoon, I went on a bicycle ride around their neighborhood. When I heard a really loud siren go off, I headed back to their house." Lucy said she found Walter sitting in his car, in the driveway, with the windows rolled down.

"Tornado warning," he replied when she inquired about the siren. "Ever see one?" he asked. She told him no. "Hop in," Walter told her.

"We went tornado chasing!" said Lucy. "What a trip that was."

Walter, a former high school basketball star, accomplished violinist, and onetime Navy officer, had always been a disciplined but sometimes unpredictable character. Every morning upon waking, he performed his calisthenics routine religiously. The generous businessman had a dry sense of humor and an abrupt manner. Dad joined and became an officer in every civic organization in town from the Chamber of Commerce, Kiwanis, and Rotary Club, to the Masonic Lodge, Elks Club, VFW, and United Fund. If he was not a member, there was not a club. He served on the school board and the city council as well as the local Bethel College board of directors. When a civic project held a fund drive, my dad usually filled a leadership role. He sang in the church choir and served as an elder and a deacon. The community recognized Walter as the epitome of civic mindedness.

Prior to marrying my dad, Helen worked for an insurance company and lived in Milwaukee where the Navy had stationed Walter. Mom had given up her career to become a homemaker, a difficult decision for her I am sure. Helen had had a taste of independence and city life. "I had to propose to your mother three different times before she accepted," Dad once told me. After moving to small-town Kansas, she, too, became active with church and civic organizations in addition to raising four children. Helen, a very classy woman, could make a fashion statement by merely throwing a colorful scarf around her neck. She had dozens of them tucked away in dresser drawers. Mom's family named Dodson, of Scottish and English descent, had settled in Arkansas and homesteaded. Her parents eventually moved to Oklahoma in order to attend the state university in Norman.

The day after the tornado chase, Lucy and I drove north on a two-lane into Lindsborg, Kansas, a Swedish community and former home of artist Birger Sandzén, a post-impressionist painter who taught for decades at Bethany College. As a kid, I used to drive to Lindsborg with my granddad and namesake, "Corny," short for Cornelius, Claassen. All of his friends and customers in Newton called him by that nickname. As a youngster, I feared people might call me Corny, too, if they knew my first name. Therefore, I kept it hidden and told my classmates and friends my name was Bill. Only years later, did I grow into the name Cornelius, learn to honor it, and respect its family history.

Just outside of Lindsborg rose a three-hundred-foot-hill, Coronado Heights. In the middle of Kansas, we called that a mountain. On top of the Heights set a native limestone, shelter resembling a miniature castle, constructed by the Works Progress Administration during President Franklin Roosevelt's New Deal era. Local legend claimed that Mexican explorer, Francisco Vasquez de Coronado, had traveled to that region in the mid-1500s in search of the Seven Cities of Gold. When he didn't find them, his exploratory party returned to Mexico.

Standing on the roof of that castle, I could see endless miles across the Smoky Valley, flat land and sky. Author Tom Spanbauer captured the vista. "There was sky between your fingers when you spread them, and sky under your arms when you lifted them up. Sky around your neck and ears and head, and sky pressing against your eyeballs. When you took a breath, you were breathing sky. Sky was in your lungs."[2] For a small-town Kansas boy, that Coronado legend conjured up all kinds of fantasies and mysteries. Of course, Grandpa Corny always added something more to the legend on each of our trips. Those visits to Coronado Heights planted seeds in my imagination that blossomed into wanderlust in the years to come.

After our brief tour of Coronado Heights, Lucy and I stopped at a bakery in town for coffee and Swedish pastry then continued onto Interstate 70 heading west. Driving across the plains of western Kansas, Lucy rambled on about all the talk she had heard regarding the amazing sunsets in Eisenhower country. Lucy declared that she had not seen one yet. "Where are they?" she kept asking. "And then there was that incredible sunset as we approached the Colorado–Kansas border!" exclaimed Lucy during a much later conversation. "It was orange and red and yellow and it filled up the entire sky," reported the New Yorker. "That's when I understood what people were talkin' about."

We stayed on Interstate 70 until reaching Limon, Colorado, then veered southwest onto Highway 24 that merged into Interstate 25 south. At the Walsenburg Exit, we turned onto Highway 160 that snaked its way westward toward the Four Corners Monument, Navajo and Hopi country. We planned to stop in Durango for a meal, then continue to Cortez, just outside Mesa Verde, and spend the night.

Early the next day, we were the first visitors on the Mesa Verde path to explore the Anasazi cliff dwellings before returning to the car by late morning to forge into Navajo territory. By early afternoon, we were descending the winding White House Trail at Canyon de Chelly, a rigorous four miles down and back up. We started out in sunshine, then encountered mist and fog so thick that we could not see a dozen feet in front of us. By the time we reached the bottom of the canyon, it had begun to snow heavily. Neither of us was dressed for that kind of weather. On the way back up the trail, huddled tightly together as we climbed, the sun peered out from behind the clouds and warmed us up.

Lucy and I continued traveling Highway 191 to Ganado, Arizona, where I wanted to stop briefly. In the summer of 1964, between my freshman and sophomore high school years, I volunteered to participate in a Presbyterian Mission Work Project on a Navajo Reservation near Ganado, home of the famous Hubbell Trading Post, a mere few hours away were the natural wonders of Window Rock and the mystical stone formation appropriately named Shiprock.

For many of the Presbyterian volunteers, it was not only our first trip away from home for an extended period but also our introduction to Native American culture. Our job was to lay a flagstone patio around the front walkway leading into a new hospital. With four adult chaperons, we spent eight hours a day working on the patio under the guidance of a Navajo supervisor. "They would drive us out to a dry and dusty arroyo in an old, rusty, red pickup," remembered fellow volunteer William Smith. "We used pry bars that slipped into the layers of rock and popped out slabs of sandstone that we took back and set onto a sand base." I remember vividly an evening orientation session with the mission doctor. As our group sat around him in a circle, the gray haired man talked about the Native American Church founded by Comanche Quanah Parker in the 1890s. The doctor told us that the church had integrated Christian and indigenous spiritual practices.

Midway through his talk, he passed around a glass jar filled with peyote buds, small, green, spineless cactus that grew carrot-like in the Rio Grande Valley of Texas and Mexico. The doctor revealed that the Native American Church used peyote as a sacrament instead of the wine and bread taken during Communion in Christian denominations. He revealed that the natural substance could be eaten, ingested in a powder form, or sipped as tea. I found his lecture fascinating. I had never heard of the Native American Church or considered the possibility of integrating Christian and Native American spiritual practices. The thought of using a cactus as the sacrament intrigued me. By the conclusion of the doctor's lecture, I knew that someday I would participate in that church's ritual. Decades later, at the invitation of its members, I joined an all-night Native American Church peyote ceremony on a Nevada Indian Reservation.

The mission grounds at Ganado had not changed much since my high school project days. When Lucy and I dropped by the administrative office we were curtly informed that all staff were now Native Americans and the records from my summer project had been destroyed. Tension in the air shortened our stay.

We briefly wandered around the complex, visited the gym where I had played basketball with Navajo kids and slept with the project crew in bunk beds upstairs above the court, then drove a few miles over to the Hubbell Trading Post where Lucy bought at least a dozen postcards with sepia tinted photographs taken by ethnologist Edward S. Curtis. The controversial Curtis, who shot his photography in the late 1800s and early 1900s, spent thirty years creating documentation that preserved the customs of the Native Americans and their cultures. For months following our trip, Lucy mailed those postcards to me, one by one, with scribbled notes. I kept every one of them.

When we got back on the road and headed for the Second Mesa on the Hopi Reservation, it had gotten dark, but a full moon and an infinite number of stars lit up the sky. We planned to travel as far as Flagstaff. Driving south out of Second Mesa and onto the two-lane Highway 87, we could see nothing but desert extending for miles on either side of the tarmac.

Lucy rewound a cassette tape she had made especially for the trip, and it began to play again. The impressive collection of blues and pop music included Etta James singing an all-

time favorite "At Last" and Linda Ronstadt with "Desperado."
Bonnie Raitt wailed through "I Can't Make You Love Me "and
"Angel from Montgomery, " then James Taylor strummed his
acoustic guitar belting out "Fire and Rain " and sweet-talking
"You've Got a Friend. " We were about a half hour out of the
Hopi Second Mesa, just as Billie Holiday began to tickle our
fancy with "What a Little Moonlight Can Do "and Lucy had
begun to hum along. That's when I slammed on the brakes,
and the car screeched to a stop.

Thirty feet in front of us, smack dab in the middle of the
two-lane road, stood a larger-than-life Native American spirit
figure. Wearing a headdress and colorful attire enveloped by
feathers, the Hopi Kachina apparition faced us straight on.
The rainbow colored figure began a ritual dance in front of the
car's headlights. One hand held a large rattle while the other
pumped to the rhythm of his moccasin covered feet moving
up and down on the tarmac. Shaking his rattle and tail feathers, the Kachina's square, mask-covered head continued to
shift from one side to the other. Lucy and I sat there stunned.
Stranger yet, he did not make a sound. All the car windows
were rolled down and there was nothing but dead silence outside. The spirit existed in a parallel universe.

I couldn't drive around it or I would end up in the sand.
Should I throw the car into reverse, turn around, and head
back north? Just as that thought occurred to me the supernat-
ural being leaped off the highway, into the desert, and van-
ished into the moonlight. Promptly, my foot slipped off the
brake and onto the accelerator. That old Chevy moved toward
Interstate 40 as fast as I could get it to go. For a time, Lucy and
I remained speechless. Then neither of us could stop talking.
"Disappeared just like that," Lucy said repeatedly.

By the time we reached nearby Winslow, Lucy and I were
ready to stop for the night. We needed down time from our
recent, other worldly, experience. After checking into a cheap

motel and unloading what we needed into the room, I got first dibs on the bathroom. When I finished showering and came out, I saw Lucy pushing the dresser in front of the door.

"What are you doing?" I asked.

"What's it look like I'm doing?" Lucy snapped back. "I don't want that thing comin' into our room."

"That's not gonna stop it," I kidded her. "If it wants to come in it'll just walk through the wall." Both of us had a hard time getting much sleep that night.

We visited Arcosanti, near Cordes Junction just north of Phoenix, the following day and took a tour. I had an interest in exploring the Italian architect Paolo Soleri's utopian city in the desert. I knew of the place because my onetime Swedish girlfriend, Alicia, had worked a three-month internship there the previous summer. The complex of energy-efficient, earth-formed massive concrete structures were built around Soleri's concept of arcology, a term he used to describe the concept of architecture and ecology working as a single integral process. Soleri had a vision of a future self-sustaining community in the wilderness.

By the end of our ten-day deadline, Lucy and I were sitting outside Guru Muktananda's Ashram in downtown Santa Monica waiting for the evening meditation to end. The tent, spanning an entire block, accommodated hundreds of devotees in one sitting. Our actor friend, Ingrid, one of the original twelve who studied with us at the Zeller's 78 Street Theatre Lab, had lived at the ashram for months. She had cut and run from New York in search of enlightenment. Ingrid penned me a lengthy letter from the ashram shortly after her arrival. "I'm feeling a little distance from the guru these days," wrote Ingrid. "I went to ask him if theater has a place in my sadhana (spiritual path). If it doesn't, what does? I'm at a point now when following the guru's teachings gives me strength. I am not at the point where I can just ask myself. My self is not clear yet. It's too clouded with fears and failures." Ingrid's emotional state seemed to be constantly fluctuating in her new environment. Lucy and I were concerned. By day, Ingrid did menial labor at the ashram. At night, she slept in a small room with three other women.

Ingrid always reminded me of a black-haired Meryl Streep but I thought Ingrid's face much more interesting, complex, with her deep, inquisitive brown eyes. She and I had worked together on a scene from Salinger's *Franny and Zooey* that we used for an audition piece.

"If Ingrid comes out wearing an orange robe with a bald head, I'm gonna get the hell out of here," declared Lucy when we left the car to search for our friend. Still a bit edgy, Lucy had not totally recovered from our Hopi Kachina spirit experience. We did find Ingrid and much to Lucy's relief our friend still had a full head of hair and wore a blouse with slacks. We shared dinner at the ashram before Ingrid walked us over to an apartment where we would be staying. Twelve hours later, I delivered the Chevy to a Nigerian man in South Pasadena and returned to the ashram just in time to participate in the evening's meditation.

When I entered the expansive, circular shaped tent, women were sitting on one side with men on other. I took a half-lotus position on the carpeted floor and joined the others in chanting Om Namah Shivaya, Hindi for "I bow down to Shiva."

Stocky, bearded, and dressed in a saffron-colored robe, Guru Muktananda, more affectionately called Baba, sat in the center of the space and spoke Hindi, translated into English by one of his assistants. Followers knew the Indian master, born in the Indian state of Karnataka at the turn of the century, for his teachings on meditation and self-realization. At the conclusion of his talk, I lined up with dozens of others for a brief audience with Baba. When my turn came, I self-consciously greeted him and knelt before the master. After he bopped me on the top of my head with his peacock feather and mumbled something in his native language, I stood up and sauntered out of the meditation center into the night. Not until departing the tent, did I realize something significant had changed. Colors were more distinct. Trees were shimmering. Everything around me vibrated including myself. According to a Baba devotee, I had been successfully bopped.

Walking to breakfast the following morning, I literally ran into Rae Allen, my first acting coach at the 78th Street Theatre Lab. Unbeknown to me, she followed the teachings of Guru Muktananda. Rae questioned why I wanted to waste my time planting trees in Oregon, and I asked her why in the world she would ever want to return to New York City. We were heading down very different paths.

When I called my parents that afternoon, they said that Susan had been diagnosed with multiple sclerosis. I broke down. Because of her age, early twenties, Susan's prognosis did not sound good. I delayed my plans for Oregon, reserved an airline ticket, and flew back to Kansas for a week thinking that I might be of some help. Having started a drug regimen, the numbness in her legs had temporarily subsided. Susan had also started to think and talk about the future. A week later, I boarded a bus in Wichita, destination Eugene, Oregon.

CHAPTER TWELVE

~

Red Star Recruit

Names tacked on the bulletin board were humorous and quirky. Red Star, Natural Wonders, and the Mud Sharks were at the top. In the middle, listed beside Cougar Mountain and Cheap Thrills, were Different Strokes, Full Moon Rising, and TNT. Near the bottom, I noticed an additional three names, Potluck, P. F. Flyers, and the Logrollers. They read like designated campsites at the Rainbow Family Gathering I had attended in a Kentucky state park. They could have been, however, a list of tribes from the annual Burning Man Festival in Nevada's Black Rock Desert. In fact, the names belonged to a dozen tree-planting crews in Hoedads, a woods worker's cooperative based out of Eugene, Oregon. The hoedad, a long-handled implement with a curved metal head, similar to a carpenter's adze, had always been the essential item in a tree planter's tool chest.

Hoedads' headquarters took up the entire second floor of an old but recently renovated building one block from the Amtrak Station and the main post office. On the first floor, around the corner from the exterior staircase, sat the Monster Cookies Shop where I had just purchased a chocolate chip monster and a cup of coffee, my breakfast on the run.

Greg Nagle, a Hoedad leader, happened to be the first person I encountered after traipsing up the stairs and into Hoedads' headquarters slinging my backpack over my shoulder. Short with tousled hair, broad shoulders, and a couple of day's beard growth, Greg strode up to me and introduced himself.

Soon, I would discover that he never just walked. Greg moved as if every destination must be an emergency and he talked that way, too. I recognized his name from an article he had written about tree planting. Rex had mailed me a copy. "I'm going to work. It's 7:00 a.m. and the grey light of dawn is just beginning to creep over the hills. Sometimes it's raining to beat hell and I just can't believe in my foggy, half-crazed mind that I'm actually going out in it," expounded Greg. "On those mornings, a long ride is the best way to prepare your mind for the inevitable. But all rides end, and the last mile up to the work site goes all too fast. Still, there is a slim hope that the ground will be frozen, or that some bizarre accident has happened to the Forest Service inspector. But no, I realize that in a few minutes I'll be strapped into a tree bag, hoedad in hand, descending into the yawning depths of an immense clear-cut. But maybe on that same afternoon I'll be flying over the slopes, slapping in my last fifty trees with the sun sinking behind the mountains. Then I'll think this job is about as close to happiness as I'll ever get."[1]

"Ya know Rex, huh?" Greg asked in a loud voice standing right beside me with hands perched on both hips. "We're on the same crew." They belonged to Red Star.

"Don't exactly know him," I replied. "Read his letter in the RFD magazine and responded." I explained that we had written a few times back and forth. I informed Greg that Rex encouraged me to come to Oregon and work with Hoedads.

"He's been down on the coast at Coos Bay," Greg informed me in his amplified tone of voice. That is when I realized the man had a hearing impairment. "He's supposed to get back late this afternoon." Greg told me that I had arrived at a good time. "Red Star's crew is meeting up here tomorrow night at 7:30 p.m.," he said. "Give ya a chance to meet everyone." The tree-planter sounded encouraging. "We leave in three days. The crew has a planting contract down at Diamond Lake,"

Greg paused for a moment, still sizing me up. "That'd be a good chance to experience Hoedad life." Our conversation lasted a while longer. Greg gave me a stack of reading material about the organization, bidding contracts, and tree-planting instructions, along with a booklet titled *Constructive Criticism* by Gracie Lyons, and told me to read the handouts before the meeting. "It'll give ya a head start," commented the tree planter. "There's a lot to learn."

When Greg asked where I would be staying, I told him that I didn't know anybody in town. "Slept in the bus station last night," I admitted. "Not sure about tonight."

"Hold on," he yelled. "Be right back." Greg strode over to an office staff member and talked with her briefly. She made a call then scribbled something down on a scrap piece of paper. He marched back over and handed it to me.

"Couple a names and an address," said Greg. "Cheap Thrills have a little house nearby. Go over and introduce yourself," he suggested. "You can get a shower and sleep on their living room floor tonight." I thanked him for his generosity, told him I would be at the crew meeting the following night, then left the headquarters in search of my temporary home.

The next day I found the public library and spent hours reading that material. Greg spoke the truth. I had a lot to learn.

I quickly discovered that tree planters had their own lexicon. Words like duff, cull, and misery whip, along with slash, topog, and peeler, populated the Hoedads' literature. The handouts talked about hi-lead, dominants, and punk whistle, as well as buck, basal area, and broadcast burn. One of the articles even referred to a cat road, gypo, and gravy cruising. I read the instructions regarding the US Forest Service inspection system, reviewed the mathematics on how to figure the number of trees in a plot according to contract specs, and learned what it meant to be a no-planting foreperson and a contract representative. I scanned the illustrations on the proper and improper way to plant with a hoedad, read the history of the organization since the early 1970s, and reviewed pages of visuals and written descriptions on tree-planting strategies spelled out in Hoedad lingo. When I began to look over Gracie Lyon's *Constructive Criticism: A Handbook,* I glanced up at the clock. The Red Star crew meeting would begin in a half hour.

When I arrived at the headquarters, there were more than a dozen members sitting in a circle kibitzing. A grisly-looking man, a life-sized Paul Bunyan, with wild hair and a full dark beard, lumbered over to me and introduced himself as Rex. With ease, my pen pal gave me a bear hug and led me over to the circle where he made introductions. There were five women and nine men including myself. They welcomed me into their circle. First impressions were good. Sexual orientation was not an issue on Red Star; there were three straight couples, five straight individuals, and three of us that were either bi-sexual or gay.

Toward the conclusion of the meeting, they invited me to work with them on their upcoming planting contract near Diamond Lake in the Umpqua National Forest just north of Crater Lake National Park. Before the session broke up, the Red Star crew informed me that they always prepared and ate their meals collectively and paid each member by the hour and by the tree. That way, every worker received an hourly minimum wage in addition to receiving pay for the number trees planted. Sounded fair-and-square to me.

A few days later, Rex and I were sitting in his renovated delivery truck driving down to Diamond Lake in a caravan of Red Star vehicles. In his homey rig, Rex had set up a bed in the back along with a small fridge and other creature comforts.

"On first sight, the Hoedads might appear to the unaware citizenry like itinerant gypsies," Wyoming reporter Bob Rogers explained. "Typical of a Hoedad band is a converted school bus, used as a central headquarters set up in remote sections of timbered forests. The bus is an office, a cook center, a meeting hall, a communications and entertainment center, a medical clinic, a prayer room, library, saloon and certified bunkhouse. Following the bus closely as it chugs its bulky way down freeways and two-laners is a caravan of well-worn pickups, station wagons and vans filled to the dome lights with all manner of camping gear, tools and supplies. The Hoedads tend to be ecology and social conscious oriented. And vegetarians."[2]

In addition to a school bus, each crew had a crummy, a rig used for transport to and from the work-site. Greg wrote about a onetime Red Star crummy in his *Whole Earth Catalog* article: "Red Star used to cruise around in a battered blue relic sporting a radio antenna and a pair of big, red stars painted on the doors. These red stars must have confused some of the locals. One night, while my crew was living it up in a bar in Montana, someone took the trouble to loosen the lug nuts on the rear wheel. That courtesy almost wiped out the whole crew off a mountain road several hours later when the wheel flew off."[3]

Months before I arrived, Red Star had purchased a yurt, along with a wood-burning stove, that we set up at each contract to provide more sleeping space. Most of the time, I either claimed a bunk in the school bus or found an empty cot in the yurt. The first few days of the contract, the crew assigned me to stay in camp and help with the cooking: oatmeal, scrambled eggs with tofu, and huevos rancheros in the morning and vegetable curries, soups, and stir-fries at the end of the day were frequent menu items. For an evening's treat, the crew would make popcorn, sprinkled with nutritional yeast. Collecting firewood and cleaning up the yurt landed on my chore list, too. I soon learned that Dr. Bronner's Peppermint Soap could clean everything from dishes and clothes to my hair and my body. I spent time writing to family and friends, too, a means to keep track of my thoughts and whereabouts. Being in the woods enhanced my ability to delve into self, similar to my experiences on monastic retreats.

I found a pair of used caulk boots, waffle-soled mountain cloggers made especially for woods work on the slopes. Soon after the crew offered me rain gear, tree bags, and a hoedad, I joined them on the slippery slopes. My first day, I spent more time falling on my butt than I did getting seedlings into the soil. It felt like I had worked at a 90-degree angle all day long. That clear-cut contract encompassed seriously steep slopes. "The land was bald, scarred as a battlefield. Limbs lay twisted on top of each other, their needles dead brown, and giant stumps loomed through the mist like so many tombstones," commented author Nina Shengold when describing a clear-cut. "The ground was a wash of mud, crisscrossed with skidder tracks up and down bare acres of mountainside . . ."[4] After weeks of planting, it seemed peculiar, like something out of whack, to return to level ground.

Planting trees required tough, backbreaking, manual labor. The crew stuffed hundreds of Douglas fir seedlings into two canvas bags that hung by straps over our shoulders. At the end of each day, for the first few weeks, my body ached everywhere; I mean everywhere. I grunted and moaned when I went to bed, and I grunted and moaned, again, when I pulled myself up in the morning. The camaraderie and support from my fellow Red Stars got me through that initiation period. Thankfully, a member of the crew introduced me to Tiger Balm, a powerful Chinese Ben-Gay. It eased the aches and pains significantly. "Don't wanna touch yer pecker with that stuff on yer hands," the seasoned planter warned me, "it'll burn fer hours." I kept his advice in mind.

Ruth, a Cajun woman from Louisiana and her French lover, Bernard, were two of the speediest planters on our crew. We soon became close friends. The fast-moving Bernard, tall and thin with a Rasputin beard, looked as if he were lightly skipping along the slopes. Ruth, more physically centered and closer to the ground like most of the women on the crew, always held a quick and steady pace.

When Red Star completed that contract and returned to Eugene, I discovered a written message at co-op central from Peace Corps: "Call the national office in DC to schedule a phone interview." A day later, in my dirt-covered, tree-planting attire, I spent an hour leaning up against a corner phone booth feeding coins into a hungry black box and answering questions posed by a Peace Corps recruiter. I had made it into their next stage of evaluation. "You'll be hearing from us again in a month or so," he told me just before we wrapped up the conversation. That night I mailed a postcard to Lisa, a close friend in New York. *"Good news from Peace Corps—acceptance into process—health project—Morocco. They'll continue to review my file."*

The Willawa-Whitman National Forest, location of my second contract, bordered Idaho and Oregon in a geographical spot called Powell Junction about sixty miles west of Missoula. Four Hoedad crews, including Red Star, worked together on that one. Some days the snow prevented us from planting but other days we slugged along the slopes pelted by ice-cold rain. Then the sun would come out. That is when it would get so hot that most of the crew, men and women alike, took off our shirts and kept right on planting. By that point, I had learned to pace myself to prevent burnout. I could hold my own.

On the Willawa contract, I had my first experience with a Thai stick, a variety of high-quality cannabis from Southeast Asia. The crew, grounded one day because the hard earth made it impossible to plant, stayed in camp. We spent some of the time cleaning up around the bus and the yurt and sweeping out the crummy. When helping each other prepare the vegetarian meals, my fellow Red Stars would frequently listen to the rousing female vocalists Cris Williamson, Ronnie Gilbert, and Holly Near, belt out "women's music" from the crew's boom box. In the evening, as we lounged in the front of the bus and shared stories, Bernard brought out a Thai stick, lit it up, and passed it around. After two hits, I jumped up and walked outside bedazzled by whatever I lay my eyes upon, the moon, the stars, the rocks. I began to talk to the trees, too, and they talked back. I had morphed into a tree-whisperer. Awhile after my exit from the bus, Bernard came out hunting for me and interrupted a tree conversation. "Better get your butt back in the bus," he yelled. "This's frost-bite weather."

On our first official day off, I joined a half-dozen other crew members in search of natural hot springs. After a mile hike into the forest, we discovered three steaming, natural pools on the side of the mountain that accommodated all of us with room to spare. We stripped down naked and soaked in that hot sulfur water for hours. Afterward, we drove into Missoula, did loads of wash, and ordered the best homemade pie ever at a little café just off Main Street. That town had the widest streets I had ever seen.

I learned four things for sure about tree planters during my first few months working with the cooperative: they had their own language; tree-planters always knew where to find the nearest hot springs; crew members could always sniff out the cafes that served the best homemade pie; and Hoedads always knew where to find the biggest and cheapest washing machines.

The night before leaving the Willawa, I wrote a lengthy letter to my mom. Feeling mellow, I wanted to keep her up to date about my tree-planting ventures and offer some thoughts about a string of subjects she had brought up in a previous letter. I kept my newly acquired tree-whispering skills to myself. Mom had a special place in her heart for the state of Oregon. She called it God's country. Her first husband, a Second World War fighter pilot killed when his plane went down into the ocean, had played minor league baseball. In the summers, his team worked out at a training camp in Oregon.

Back in Eugene, following the Idaho contract, coop members prepared for one of Hoedads' marathon quarterly meetings where I would witness democracy at work. Hoedads' process reminded me of the weekly community meetings on Israel's Kibbutz Maabarot. "The most important decision-making body is the quarterly meeting. General meetings are the place to see the real dialog," Greg had written. "We go on for two long days, plodding through an endless agenda. But we always manage to grind to a finish by the night of the second day. On the night of the first day, we throw a party with a hired band and at least ten kegs of beer."[5] The coop incorporated crew-feedback guidelines spelled out in Gracie Lyons's booklet *Constructive Criticism: A Handbook*. The cooperative used her "crit-self-crit" technique as an integral part of the dialectic. "The overall goal of criticism and self-criticism is to strengthen us for victory in the class struggle," explained Lyons.[6] Whether or not an individual believed in the class struggle, the power of the technique was undeniable. Hoedad members considered the quarterly meeting, held in WOW Hall, an extension of our work.

Once owned by the Woodsmen of the World, WOW Hall had a Grange Hall feel to it, a big, open space with bleachers on two sides and a stage up front. Hoedads had donated a good amount of money to prevent demolition of that structure in downtown Eugene. "To save it from burger kingdom," I had read in one of the coop's publications.

Before traveling to my final contract of the season, situated in Wyoming's Bighorn Range, I received my Peace Corps acceptance letter. The assignment in Morocco, a country I had requested, would begin in less than two months. Soon, I received a plane ticket to the training site in the mail. Just a few days before departure, however, I got a disheartening phone call from Peace Corps headquarters. A talking head, in the nations' capitol, informed me that they had canceled the project with no explanation, and told me to return the plane ticket promptly. By then, I had given notice to Hoedads, moved out of an apartment, and said my goodbyes to family and friends. I heard tell about Peace Corps projects canceled at the last minute, but, of course, I never expected that to happen to me.

"Will I be reassigned to another project in Morocco?" I asked.

"You'll be reassigned to another project," replied the man. "But we can't promise it'll be in Morocco."

I fell silent for a moment. I needed to hold back my anger. "How long will I have to wait?"

"Usually three to six months," he answered. The conversation ended shortly after that.

Within a week, I wrote him a letter just to make sure he hadn't forgotten me. I reminded him of my past work experiences that were relevant and reiterated my desire to work in Morocco. Months later, the Peace Corps finally assigned me to work with water development projects in Kenya, a country that I had not mentioned as a desirable work assignment on my application. Kenya had not been my first, second, or third choice as a possible work site. I accepted the assignment because I simply could not afford to wait any longer. Training would begin May 1982.

The Peace Corps Training Assignment criteria sheet arrived in the mail. "As a volunteer you will advise and assist local self-help water committees in the planning and construction of their systems. You will then train local people in routine maintenance and minor repairs. In addition, you should introduce, where feasible, improved methods of water catchment, collection, and storage, and also assist in the development of environmental sanitation and health education programs within the community." I sent a copy to my family.

CHAPTER THIRTEEN

~

Elephants, Giraffes, Hyenas, Oh My

Personal Journal
July 4, 1982

Now at the Lugari Farmer's Training Center thirty-eight miles from the Ugandan border. In my third month of Peace Corps training.

Early this morning, Kamba tribesmen slaughtered three goats. All night long, the animals bleated incessantly as if they knew what was coming. I witnessed the first killing but didn't stick around for the other two. There will be roasted goat meat at the celebration scheduled for later this afternoon.

Three Kamba tribesmen tied the goat's front and back hooves together, lay the animal on his back, and slightly twisted his neck. Grasping a long, sharp knife, a Kamba leader approached the goat then plunged it into his jugular and swiftly sliced across the remainder of his throat. The goat jerked once, emitted a muffled gurgling sound then fell limp. His eyes remained open as if he was still alive.

The four men heaved the body up and hung it from a nearby tree for skinning. They made incisions just above each of the hooves then a long, shallow-cut through the skin from the anus down to the neck and then began to peel. "Can't cut the pelt," commented a tribesman standing beside me. "Have to be patient." I had met him earlier in the morning. Finally, they peeled the pelt from the body with the head still intact.

Then the slaughterer cut deeply into the torso beginning at the base of the penis, where he severed the testicles and down through the belly until the guts spilled out almost intact. The bloody mass landed on a piece of a plastic spread out on the ground below. "Pancreas has to be removed," my fellow spectator informed me again. "Poison inside."

Before the afternoon feast began, tribesmen placed a large clay vessel, filled with a fermented corn drink, above a fire. When it started to boil, each volunteer received a reed through which to sip the warm drink. The tangy, sour mash had a bite to it, definitely an acquired taste. It did not take long to feel the effects of the celebratory drink. Then the tribe members invited us to chant and step to a rhythm set by them. Soon, we were chanting and dancing in a conga line around the trunk of a tree. The scenario could have been a scene out of <u>Keep the River on your Right</u>, an extraordinary Amazonian adventure written by my friend, Tobias Schneebaum. Except in Schneebaum's case, he lived with cannibals. Soon, one of the tribesmen began to share traditional Kamba creation stories and long held spiritual beliefs explaining that his people had originated from the trees.

After listening to the stories, I needed time to myself so I left the training compound and took a long walk down a one-lane dirt course. Aloe Vera plants were growing abundantly on both sides of the road.

I passed Kenyans along the way. "Jambo, jambo, bwana," they would say, "habari." They greeted me in Swahili. "Hello, hello, mister, how are you?"

"Nzeri sana," I usually replied. "I'm very good."

Sometimes, after passing by, I would turn around and see them looking back at me. I could hear them thinking. Who is he? Why is he walking on this road? Will he be here long? I was asking myself the same questions.

Hearing faint cries of "Jambo, jambo" from a distance, I noticed clusters of children through rows of corn. They gathered beside thatched roof mud huts, looking in my direction, jumping up and down, and waving eagerly. Their excitement gave me a boost of energy and the feeling that maybe, just maybe, I was welcome in their world.

I continued to walk the deeply rutted lane then veered off into a wooded area planted years ago with columns of tall, aromatic eucalyptus trees. I began to walk down one of them appreciating the silence, the still air, the soft cushion under my feet. It was a walk into nirvana.

Was it the walk that prompted my journal entry? Perhaps it was my recent interactions with fellow volunteers Dan, John, and Mark. There always seems to be a subtext in our communications. You know, so many things that could be said, could be shared, but they are not.

Again and again I observe how men desire and need intimacy, and nurturing, from one another but it's usually withheld in our day-to-day interactions in the United States. Any attempt at intimacy, within our cultural framework, so often becomes superficial.

In Kenya, it is common for men friends to hold hands. I appreciate and honor that practice. For me, holding hands always feels like a very intimate act, maybe even more intimate than making love. However, even I had to get used to it because of my cultural upbringing. In the beginning, I felt very self-conscious when a Kenyan man held my hand as we walked and talked. It is ironic that such a custom has survived in an African society that adopted so many of the rigid and defined roles imposed upon them by the British colonialists.

Does hand-holding, that skin-to-skin physical contact, allow for a greater intimacy among Kenyon men friends? Are their relationships deeper and more satisfying because of that physical contact? What have they learned through that custom that men in the West are missing?

Peace Corps training began in Oklahoma's Choctaw Nation, in the southeastern part of the state, hot and dry red-soil country. There the Native American Church thrived, and its use of peyote as sacrament still existed, even in that red state where extreme right-wing legislators dominated the government. For more than one month, we were living in the sleepy town of Antlers and housed in a facility originally constructed for senior citizens. We had thirty trainees in the group: five women, three retirees, two of us in our early thirties, and the remaining volunteers in their mid-twenties.

We attended technical classes, participated in cross-cultural simulation games, and watched training films on appropriate technology water projects. Divided into work groups, we were assigned hands-on building projects like concrete block latrines and simple water catchment systems. The films emphasized that bringing accessible water into a village would dramatically change the social structure of the community. Onetime long distances to water would become mere walks to the center of the village. If, for centuries, women and children had spent half their day retrieving water miles from where they lived then what would happen when that activity was no longer necessary? Even appropriate technological water projects could do more harm than good. That thought stayed with me throughout the training, from Oklahoma to Kenya.

"The key to organizing success is not possession of the technical knowledge as much as it is the ability to create an environment where the information is easily exchanged in the work place," repeated our trainers, week to week. I needed to hear that.

Prior to arriving in Oklahoma, I had recorded a comprehensive list of questions about international aid programs in my journal. I found it in a progressive independent publication critical of US development projects. *"Whose project is it? Does it belong to the donor agencies, or does it originate with the people involved? Does it reinforce the economic and political power of a certain group, or does it generate a shift in power to the powerless?*

Does it take away local initiative, or does it generate a process of democratic decision-making and a thrust toward self-reliance? Does it reinforce dependence on outside sources of material and skills, or does it use local ingenuity, local labor, and local materials? Does it merely help individuals adjust to their exploitation, or does it encourage an understanding of that exploitation and a resistance to it? Will success be measured by the achievement of the preset plans of outsiders or by the communities themselves?"

I had always understood that Peace Corps founders never intended the organization to be a significant player in the world of international development. Peace Corps was first, and foremost, an extension of US foreign policy. Training reinforced that understanding. In most cases, volunteers derived the primary benefits from the program. What we observed and learned from the people with whom we worked, then took back to our respective communities, might ultimately be worth everyone's efforts.

The in-country training cycle extended for more than two months, beginning with a week-long orientation session in Nairobi. We then traveled to the Lugari Farmer's Training Center, northwest of the capitol, near the Ugandan border. I quickly discovered that the Lugari site, a training center throughout the week, became a sanctuary for evangelical Quakers on Sundays. Much to my surprise, Kenyan Quakers were holy rollers, and their services lasted for hours. They moved, shouted, and sang with spirit. I soon ascertained that the largest growing communities of Quakers were Third World evangelicals. Despite that, the glue that held all Quakers together, worldwide, would continue to be their commitment to pacifism.

A typical day of training began at 6 a.m. with a cold shower and coffee and concluded with dinner at 7:30 p.m. The daily schedule included hours of Swahili language training, additional technical instruction, cross-cultural orientation, and home-stays with nearby farm families. Our trainers were skilled, attentive, and conscientious. At the conclusion of our first week at Lugari, we divided into groups according to language comprehension and retention ability. Trainers placed me with the slow learners.

Swahili was the national language of Tanzania, Uganda, and the Democratic Republic of the Congo, in addition to Kenya. The British first recorded the language using the Roman alphabet. Thus, for an English speaker, Swahili words were pronounced phonetically just as they were written. Despite that advantage, I remained a frustrated slow learner.

On the last weekend in July a fellow volunteer, named Josephine, and I decided to hitchhike to the Mt. Elgon National Reserve that bisected the border of Kenya and Uganda. We had read that elephants and buffalo, antelopes and leopards, in addition to hyenas, miniature deer-like creatures called dik-dik, and a wide variety of monkeys inhabited the reserve. Salt deposit caves, where the animals fed, were located there, too. We wanted to reach those salt caves, observe, and photograph the animals. Though similar in age, Josephine had considerably more international experience than I. Trainers frequently referred to her as confident and strong.

We departed Lugari early on a Saturday morning hitchhiking on a paved road that ended in a village near the Ugandan border. Surprisingly, we reached that village with a mere two rides, but unexpectedly had to schlep for miles, under a heavy downpour, on a muddy road that led to the lodge and the reserve entrance. By nightfall, Josephine and I finally reached the locked entrance gate and the lodge, the onetime home of British Lord Depy and family. We were drenched. Having nowhere to stay, we entered the lodge, sat down at the small bar, and ordered two cold Tuskers, a popular East African beer.

Soon we were engaged in a conversation with Gitan, a Kenyan agricultural student and a member of the Kikuyu tribe, the largest ethnic group in the country. He had recently completed his practicum. We quickly discovered that Gitan had two favorite phrases, "in a big way" and "permanently assured." When we told him that we were homeless, Gitan offered to take care of us "in a big way" by inviting us to stay overnight with him and his three roommates. "You can be permanently assured that you will be in good hands," said Gitan. After another round of Tuskers, we followed our host a mile back down the road and arrived at the small, three-room student quarters at their agricultural learning center.

Gitan's fellow students gave us a grand welcome, fed us dinner then launched into a barrage of endless questions. Because Josephine and I were exhausted, it felt painful to stay seated upright and wide-awake, but we could not end the conversation out of courtesy and respect for our hosts. At about 1:30 a.m., Josephine and I caught our second wind and stayed awake for another hour until our hosts finally granted that it was time to sleep. They quickly made up two beds for us in one of the rooms, devised alternative arrangements for themselves in the front room, and bid us goodnight.

Early, we awoke to a blaring radio broadcast on the Voice of Kenya announcing a military coup led by Air Force officers. The rebel speaker instructed all citizens to remain in their homes under an around-the-clock curfew. For the next few hours, Josephine and I listened intently to the broadcasts and the students' reactions. Although we were in the countryside, all of us were uneasy by what we heard. Since Kenya's independence nineteen years before, the government had remained stable. By midmorning, however, President Daniel arap Moi had come on the air and announced that the coup had failed, but he imposed a curfew for all citizens until further notice. At that point, Josephine and I knew we would be staying with our hosts for at least another night.

"The strange and violent 72-hour outburst beginning on August 1, was led by discontented enlisted members of the country's 2,200-member air force in an effort to overthrow the government of the President Daniel arap Moi, 57. It came as a particular surprise to Kenyans, who are proud of their country's reputation as a model of African capitalism and stable black self-rule in the midst of turbulence. Suddenly, Kenya was revealed as a country racked, beneath its placid surface, by savage and dangerous political and economic tensions." The *Time Magazine* article explained that a day after the attempted coup there were blocks and blocks of boarded-up downtown shops concealing "shattered windows and vacant shelves left behind by an orgy of looting." The Indian merchant class in the country, oftentimes resented because of their ill treatment of native Kenyans, owned most of those shops. "All told, at least 129 Kenyans were dead and an additional 100 missing last week after the suppression of the bizarre coup."[1] The article never appeared on Kenyan newsstands. Government censors removed it from that issue of *Time*.

"The park entrance will be closed," Gitan had told us but Josephine and I were determined to find a way in for the day. Under periodic heavy rainfall, we returned to the lodge, found the entrance gate locked, and no reserve personnel on duty. With no one in sight, Josephine and I merely walked around the gate, crawled under a fence, and, voilà, we were inside the reserve. Officially, visitors could only enter in land rovers because of the danger factor, but that did not stop us. With two bottles of water, a couple of sandwiches, a flashlight, cameras, rain ponchos, and two Swiss Army Knives, we began our adventure. She and I intended to reach the salt caves by early afternoon then turn back, but hiking the one-lane muddy road required much more time and effort than anticipated.

An hour into our hike, we suddenly felt the earth vibrate and heard a crashing sound coming from the jungle just ahead and to our left. Josephine and I backed down the road and hid behind jungle brush on the other side. The earth continued to vibrate as if giants were lumbering toward us, and that is exactly what they were. Soon, two adult elephants and a calf, a baby elephant, were standing in the middle of the road spraying one another with water from the puddles. Luckily, we had positioned ourselves downwind so they did not pick up our scent. When finished bathing, they continued with their journey crashing and smashing their way back into the jungle.

Continuing our trek, we encountered dozens of dik-dik that leapt through the jungle like oversized rabbits amidst the multitude of monkeys swinging from tree branch, to vines, to the earth, and then back into the trees again. Their anxious, high-pitched chatter pierced our eardrums. Sometimes horned antelopes ambled near the dirt road with confidence but always on alert.

As the afternoon wore on, we began to hear hair-raising sounds, the eerie and bloodcurdling howls, and shrieks, of hyenas roaming in packs but hidden in the jungle. They freaked me out. That's when I spoke up and said we needed to return to the lodge.

"We'll be fine," responded Josephine. She did not want to turn back.

Documentaries about those flesh-eating dogs, which I had seen over the years, were replaying in my mind's eye. Josephine's insistence that I keep going was like asking someone who had just watched the movie *Jaws* to jump into the ocean for a casual swim. What I could not see became much more threatening than what I could and I said so.

"I have done everything I've ever wanted to do," Josephine declared. "If I die now, so be it."

Well, I told her that I had not accomplished all the things I had ever wanted to do. "I'm heading back." Against her wishes, she finally agreed to return with me.

Dark by the time we reached the entrance gate, Josephine and I crawled back under the fence, walked to the lodge's bar, ordered a Tusker each, then hiked back down the muddy road to the students' quarters for another long night of questions and answers. During our conversation, Gitan revealed compelling family history. His father had become a Mau-Mau activist from 1951 to 1954. The Mau Mau, a militant nationalist movement and peasant revolt led by Jomo Kenyatta, opposed the British colonial state. Members of the Kikuyu ethnic group were the predominant fighters and supporters of the movement. "Jomo Kenyatta was imprisoned by the British colonial government during the fight for independence," James Verini wrote in a *New York Times Magazine* article. "After Jomo was freed and elected president of an independent Kenya in 1964, however, his revolutionary impulses didn't persist. He stocked the government and businesses with family members and fellow Kikuyu and 'operated with little concern for the niceties of law,' the historian Charles Hornsby writes, 'traveling with his inner circle from residence to residence like a medieval monarch.' . . . His family is believed to be the country's largest land holder."[2] Before our morning departure, Gitan invited us to spend Christmas with his family, a most generous offer.

By the end of the day, Josephine and I were back at the training center chastised for not contacting staff by phone. Neither of us had even thought to use a phone at the lodge or the training center, a serious over-site on our parts. Our instructors thought we had been disappeared, as in killed. We would repeatedly hear about our bad judgment for days to come. Once the political scene calmed down, I decided to take a weekend day trip into the savanna by myself. I had spotted a herd of twiga, Swahili for giraffe, a half mile inland from the road, during the return trip to Lugari from Mt. Elgon. When I inquired about the twiga with locals, they informed me that money from the British Rothschild family maintained the herd in protected areas. The animals stayed within a corridor, like a pilgrimage path, which they traveled up and down year round. There were male and female herds.

Filling my day-pack with a canteen of water, food, and a camera, I caught a ride to the main highway and then waved down a matatu, one of thousands of Toyota minibuses that operated in the cities and the countryside. In less than an hour's ride, I spotted the herd and told the driver to stop and let me out. That afternoon I communed with dozens of twiga and their calves. Unique in their coloring, the orange and brown patches that covered them faded to white on their lower legs giving the impression that the long-legged animals were wearing white stockings. "A giraffe is so much a lady," commented *Out of Africa* author Karen Blixen (Isak Denison), "that one refrains from thinking of her legs, but remembers her as floating over the plains in long garbs, draperies of morning mist as mirage."[3]

The graceful animals had two gaits, an ambling walk and a gallop. Their necks moved in synchrony with the legs and helped them maintain balance. "Giraffes walk differently from most other four-footed animals. The legs on the right side of the body move forward, then the legs on the left side move forward," revealed a *San Francisco Chronicle* article. "This keeps them from tripping over their own feet, since they have short bodies and long legs. A walking giraffe takes strides up to fifteen feet long."[4] An adult giraffe can grow to be sixteen feet tall, weigh up to three thousand pounds with a neck that can extend six feet or longer. Even though the twiga gave me great leeway in wandering amongst them, observing and taking scores of photographs, I soon discovered that an invisible boundary existed between us. When I crossed that line, the adult females promptly lined up in front of their offspring, in a defensive posture, and proceeded to snort. The snort was the giraffe's way of saying "Back off, buddy."

Our volunteer crew returned to Nairobi, upon the completion of the Lugari training, for a week of assignment preparation and the official swearing-in ceremony. On our first free day, I set aside time to track down Kenyan author Ngugi wa Thiong'o at Nairobi University. I had read two of his books: *The River Between* and *Detained: A Writer's Prison Diary* prior to beginning my Peace Corps training. In the late 1970s, after Amnesty International declared Thiong'o a prisoner of conscience, my local Amnesty International group wrote letters to Kenyan authorities and influential international figures to advocate his release. *Detained* described in detail the year he spent in a Kenyan prison because of his "subversive" writings. Thiong'o had written and produced a play critical of the Kenyan elite. Both President Jomo Kenyatta, and then Vice President Daniel arap Moi, had supported Thiong'o's imprisonment.

Taking a short cut, I began my walk to the university. On the path but a short time, I noticed a Kenyan man, who seemingly appeared out of nowhere, walking a short distance in front of me. Startled, I turned around and spotted another man following me at about the same distance. It felt like a set-up I had read described in a traveler's guidebook. Sure enough, the man in front soon dropped a thick roll of bills onto the ground, as if they had fallen out of his pocket, and kept right on walking. I turned back around to look at the other man who was motioning for me to pick up the bills. "Pick'em up," he said in a loud whisper, "pick'em up." If I picked up the bills and tried to return them, the two men would apprehend me then threaten to take me to the police for theft unless I paid them off. I ignored the man's suggestion, promptly crossed the street, and continued on my way at a fast pace. When I glanced back, the scammers had disappeared.

Reaching the university, I found it deserted. Authorities had probably closed it because of the attempted coup. I knew that many students had been arrested, held for questioning or worse. Regardless, I did track down the English department and found an administrator doing paper work in her office. When I inquired about Thiong'o, the woman acted as if she didn't know the man. When I persisted, she finally told me that he had left the country, did not know when he might return, then curtly wished me a good day. I learned that he had fled the country with his family because of death threats.

"In the course of two lifetimes, Kenya has gone from a state of tribal warfare, through colonialism, past independence, to its current incarnation as a nation ruled by autocracy and paranoia, its wildlife crudely marketed as little more than a series of giant zoos prowled by zebra-striped minibuses," declared the frustrated adventurer and noted journalist Jon Bowermaster. "Men whose grandfathers never saw a white man are now entrepreneurs in a booming souvenir economy. Since winning its independence, in 1963, Kenya has wrestled with political freedom only to fail miserably with the whole world watching."[5]

On my return to the hotel, I decided to stay on a heavily trafficked street and detoured into an outdoor market to pick up some fruit. I had barely started shopping when a woman standing twenty feet away began to scream "Mwezi!" the Swahili word for thief. "Mwezi!" the woman continued to scream pointing at a man backing away from her. Everyone in the market immediately stopped whatever they were doing and turned their attention in her direction. Within seconds, dozens of shoppers converged on the accused and began to punch, kick, and eventually throw him to the ground, mob justice. Bleeding from his head and mouth, the alleged thief curled up into a ball to protect himself from the ongoing blows. If two police officers had not interceded when they did, and hauled the bloodied man away, he would have been dead within minutes. The brutal scene left me shaken. In a land where the majority of people lived on the margins, thievery had become a crime the equivalent to murder.

Back at the Peace Corps Office, where I took time to process what I had witnessed, I found a letter in my mailbox from Charlotte, a New York friend who had facilitated my Amnesty International local group on Manhattan's Upper West Side. She worked in the publications department at the United Nation's Habitat office. Charlotte, too, had joined Peace Corps decades earlier and been placed in Morocco. In fact, she had written one of my recommendations for the program. Surprisingly, her letter had a Nairobi return address. I discovered that between the time I had left New York and received my Kenyan assignment, she had applied for a two-year stint with Habitat Africa and assigned to their office at the Kenyatta Conference Center in downtown Nairobi. When I called Charlotte, she invited me for a day trip out to the Ngong Hills with friends and her eight-year-old son.

Years past, the Ngong Hills were in the country. Karen Blixen could see them from her struggling, six-thousand-acre coffee plantation in the early twentieth century. By the time I arrived in Kenya, however, Nairobi's urban sprawl had already incorporated them. From atop the hills, a visitor could see out over the Serengeti Plains that spanned twelve thousand square miles. The Plains hosted the largest annual terrestrial mammal migration in the world.

I met Charlotte, friends, and her son at her temporary home where we had lunch and then left for the day's trip. Arriving at the entryway to the parking lot, a tall, lanky Kenyan guard met us with rifle in hand. "Last week, three people were attacked by men with machetes," he warned us. "Two cut very badly and in the hospital," the guard said shaking his head. "Not a good time to be in the Hills." When he realized that we were going to stay, he warned us not to go beyond the second hill. "Attacks were on hill three and four," he informed us.

With clear skies and cool temperatures, we set off on our hike. Passing over hill one and then two, we were the only visitors hiking the trail that day. Clearly, others were smart enough to heed the guard's warnings. Not paying much attention to how far we had gone, our group continued on to hill three chatting and enjoying the extraordinary Serengeti vista spread before us. When arriving on the top of hill three, however, I noticed two Kenyan men sitting with their backs to us. It looked as if they were having a friendly conversation so I wasn't alarmed until they jumped up, abruptly, with machetes in hand, and began to circle our group slapping us on our arms and legs with the sides of the long, sharp, lethal blades.

"Git down!" yelled the taller man wearing a torn T-shirt, baggy pants, and sandals. "Git down!" he repeated. His eyes were bloodshot. Maybe the Kenyan had been drinking and smoking chamba, called Malawi Gold, marijuana sometimes laced with something stronger. All of us, except Aaron who lagged behind, followed his command and hastily lay down on our bellies. Because the men had not seen him, Aaron hid in the brush on the side of the hill. "Yer money!" demanded the other Kenyan, "Rings and watches, too." His puffy red eyes matched those of his partner. We emptied our pockets and removed watches and rings. "Stay down!" yelled the tall man. "Stay down." Both men continued to swing their machetes and circle us as they quickly snatched up their newly obtained treasures, then fled into the brush covering the side of the hill. Shaken, we quickly scrambled back to hill two, then one, and made it to the car. The guard had left. Free time in Nairobi had been informative to say the least.

After the swearing-in ceremony, I wrote a letter to my family with the details. I had been assigned to work under the sponsorship of a comprehensive development group funded by the European Economic Community. Most of its employees were either British or German and based in Machakos, the first capital of Kenya, located an hour south of Nairobi. I would be living and working near the mountain village of Kilome, a region dominated by the Kamba tribe, two hours outside of Machakos. The Kamba were the second largest of the nine Kenyan ethnic groups.

Interestingly enough the Quaker school, Friend's World College, whose main campus happen to be located in Huntington, Long Island, had its East African Center just outside of Machakos. Some of their students would spend a school year abroad in East Africa. Because my language skills were still basic, I arranged to join their month-long Swahili review course in Lamu. An island on the northeastern coast of Kenya, Lamu had a rich Arab and Muslim history because of trade routes on the Indian Ocean. I would begin the course soon after establishing living arrangements a few miles from Kilome.

When I first arrived in the onetime capitol of Machakos, for introductions, I noticed a mosque in the middle of the city. Although I knew that a significant Muslim population inhabited the Kenyan coast, I had no idea that the Islamic influence had moved inland as well. Strolling by the place of worship, I noticed men washing their hands and feet preparing for afternoon prayers. Because I had never been inside a mosque, I naively decided to join them. Acting as if I belonged there, I proceeded to sit down next to one of the faucets, removed my shoes and socks, washed my feet and hands, splashed the cool water on my face and followed two men into the mosque barefooted. No one looked up as I joined the line preparing for prayer. Having no idea about the prayer ritual, I simply followed the lead of the man standing, kneeling, and bowing next to me. Instead of speaking words, I quietly hummed to the cadence of the other men in prayer. When they moved down to their knees and bowed to the floor with outstretched arms, I followed suite although a few seconds behind everyone else. At the end of prayer, I exited the mosque with the other men, pulled on my socks and shoes, and started to walk away.

To my surprise, one of the worshipers approached me from

behind and placed his hand firmly on my shoulder. When I turned around to face him, he asked me in English if I was Muslim. I told him no. The light-skinned, brown-eyed man, about my size and probably about my age, dressed in white and wearing a colorful taqiyah, a skullcap, stood in momentary silence. Then in a quiet but angry voice, he responded to my admission with words clipped and sharp: "If you ever enter the mosque again," the man could hardly contain himself, "you will risk physical harm." Then he turned around and stomped away.

Late that night, I could not sleep. My lime green room, in the cheap hostel, had only a small window and no fan, and I continued to obsess over my afternoon experience at the mosque. Clearly, I needed to learn more about being an outsider in the Islamic world. In the past, I had experienced many different religious and spiritual practices in communities unfamiliar to me. Most of the time, they had welcomed me into their services. I had never been physically threatened. Finally, I pulled on my clothes and took a walk. The cool night air helped clear my mind. The wind blew up the dust around me like miniature tornadoes as I wandered down the deserted main street. When passing a stationary shop, I peered into the soot-covered display window out of curiosity and surprisingly recognized greeting cards for sale. Peter McWilliams, a man with whom I had a short-lived relationship in New York in 1978, had written and produced them. I remembered visiting Peter's production room for the pastel colored greetings, with Rod McKuen-like poetry enclosed, and meeting his part-time employees. Businesses in the First World were always marketing in the Third World what they could not sell in their own world be it greeting cards, Nestlé's infant formula, or Monsanto's Roundup herbicide.

Peter, a longtime devotee of Maharishi Mahesh Yogi, the Beatle's guru, and onetime teacher of transcendental meditation, later became a follower of Werner Erhardt and active in the Erhard Seminar Trainings, better known as EST. He had also been a photographer and a best-selling author. In the last few years of his life, Peter, who died from AIDS, became a leading activist, respected spokesman, and influential vocal advocate for the legalization of medical marijuana. He openly used cannabis to stave off overwhelming nausea and improve his appetite. Because of his intrepid support for medical marijuana, the legal authorities arrested Peter and threatened him with a prison sentence unless he agreed not to use the substance. With no other option, he accepted their plea bargain that included frequent urine tests. Not long after the court imposed sentence, Peter died alone in his Los Angeles home.

I boarded a crowded bus to Kilome, the following afternoon, and arrived unannounced contrary to the advice of Peace Corps staff. The village had one main dirt road with rows of small, wood plank, single room shops called dukas on either side of the two-block-long shopping area. My first order of business would be to find a place to stay overnight. At the chi shop where I stopped for fried bread, which tasted like a sugar donut, and cup of tea with milk, the proprietor informed me that he knew of only one place in the village to stay. "There are five rooms behind the tailor's shop," the bearded man told me pointing across the street and down the block.

At the tailor's shop, the proprietor informed me that he had one room left. "University students staying in the other rooms tonight," he said. "They're on a school tour." The tailor pulled a key off a nail behind the counter then led me outside and around to the back of his shop. The simple room had a bed, a chair, and a small desk with a kerosene lamp and a bucket of water. "There's no electricity at night," he informed me. "You can wash in the sink outside by the chou, the outhouse." There were bars across the small window that looked out onto the valley below and the wood plank walls between the rooms that reached only as high as the rafters did. That meant that every tenant could hear every other tenant's movements and conversations. I anticipated a noisy night. Before leaving, the tailor informed me that he hiked back to his home in the countryside in the evening. "Most people live outside the village."

By the time I had settled into the room, walked around the village, and grabbed a bite to eat, the sun had receded behind the mountains. The only light in the village came from fires burning in metal barrels and flashlights. For a time, I joined a small cluster of men perched on logs by one of the barrels and mostly listened to their conversation. They spoke Swahili with a smattering of English possibly for my benefit. Upon returning to my room, I could hear the students' conversations in the other rooms and smelled chamba. When I smoked some of the weed, covertly, with a fellow volunteer the week before, I came to realize how potent it could be.

Hour after hour, the conversations grew louder and the smell of chamba more pungent. When I heard bottles break on the concrete floor, I knew the students were drinking alcohol as well, bad idea to mix the two. Finally, in my elementary Swahili, I raised my voice and asked them if they could please lower their volume. Initially, the students did quiet down but then someone replied with one word, "Mazungu", meaning white man, and their voices began to grow progressively louder with a repetitive chant of "Mauaji mazungu!" I knew what they were saying. "Kill the white man!"

I visualized a replay of the machete-wielding thieves in the Ngong Hills and the incident in the marketplace less than two weeks before. As the chanting increased in volume, I got out of bed to check the two locks on the door then tested the bars on the window. Could I remove them and escape if necessary? The bars would not budge. I felt trapped. Operating on fear and high anxiety, I mounted the desk with a small chair to see if I could swing up into the rafters if need be. I could not reach them. I was sweating despite the cold night air. Eventually, the chanting students left their rooms and began pounding and kicking on my door. Were they going to break it down? Did they have machetes? Their chanting, pounding, and kicking seemed endless. Finally at a certain point in the chaotic chamba and alcohol-fueled scenario, something snapped apart in my mind like a rubber band stretched too tight. I felt it. Resigned to whatever might happen, I sat on the bed, closed my eyes, and just lay back. When I awoke in the morning, the students were gone.

By noon, I had walked a few miles to the village of Nunguni where I met a volunteer German couple employed at a nearby health clinic. When they invited me to stay with them until I managed to find a living space, I did not hesitate to accept their hospitality. Within a few days, I had secured a temporary living space, adjacent to a secondary school, constructed of cement blocks and tin roof. A rainwater collection tank and outhouse were in the back. Soon after, I left for my month-long Swahili course on the Muslim island.

Personal Journal
November 23, 1982

It's Saturday night in Lamu. The early evening prayer call just finished, the dhows (small fishing boats with nets and sails) anchored, and the hewa (weather) has begun to cool off. I can hear flute music. There are no automobiles on the island, simply carts pulled by pundas (donkeys) or watatos (people). A traveler arrives here by way of a ferry and then walks. The island is seven miles long and four miles across. Settled by Arab tradesmen, they brought Islam and their architecture with them. It is unlike any other place in Kenya so I am told. Except for the language, it feels like I am somewhere in the Middle East.

I have recently recovered from sunstroke. Nancy, a fellow volun-

teer, and I were flat on our backs with fevers and nausea for a few days. Nancy was in worse shape than I. Initially, we thought she would have to go to the hospital. We had no appreciation for the power of the sun when we took a long hike along the beach. Only when we turned around and began to walk back into town did we begin to feel the intensity of the heat. By then, we had finished our water.

Now in my fourth week of the Swahili course. I discovered that one of my teachers, a longtime fisherman born here on the island, is the brother-in-law of the woman that lived in the apartment directly above me in Eugene, Oregon. Who'd a thought!

Next Sunday, I plan to catch the ferry to the mainland and then board a garila busi (bus) for the southern coastal city of Mombasa, the second largest urban scene in the country and an important port for trade. There is also a strategic US naval base there. The ride usually takes a day and breakdowns along the way are frequent from what I've experienced. Baboons, elephants, and wild boars often block the poorly maintained road. From Mombasa, I will board the antiquated but well maintained train destined for Nairobi. It is a flash from the British colonial past. The sitting cars have wood paneled interiors, sectioned compartments, and the dining car provides meals served by men in white coats and dark pants. It is the kind of train where I would expect to encounter the travel writer Paul Theroux.

After a few days in Nairobi taking care of business, I will return to Kilome and begin to settle into my temporary living quarters adjacent to the secondary school complex in Nunguni. The cool weather in the mountains will be a welcome relief.

The night before leaving Lamu, I developed stomach cramps and diarrhea with vomiting. Had to be food poisoning from the meal I had eaten in the small duka near Nancy's apartment. I delayed my return trip for a day. The vomiting stopped that afternoon, but the diarrhea persisted. Luckily, I had a reserve of Lomotil, an anti-diarrheal, that I took in the evening before departure.

Although I had anticipated problems, like being tossed off the Mombasa bus for shitting my pants, and left at the mercy of the baboons, elephants, and wild boars, I made it to the city without incident. Due to the Lomotil, my digestive system shut down for two days but the symptoms returned after I reached Nairobi and the medication wore off.

After a thorough examination, a Peace Corps doctor determined that tainted food particles had lodged in my gut, so I went through a series of enemas at his office. That did the trick. Two days later, I boarded a bus for Kilome, walked the few miles to Nunguni, and began to settle in.

Weeks later, I returned to Nairobi with an excruciatingly painful tooth abscess. I felt every bump on that road back into the city. Following the dental treatment, including a root canal, I spent some down time in the capitol. By that point, I had concluded that either a powerful village shaman had put a very dark spell over me or I simply had an endless supply of bad karma.

Early in the New Year, 1983, I withdrew from the Peace Corps and scheduled a flight back to the States. "The drums mute, the faces blur, the African landscape and your days in it have been left behind," wrote Richard Critchfiled. "Yet just as real as when you walked the hills of Machakos, a mile high in the sky, is the sense of empty, limitless space. Karen Blixen put it just right in *Out of Africa* 'Looking back on a sojourn in the African highlands, you are struck by your feelings of having lived for a time in the air."[6]

The second I stepped off the plane at New York's LaGuardia Airport, I knew I had made the wrong decision. Totally disoriented, I spent a week in the city then flew to the West Coast to visit a close friend in Sacramento. I had no idea where I fit into society and no immediate plans for the future. That was when I began to have anxiety attacks. At first, they only lasted for brief periods throughout the day. But week by week, they became more debilitating. Returning to Eugene, I registered to audit a few college courses and find work. I thought that might help focus my thoughts. Unfortunately, it did not.

Part Three

~

CHAPTER FOURTEEN

Don't Think, Do It

My entire body began to shake uncontrollably and my vision blurred. I felt intense nausea. Slamming the textbook shut and stumbling out of the classroom, I struggled to get to the mental health center on campus.

In a matter of minutes, the receptionist had shown me into the doctor's office. Immediately, he gave me an anti-anxiety medication, and a prescription before scheduling an appointment for me with a clinical social worker in downtown Eugene the following day.

At the conclusion of our initial meeting, the therapist agreed to work with me during the following four weeks. Each session, he integrated an effective hyperventilation exercise into my therapy where I would lay on the floor, flat on my back, and emote as he asked me questions. Luckily, his office walls were sound proof. I left every session with a hoarse voice. I felt an overwhelming sense of guilt for not completing my Peace Corps assignment and began to obsess over every bad decision I had ever made. Day after day, I became caught-up in a circular way thinking-everything bad, nothing good.

Although I thought it probably futile, I made an effort to get back into the program. I contacted Peace Corps and requested reinstatement to my Kenyan assignment. Calling their office numerous times, I talked with a number of staff members then mailed them letters. My attempts were unsuccessful.

Soon, the medication ran out and the therapy came to an abrupt halt. The sessions were simply too expensive. I had no health insurance. Ongoing anxiety attacks and long stretches of nausea became predictable daily events. To numb the psychic pain, I began to drink bottles of cheap wine. Like Brick, the troubled newscaster in Tennessee Williams's *Cat on the Hot Tin Roof*, I drank until I could hear that click in my head, when I had enough of that stuff to make me feel peaceful. There were also dramatic mood swings, heavily weighed on the side of anger. I felt anger primarily toward self, but I frequently flipped out when I witnessed friend or stranger wasting water or food, but especially water. Water had always been a precious commodity in rural Kenya.

I could not retain what I had just read, my attention span became shorter and shorter, and I lost any sense of self-confidence. It became impossible to watch television or view a film; images moved too quickly to follow. They made me nauseous. Everything came at me all at once. My emotional and psychological filters had dissolved and I began to hear the subtexts of my conversations and those of people around me. There were two conversations going on at once, the spoken and the unspoken. By losing one set of mental abilities, I had acquired another.

With the help of a Hoedad friend, I rented an inexpensive room in a two-story house on East 13th, near the university, with a shared kitchen and bathroom. Although two other men lived in the house, I stayed mostly to myself. My Livingston College classmate, Ann, who had worked on an Israeli kibbutz and hitchhiked with me across Greece and into Italy, lived in Portland but visited me frequently. Although she worked for Legal Aid in the city, her lover attended the University of Oregon in Eugene. Without her help and constant attention, I could not have recovered on my own. Gradually, I began to seek out places of retreat, both religious and secular, where I would be welcomed into quiet and supportive communities. I scheduled my first retreat at the Mount Angel Benedictine

Abbey, midway between Eugene and Portland, a small step toward piecing my life back together again.

As the weeks passed, I arranged another retreat at a Trappist monastery, Our Lady of Guadalupe, near the coast, began sitting meditation with a small group in Eugene, and started to attend Silent Meeting with the Quakers on Sunday. An acquaintance invited me to participate in a ten-day silent Vipassana meditation retreat at Breitenbush Hot Springs in the mountains a few hours east of Salem. Ruth Denison, an internationally recognized Buddhist teacher, led the group and met with me daily. Our conversations were brief but her feedback would be invaluable.

Born in Germany, Denison had studied with the revered Myanmar Buddhist teacher U Ba Khin. Although she had established her own Vipassana Center in the Mojave Desert, in Joshua Tree, California, Denison traveled the world to facilitate such retreats. The only talking permitted over that ten-day period occurred during those brief individual daily conversations with Ruth. I felt completely at ease communicating with the other participants without words. I knew the potential healing power of silence.

Months into my recovery, a wild and woolly Red Star comrade invited me to attend an improvisational performance by a local group called Theatre of Life, a company directed by Denise Taylor. They were appearing at the WOW Hall where Hoedads held their quarterly business meetings. I had heard about the company and wanted to see the group in action. The improvisers were spellbinding like nothing I had seen before on stage. By the end of their performance, I knew I wanted to be part of what they were doing. If I belonged anywhere, I belonged with them.

"Improvisation has long been part of the training of artists of all persuasions. Let go. Play with it. Don't think. Use what you have. Make it up as you go along," explained performance artist Barbara Dilley.[1] Even in my befuddled state of mind, I could do those things. They were all aspects of the performance that I had witnessed that night in WOW Hall.

After the show, I introduced myself to Ms. Taylor. We talked briefly about my theater background and improvisational experience. I told her that I wanted to attend her rehearsals, and she gave me permission to join them the following week. "You came in late your first night," Denise recalled in response to questions I posed years later. "I think it was raining, and you had a hard time finding us. I told you that you could observe, but would not be able to work out with us because you'd missed too much of the class." She clearly remembered my response. "You said you just needed to be with people who were focused on the moment to moment." The following rehearsal, Ms. Taylor allowed me to participate. A few weeks later, she invited me to join the group.

Unlike the more conventional improvisational performance that went for the laugh, Taylor's technique evolved from an organic process, growing out of the actors themselves rather than imposed by someone else's script or audience suggestions. Each performer used what he or she brought into the moment. Our rehearsals and performances sought honesty and vulnerability, playfulness and dead seriousness.

Denise, a striking woman with close-cropped brown hair, piercing blue eyes, and a velvety smooth voice, had studied Afro-Haitian and Jazz Dance at university. "I had my first spiritual experiences in those classes," Denise revealed to me. "The live drummers would take us with them till we were all in a-frenzy. I'd be exhausted, but dancing anyway." After completing her master's degree, she studied performance improvisation for three years with Ruth Zaporah's Action Theater at the teacher's Berkeley Skylight Studio.

"Students, whether dancers or lawyers, actors or business people, whether they're wearing layered threadbare dance clothes or swanky sweat pants, whether they're in their glistening twenties or their cynical fifties, they all come into the improvisation practice because they want a fresh introduction to life," expounded Ms. Zaporah, "just as I did so many years ago."[2]

I asked Denise what in Ruth Zaporah's work appealed to her. "Ruth's absolute presence when she performed and the authenticity of what she did when she performed," Denise replied. "Ruth was a very good teacher, very specific in her feedback." Denise Taylor's Theatre of Life became an extension of Zaporah's Action Theater. Techniques practiced by Denise in Theatre of Life had been developed by Zaporah. "I always started with a mindfulness meditation session, maybe fifteen or twenty minutes," she told me when I asked Denise to describe her typical rehearsal process, "then a kind of check-in for me to get where people were coming from on that particular day then a warm-up. Sometimes I led it. Sometimes they could do their own private warm-up knowing what their bodies needed. Then we would do scores."

Denise described that the scores "came in threes: movement, sound, and language but stillness and silence always added more options. With any of these scores, the improviser could develop, transform, or drop the movement images, sound images, or language images." I asked Denise how she determined the initial scores given to the actors. "Often I'd create scores based on what people in the company were struggling with in the moment."

Theatre of Life resonated with my state of mind, wide open and vulnerable. Without censors or filters, I felt comfortable in the unpredictability of it all. I welcomed the opportunity to develop a performance piece in the moment. During those rehearsals and performances, I felt like a whole person again.

Everyone in the company had a day job, and each member was an artist in their own right. Theatre of Life had simply become one of their art forms. Within our group of a dozen men and woman, Alioto Alessi and Karen Nelson were fast becoming respected teachers of a movement form called contact improvisation, a subculture in the world of contemporary dance. Alioto and Karen brought their contact improvisational skills into our rehearsal process and we began to integrate them into Theatre of Life. Meanwhile my performance vocabulary expanded beyond my imagination.

"Begun in 1972, contact improvisation challenges easy definition. In addition to identifying it as experimental dance, practitioners have called it art-sport, folk dance, meditation, therapy, play, and a technique for choreography," explained contact improviser Cheryl Pallant. "However, when dancer Steve Paxton founded the form, his intention was to explore the specific movements arising from the pairing of bodies in motion; he was investigating the perception and performance of dance." [3]

Contact improvisation demanded my full attention and engagement just like Taylor's Theatre of Life and Zaporah's Action Theater. Each of those creative outlets entailed moment-to-moment intimate, physical, and often sensual improvisational work. They required trust in the moment and in my fellow performers.

"Contact improvisation is most frequently performed as a duet, in silence, with dancers supporting each other's weight while in motion. Unlike wrestlers, who exert their strength to control a partner, contact improvisers use momentum to move in concert with a partner's weight, rolling, suspending, lurching together," pointed out dancer Cynthia J. Novak. "They often yield rather than resist, using their arms to assist and support but seldom to manipulate. Interest lies in the ongoing flow of energy rather than on producing still pictures, as in ballet. The dancers in contact improvisation focus on the physical sensations of touching, leaning, supporting, counter-

CHAPTER FIFTEEN

~

Blue Plate Special

"In the 1960s and 1970s, the opposition to American policy in Vietnam was centered on the nation's college campuses," Jeff Landers reported in a provocative newspaper article that appeared in the *Lake Oswego Review*. "Today there is a new trouble spot–Nicaragua–and once more a significant number of Americans are taking a stand against their government's involvement. But the enclaves of the most important opposition are not student unions but fellowship halls.

Church leaders are taking strong stands in condemnation of America's covert campaign against Nicaragua's Sandinista government. From this Christian [and secular] well of opposition has sprung an organization called Witness for Peace, and among the witnesses is a Lake Oswego man, Bill Claassen.

Witness for Peace, an interdenominational group formed in late 1983, provides an American Christian [and secular] presence along the dangerous northern border of Nicaragua. Witnesses pay their own way to serve in two-week shifts, talking to the people and touring the countryside. When one group's tour of duty is completed, another group is rotated in.

Claassen, 36, visited Nicaragua from June 6 to 23, in a Witness for Peace group of 20. Ranging in age from 15 to 70, they shared a desire to spend time in the conflict zone, meet with victims of the fighting and report back to others on what is happening there."[1]

Weeks before Jeff Lander's article appeared in my local newspaper, our Witness for Peace delegation had been sitting on the front porch of a small house in a Managua barrio listening to Cora Ramos's devastating tragedy. She told us that in the middle of the night, a grenade had exploded in her front yard, and Contra soldiers aimed rifle fire at her family's three-room adobe hut. The surprise assault lasted only a few minutes but left Cora's parents dead. Despite bullet wounds, Cora, her two-year-old daughter, and Cora's younger sister escaped into the jungle. During the seemingly endless rain-soaked darkness, the daughter died in her mother's arms. Cora's father, a community activist and the president of a local agricultural cooperative, was on the Contra hit list. Contra had become the name of three ragtag rebel groups that opposed Nicaragua's Sandinista Government. Largest of the three, the Nicaraguan Democratic Front (Federación Democratico Naciónal), had thousands of armed men based just inside the Honduran border. From there, the notorious rebel group launched merciless attacks on towns, villages, and farmer's cooperatives across the border in northern Nicaragua.

Our Witness for Peace delegation had flown out of Portland's International Airport a few days before our meeting with Cora. We traveled to Central America with the intention of investigating the impact of US foreign policy on Nicaragua. With close to two dozen people, our rainbow delegation represented a cross–section of America. We embodied a range of ethnic groups, professions, ages, and sexual orientations, with an equal number of men and women. Delegate's spiritual and religious practices ranged from Roman Catholics and Buddhists to Unitarians and Pagans. The initial leg of our journey involved a layover in Mexico City where we participated in an orientation session at the Quaker House of Friends, called Casa de Los Amigos. On our first morning together, we sat in a circle and introduced ourselves.

Kim and Martha, a Japanese American couple and the oldest members of our delegation, sat to my immediate right.

When teenagers, they were detained in an Arizona Japanese Internment Camp during the Second World War. The reserved, gray-haired Kim let his wife do most of the talking. Bubbling with energy, the thin, black-haired woman exuded warmth and empathy. Although amiable, Kim seemed to be distant at first but he became more engaged with the group as the days went by.

Early in our introductions, I discovered that the couple knew my Aunt Barbara Smucker, a noted author of children's books, and my Uncle Don, a theologian. Martha told me that the two couples had shared a cul-de-sac in Lake Forest, Illinois. At that time, Kim, an architect, commuted into Chicago for work. Martha, a full-time homemaker, had become a community activist involved with a wide range of issues. "Your aunt and uncle are our closest friends," remarked Martha as she placed her hand gently on my shoulder. "We're so pleased to be with you on this delegation."

On the other side of Kim and Martha sat a tall, gregarious, African American man, Richard. A Vietnam Vet with combat experience, he introduced himself as a freelance photojournalist based in Portland. Richard told us that he had served in the Air Force for two decades. Since his departure from the military, he had become active in a local chapter of the Black United Front and Jesse Jackson's Rainbow Coalition.

An olive-skinned Italian American, John, sat beside Richard. Both men had full mustaches, but their personalities were distinctly different. John seemed self-contained, serious, and aloof. He spoke Spanish fluently and taught English literature and grammar in a migrant education program for farm worker youth.

John, and three other delegation members, Guadalupe, a special education teacher's aide from New Mexico, a Eugene nutritionist named Pam, and a Denver community organizer, Ana, born in the Dominican Republic, served as our translators for the following two weeks. We were lucky to have four fluent speakers in our delegation.

On the other side of Richard sat a Native American man, Robert, an assistant professor of cultural anthropology at Oregon State University. He tended to be the more reserved member of the delegation.

To my left was Heike. Born in Germany at the beginning of the Second World War, she shared some of her personal background. "I have vivid childhood memories of the total destruction of my hometown in Germany." Heike's short, feathered, brown hair and wire-rimmed glasses highlighted the angular features of her face. She looked more like an academic than a nurse.

Alan stood directly across from me in the circle. Bushy-haired, disheveled, and unshaven, he had long been a highly respected KLCC Public Radio news reporter working out of Springfield, Oregon, for more than a decade. Alan produced a daily, in-depth news program called the *Blue Plate Special*; the local equivalent of Amy Goodman's daily radio news program, *Democracy Now*. With a mike in hand, he recorded our morning session in preparation for a *Blue Plate Special* covering our two-week experience.

A high school sophomore and the youngest member of our delegation, named David, helped Alan with the production equipment. Tall, skinny, and awkward with tousled brown hair, David quickly became the consummate volunteer. The eager, inquisitive teenager cheerfully offered his assistance whenever needed. His no-nonsense mother, Marion, a staff member of Eugene's Clergy and Laity Concerned, had taken on the responsibility of being our delegation's coordinator.

Each of us worked on Central American issues in our respective communities. Once established in Lake Oswego, I became active in Portland's Sanctuary Movement based out of Saint Andrew's Catholic Church, a tightly knit, multicultural, and politically active parish. Saint Andrew's congregants had agreed to house political refugees, from El Salvador and Guatemala, on church grounds. The refugees were on their way to Canada seeking political asylum, via an underground railroad, organized by faith and secular communities around the US. At the time, President Reagan's administration refused to recognize political refugees from either of those countries. Instead, they provided covert and overt aid to prop up extreme right wing, military-controlled governments throughout Latin America.

Most recently, I had provided transportation, from Portland to Seattle, for political refugees traveling that Underground Railroad from Mexico, through the United States, and into Canada. When the Reagan Administration began to prosecute individuals providing transportation for the asylum seekers, I joined more than one hundred Portland sanctuary activists at a local church to observe A Day of Shared Responsibility. "About 125 persons gathered for the observance which expressed solidarity with the sanctuary movement workers Stacy Lynn Merkt and Jack Elder, who were sentenced in Texas Wednesday to prison terms for illegally transporting Central American refugees," disclosed an *Oregonian* reporter. "Portland demonstrators also delivered petitions with about 650 signatures supporting Elder and Merkt to U.S. Attorney Charles Turner after a short march through the South Park blocks to the Federal Courthouse."[2] Involvement with the Sanctuary Movement prompted my participation with Oregon's Witness for Peace delegation.

Our delegation members were well informed, politicized, and ready to experience Nicaraguan culture. Following orientation, we flew out of Mexico City and landed in Managua.

"Modern Nicaragua, that is to say the revolution (Sandinista) that seized power in mid-1979, was shaped by U.S. military occupation (1911-33), and then by the U.S. created and supported Somoza family dynasty (1934-79)," revealed historian Walter LaFeber. "The family seized most of the wealth, including a land area equal to the size of Massachusetts. Meanwhile, 200,000 peasants had no land."[3] The Somoza dictatorship had played a pivotal role in Washington, DC's, diplomacy toward Nicaragua because of its willingness to follow orders without question. The press widely reported that President Franklin D. Roosevelt once remarked, "Somoza is a son of a bitch but he is our son of a bitch." In the mid-1930s, Anastasio Somoza Garcia had deposed the political leader of the country and soon thereafter became Nicaragua's new president with the support of the National Guard and a rigged election. Thus began a family of dictators, Anastasio and his two sons, who ruled for more than four decades. During that span of time, the Somoza controlled National Guard morphed into a brutal military force responsible for maintaining the status quo and keeping the family in power.

Upon landing at Managua's chaotic airport late at night, our delegation met three, long-term, Witness for Peace volunteers who helped us wade through the bureaucracy. To my surprise, I discovered that an acquaintance of mine, Larry, had become a long-termer. When I lived in New York, Larry and I resided in the same Upper West Side neighborhood. He dated a good friend of mine, Sandy, with whom I had participated in the UN Student Internship Program in 1976. Five years later, in 1981, Sandy had strongly encouraged me to attend Jesuit Dan Berrigan's Plowshares-Eight fundraiser then participate in the next day's civil disobedience action at the Army Recruitment Center in Time Square. Larry and I would occasionally run into each other at the popular Hungarian Pastry Shop across the street from the prodigious St. John the Divine Cathedral on West 112th and Amsterdam Avenue. I was pursuing an acting career while Larry spent his workdays in a mind-numbing government job. He complained about it frequently.

"What a surprise to see you here!" I exclaimed shaking his hand firmly. "Where have you been for the past five years?" Larry's prominent forehead, height, and large framed glasses, reminded me of Garrison Keillor, the host of National Public Radio's *A Prairie Home Companion*. He informed me that he had taught Latin American immigrants in New York City at a community-based educational institution. Then, my acquaintance had the opportunity to work with Salvadoran refugees in Honduras and participate in Nicaraguan work projects prior to joining Witness for Peace.

He asked me the same question. "After leaving New York, I moved to Oregon and worked for a tree-planting cooperative," I told him raising my voice above the din of the airport. "Later, I joined the Peace Corps." I paused to look over at the luggage claim area to see if my backpack had arrived yet. It had a bad habit of getting lost in airports. "When I returned to the States, I moved to Portland and started working as a trial assistant with the Public Defender's Office. I'll begin law school in September." Once our luggage had arrived, the delegation boarded a rickety school bus headed for Managua. Within an hour, we had settled into a simple guest-house near the Witness for Peace headquarters.

Our intense and emotional first week-long schedule of meetings and question-and-answer sessions began with Cora Ramos and concluded with the Roman Catholic Archbishop Obando Bravo, who opposed the Sandinista Revolution. In between, we met with newspaper editors and economists, church representatives and opposition political party leaders, US Embassy representatives and labor union officials in addition to business and educational leaders. Our meeting with Ernesto Cardenal, Nicaragua's Minister of Culture, stood out in my mind. The onetime Dominican priest had become an internationally recognized poet and a leading advocate of liberation theology, a Christian theology focused on the oppressed.

In the late 1950s, Cardenal had entered the Trappist Abbey of Gethsemani in Kentucky and studied under Father Thomas Merton. They became close friends and remained in frequent contact until Merton's accidental death in the late 1960s. I had read published letters exchanged between the two men, a correspondence that spanned decades. I felt as though I already knew him. "Ernesto Cardenal is a poet and a priest, a revolutionary and a mystic. His poetry speaks of Marilyn Monroe and Charles Darwin, of Spanish conquistadors and pre-Columbian gods," disclosed a *New York Times* reporter. "Science saturates his writing. He has been fighting for change since the 1950s, in an early aborted revolt against the brutal, kleptocratic Somoza dynasty, in his poetry and then as part of the left-wing Sandinista uprising, in 1979, that overthrew Anastasio Somoza Debayle. He was long at odds with the Vatican hierarchy, staying faithful to the doctrine of liberation theology as Pope John Paul 11 and Benedict XV1 remade the Roman Catholic Church in their conservative mold."[4]

At the end of the first week, our delegation boarded a small white bus and began the arduous journey north into Nicaragua's mountainous interior, the Department [State] of Jinotega, destined for the Ernesto Acuño Farmer's Cooperative. Marion, David's mother, maintained the front row seat as the bus weaved its way along a narrow dirt road through the lush green jungle. After spending the night in the town of Jinotega, we arrived at the cooperative the following afternoon. Just before reaching our destination, I got off the bus with the others and peered down at the cooperative tucked into the valley below. Low-lying clouds floated over surrounding mountaintops like billows of smoke. Jungle and vegetation surrounded the three dozen dwellings, covered with corrugated tin roofs, adjacent to cultivated fields. Ernesto Acuño would be our home for the next five days.

Clusters of children ran up to the bus as we drove into the

cooperative. Some of them carried baby brothers or sisters while others held their mothers' hands. Their dark eyes followed the movements of our group. The children's clothing hung loosely on their thin frames. Most adults kept more of a distance. Our rainbow delegation must have appeared strange to the welcoming committee of campesinos, farmworkers. We greeted our hosts and then casually began to unload the bus. There were backpacks and sleeping bags, cameras and tape recorders, and supplies that we had brought for the cooperative's school.

I had barely finished unloading my pack and shoulder bag, along with some of the school supplies, when a skinny little boy, in a yellow T-shirt and green baseball cap, grabbed my hand. I had a hunch he had chosen me to stay with his family. "Hola," he said looking up at me, and smiling, with inquisitive brown eyes.

"Hola," I replied holding his small hand in mine and feeling a bit awkward. I told him my name, Guillermo, in Spanish and asked for his, "Como se llamo?"

"Pablo," he replied.

My new friend pulled me to an older couple shyly standing behind the crowd and introduced me to his parents. They shook my left hand because the little boy would not let go of my right one. Pablo's mother, Maria, did not stand much taller than he did. She had pulled back her shiny black hair into a ponytail and secured it with rubber bands. Maria wore a faded light blue dress spotted with orange geometric designs and a pair of black plastic shoes that looked uncomfortable. Tómas, his father, stood a head taller than his wife. He had just come in from the fields in his mud-covered boots, stained work pants, and loose-fitting, long-sleeved, work shirt.

Still holding my hand, Pablo led the way as we walked toward their house. Pigs, cackling hens, and scrawny dogs wandered in and out of the muddy clearings between the simple abodes. My escort did not let go until we reached our destination. The family home, a rectangular, wood frame room, had a concrete floor. Inside were three large, sturdy, wooden crates with closed lids, two plastic chairs, burlap bags filled with grain, and a hammock attached to opposite walls. A stack of folded blankets and bedding sat in one corner. A makeshift crib, holding their crying, six-month-old baby boy, sat in the opposite corner.

"Suffering from diarrhea," Maria told me in Spanish. Immediately, I thought about their polluted water. She beckoned me over to the corner behind the door that led out into the kitchen and eating area. "This is where you will sleep," she said pointing to a raised platform with bedding. I assumed that Thomas and Maria slept there. When I told her I would sleep on the bags of grain, Maria insisted I take their bed. Attached to the one-room abode, like a carport to a house, the kitchen held a plywood table covered with a blue plastic cover and two wooden benches sitting on a packed earthen floor. A stone grill sat in the opposite corner.

Before eating dinner with our host families, the delegation met with a community leader, Lorenzo, for a brief orientation session. He wanted to share the community's history. Lorenzo informed us that a farmer named Ernesto Acuño had lived in the area before the 1979 Sandinista Revolution. "Señor Acuño was a community activist, a union organizer, and an advocate of agricultural cooperatives," the coop leader told us. The late activist believed that cooperatives were a practical way for campesinos to become their own bosses. Someone asked what happened to Acuño. "Killed by the wealthy landowners," replied Lorenzo.

Lorenzo informed us that all thirty families in the cooperative were former migrant farm workers. Eking out a living, much like the Mexican migrant farm workers in the United States, the coop workers used to move from one large plantation to another. In the early 1980s, according to Lorenzo, the coop began the physically demanding work of clearing the deserted plantation. By a few years later, they had planted seventeen hundred acres of corn, beans, and coffee. Every year the members devised a production plan and elected their leaders, much like the members of Kibbutz Maabarot in Israel and Hoedads in Oregon. "Aqui todos trabajamos para todos," Lorenzo said proudly. "Everyone here works for the good of all."

When I returned to my family, the sun had disappeared, and Maria stood over the grill cooking the evening meal of rice and beans with corn tortillas. Blue smoke, filling the kitchen, would gradually escape through a glassless window near the grill. As we ate, Tómas asked if I felt comfortable, and I assured him that I did. Little Pablo sat close to me with obvious curiosity. I appreciated that he had taken such a liking to me. I seldom had the pleasure of a child's company. Following the meal, Maria served lukewarm coffee in a tin cup. Should I drop an iodine tablet or two into the cup to purify the water? Their baby boy began to cry again. Question answered. I discreetly slipped two tablets into the black liquid and let it sit for awhile. After Pablo went to bed, Maria lit an extra oil lamp and set it in the middle of the table where we continued our stilted conversation. During the long periods of silence, I began to drink the strong, bitter coffee. I knew enough Spanish to ask and answer elementary questions. My comprehension, however, fared better than my speaking skills. Tómas offered me rolling papers and tobacco from a plastic pouch, which I gratefully accepted. In a universal bonding ritual, we rolled cigarettes and shared a smoke.

After the baby stopped crying, it began to rain so hard that the drops sounded like pebbles on the metal roof. Soon their sound became soothing white noise.

As I prepared to go to bed, Tómas got ready to go on watch. "I go on guard every day and night," he told me. "So does my oldest son." I did not know they had a third child. I understood that every male over the age of twelve and some females were responsible for two hours of daytime and nighttime guard duty every twenty-four hours. The rigorous schedule had enabled the cooperative to survive two Contra attacks. The last one had occurred in November, less than eight months before. Tómas pulled on his rubber boots, slung an ammunition strap over his shoulder, and picked up his automatic rifle. After covering himself with a sheet of clear plastic, he disappeared into the wet darkness.

As I unrolled my sleeping bag on the platform bed, I could hear Pablo whispering something to his mother. They were sleeping on the feedbags, now covered with bedding. Shortly after I slid into my cocoon, folded over one of my boots, and placed it under my head, Maria extinguished the flame in the oil lamp.

Morning at the coop began at dawn as the roosters' crowed announcing a new day followed by a chorus of barking dogs and the screeching of wild monkeys who inhabited the surrounding jungle. By the time I slipped out of my bag, dressed, and pulled on my boots, the kitchen had filled again with the blue smoke. My eyes began to water.

Pablo joined me on the bench and began to mimic every gesture I made. Then, I mimicked what he had just mimicked. Our breakfast table improvisations became a two-character, one-act play as we laughed and tried to outdo one another. Meanwhile, Maria tolerated our bad table manners and appeared to enjoy our creative antics. She served beans and tortillas topped with a fried egg, a valuable source of protein there at the coop. When Maria poured me a steaming tin cup of coffee, she smiled, knowingly, and set it down on the table. I had not been as discreet as I had thought.

Before leaving for my morning work assignment, I went in search of nurse Heike and told her about the baby's diarrhea.

After she retrieved re-hydration packets and Pepto Bismol from her first aid kit, we returned to my house. "Gracias Guillermo," said Maria as I walked out of the kitchen. Heike stayed behind with Pablo's mother.

For our morning task, we weeded the cornfields. It felt good to contribute at least something to the workday. When yanking weeds out the moist soil, I carried on a conversation with one of the campesinos who assured me that coop members were always on guard watching the fields. Until his remark, I had not thought about the possibility of a daytime Contra attack. In the late afternoon, our delegation met with the preschool teacher and women leaders of the cooperative in the one-room, wood frame, schoolhouse where someone had painted a Sandino silhouette on an exterior wall. Augusto Cesar Sandino, a Nicaraguan revolutionary and national hero, had fought the American Marines who occupied Nicaragua in the 1920s. A symbol of resistance to US domination, Sandino had died at the hands of Somoza's National Guard.

As the women talked to us, they used a blackboard on an interior wall. The teacher, Señorita Arenaño, described the daily schedule for the preschoolers and the programs designed for the older children.

"Now the women in the co-op are free to spend part of the day working in the fields," she informed us. "This is important because some of our men had to leave the fields to serve in the military."

Abruptly, the cooperative president Marcos Castro, dressed in green khakis and a cap, rushed into the schoolroom interrupting her talk. Out of breath, Marcos looked worried. "There are Contra forces, possibly as many as four hundred, only a few kilometers away," he informed us with a sound of urgency in his voice. "All work in the fields has been canceled." He said that everyone must stay within the boundaries of the trenches that surrounded the cooperative.

The bearded Marcos tried to reassure us that cooperative members had become better trained and armed since the last Contra attack in November. He said that the community expected back-up support from regular Sandinista Army units soon. "Sleep in your clothes tonight," Marcos told us then hurried out the schoolhouse door. We soon dispersed and returned to our families for an early dinner.

Pablo did not greet me when I entered the kitchen. Instead, the little boy remained quiet and stayed close to his mother where he felt safe. Pablo's eyes showed his fear. The memory of the last Contra attack remained fresh in his mind. While Maria prepared the meal in silence, I began to feel pensive. After pulling a paperback out of my shoulder bag, I made myself sit down and read at the kitchen table.

Tómas arrived just as Maria began to serve supper. I noticed their furtive glances, a silent language. They kept their thoughts to themselves. In the moment, I imagined that restraint for Pablo's benefit, but perhaps they were also thinking about me. I usually welcomed the silence, but that evening it felt foreboding. In the dim light, we ate supper without an exchange of words.

After finishing the meal, their oldest son trudged into the kitchen, with rifle in hand, and spoke to his father in a muffled tone of voice. He could not have been older than fourteen or fifteen. I felt the tension. Tómas quickly gathered up his gear and disappeared into the night with his eldest son to stand guard duty in the outlying trenches. Despite the early hour, Maria informed me that we should go to bed. I assumed that she wanted to extinguish the lamp and move inside the house to prevent the possibility of becoming easy targets. I went to bed fully clothed with my flashlight within arm's reach. The sleeping bag remained unzipped, and I lay awake staring into the darkness.

"The Contra usually attack early in the morning," a coop

member had told me earlier in the day. "Everyone must be prepared just in case." Leaders had given straightforward instructions to the mothers: if attacked, grab the children and run to your assigned shelters, which they had built of sandbags and dirt at strategic points inside the trenches.

Sometime during that endless night, Tómas and three other men entered the one room house quietly. I could only see shadows, but I recognized his voice. Maria got up, said something to her husband, and then returned to her makeshift bed with Pablo. Thank God, the baby remained quiet. After hearing the creaking noise of the wooden crate lids opened, supplies withdrawn, and rifles loaded, I realized what they contained. If the house became a target, it could blow sky high! The men left hurriedly.

Soon after their departure, the silence split apart with the cracking of automatic rifle fire. "Mama, mama," Pablo yelled out. The baby began to cry, too. I threw back the top of the sleeping bag and sat up with flashlight in hand. At any moment, I expected to hear the command "Run for shelter!"

We waited endlessly in the dark. I sat on one side of the room. Pablo, Maria, and the baby, who had gone back to sleep, were huddled in a corner on the other side. There were no more shots. At dawn, the community moved about cautiously. The crowing and the screeching only multiplied the tension, but I noticed that the dogs were strangely mute. In the smoky haze, Maria stood silently at the grill preparing breakfast while Pablo continued to remain at her side. Just as she placed my plate on the table, mortar fire exploded in the distance followed by ear-splitting sounds of automatic rifles. Pablo clutched his mother's dress.

A Witness for Peace volunteer ran by the house and stuck her head inside the kitchen. "We're meeting down at the schoolhouse," she yelled, "now!" Maria rushed into the house, picked up the baby, grasped Pablo's hand, and ran toward their assigned shelter. I grabbed my shoulder bag and headed in the opposite direction.

The rifle fire became deafening. Mortar shells were exploding just over the hill. Two women met with our delegation at the schoolhouse for reassurance, I guess. They claimed that they could distinguish the sounds between the mortar fire of the Sandinista Army and that of the Contra. "Watch the horizon," the one dressed in green fatigues advised us. "If you see smoke, the Contra won the battle. They'll burn down the cooperative and then come after us!" They told our delegation to sit and wait.

I expended some of my anxiety by making sure that each delegate had seen the trap door. Set into the wooden floor, it showed a narrow staircase down into a deep, dark, and damp underground tunnel that opened above ground somewhere outside the surrounding trenches.

With idle time on my hands, I began to think about the phone call from Camille I had received at the Public Defender's office just a few days before my Nicaraguan departure. Camille, a woman I was dating, taught at Portland State University. We had met at a contemporary dance performance there. Colorfully dressed, she had pulled back her hair and tied it with a beautiful silk scarf. Camille looked like a gypsy, a free spirit, which drew my attention. It came as no surprise to learn that she had grown up on a commune. The two of us enjoyed one another's company, but neither Camille nor I were seeking a long-term commitment. She had gone through a difficult divorce the previous year.

A few months before meeting Camille, I had ended a brief relationship with Mario, a big man with a shaggy mustache and a kind and thoughtful demeanor. He, too, had finalized divorce papers the previous year before moving to Portland from a Midwestern city. I had met Mario when we were signing up for a climbing course with Mazamas (mountain goat), a century-old mountaineering club headquartered in the city. Because he worked for the city's Parks and Recreation Department, Mario knew every hiking trail, cross-country ski route, and outdoor program in the region. He was seeking a long-term commitment that I could not make.

When I answered Camille's call, I did not receive her usual cheerful greeting. All I heard were four earth-shaking words, "I think I'm pregnant." Wow! I had not received a call like that for more than a decade. Camille had missed her period and scheduled a doctor's appointment for the following week. The thought of having a child with her gnawed at me. Before our brief phone conversation ended, we agreed to meet the day after I returned to Portland from Nicaragua.

Putting my mind to something else, I began to write in my journal. Within the tense setting of the schoolhouse, most delegation members gathered in small groups; some stayed to themselves. Each of us had our own particular way of dealing with the unknown. Martha and Kim sat close to one another scribbling in their journals. I checked in with them periodically because they already felt like family to me. The restless freelance photographer, Richard, darted in and out of the schoolhouse despite our instructions. The former military man wanted to capture the experience on film. Alan had brought his professional equipment with him and started recording the sounds of the automatic rifle fire and mortar explosions. The talented reporter planned to use the recording for background noise in his radio feature to air back in Oregon, that is if he made it back to Oregon. High school sophomore, David, and his mother sat in a corner talking quietly.

Aside from my anxiety-driven guided tours to the underground shelter and the troubling thought of possible fatherhood, I made frequent dashes to and from the outhouse. My digestive system had begun to rebel. Food, nerves, the water, or a combination of all three had taken their toll. My gut ached, and I had a mean case of diarrhea. The nearest outhouse, constructed on a mound of earth and recently painted white, sat in an open area near the schoolhouse, an easy target. Throughout the day, during fleeting moments of my sometime dark sense of humor, I envisioned the bold headline in my hometown newspaper: "William Claassen Dies in Outhouse."

The delegation had purposely parked our white van near the latrine so it would be visible from a distance. If the Contra knew that a Witness for Peace delegation was present, perhaps they would not attack. They were aware that bad publicity for them, back in the States, could jeopardize President Reagan's Administrations' covert and overt funding for their cause. An ignorant and uninformed Ronald Reagan had once compared the Contra terrorists to America's Founding Fathers.

By mid-afternoon, we had to confront our collective anxiety when Marion called us together for a meeting. "Marcos has informed me that we can still leave by bus and get through the mountains safely," she revealed. "We can still get out." Marion took a moment to look at each volunteer in the circle and allow time for her words to sink in. "But we must make our decision within the next hour." Tensions were high, and our allegiances strained. We agreed to move around the circle and permit each person to have his or her say, and no one could respond until everyone had a chance to speak. We intended to reach consensus. Some of us expressed our opinions quietly while others revealed their raw emotions, and a number of folks spoke with resolve. Our session reminded me of Quaker business meetings, ruled by consensus decision-making, that I had attended. Although frequently tedious, the process usually paid off.

"We should leave," declared one person in the group. Immediately, the speaker had everyone's attention. Yesterday, that delegation member had rejoined us after spending two days with the long-termer, Larry, at an evacuation camp northeast of Ernesto Acuño. The individual had volunteered to help interview survivors of a recent Contra attack at the Jacinto Hernandez agricultural cooperative in the state of Jinotega. Of course, the horror that they witnessed colored the delegate's resolve. Larry commented that driving into the evacuation camp "felt like driving into the heart of darkness."

In the emotionally charged atmosphere of the evacuation camp, the two American volunteers heard survivors reveal that the Contra burned down their houses, the warehouse, their Catholic chapel and Evangelical church, their crops then slaughtered all their livestock. The terrorists had also killed eleven people, including a two-year-old and a teenager, a member of the volunteer defense team. The Contra also seriously wounded a half-dozen adults and kidnapped nine people. "I keep seeing mud-and-mucus-stained faces of the children who'd lost everything," admitted our fellow delegate.

After each person had stated their opinion, the discussion began. Some people spoke about families at home and the responsibilities to them, and others talked about our commitment to host families at the cooperative. Most of us expressed fear. Within the hour, we had reached a consensus. Witnesses for Peace would stay. The decision provided significant relief because each of us had realized the opportunity to speak and determine our immediate future.

Abruptly, the rifle fire and mortar explosions ceased. Some delegates cautiously walked out of the schoolhouse to look at the horizon, no smoke. Two hours more of silence eased tensions even more. When we saw members of our host families leave their rifles by the side of the homemade baseball diamond, pick up bats and gloves, and begin to play a game, we felt relieved.

Marcos returned to the schoolhouse and told us that we could return to the families for dinner. At the house, I ate part of a tortilla, half of a small banana, and drank a few sips of water from my canteen. I did not want to have to scramble to an outhouse in the middle of the night. Despite the fact that the village remained on high alert and the campesinos had not been able to work the fields for two days, the families were determined to celebrate the Feast of Saint Anthony in their small chapel. Saint Anthony, a member of the Franciscan Order of monks in thirteenth-century Italy, was the Roman Catholic patron saint of the poor. His feast marked an important religious event in the coop where the adults recognized some children for completion of a catechism class. Colorful jungle wildflowers, set in glass jars, and flickering votive candles sat on an altar surrounded by simple paper decorations cut out by the children. The community had transformed the small abode into a comforting space for worship where we released tension and anxiety in song, testimony, and prayer. "A few yards beyond the house and the flickering light of the candles were the coffee bushes, the profound darkness of the mountains, and somewhere within a few kilometers, the Contra. Everyone knew that the Contra usually travel by night and attack at dawn, but their proximity didn't keep the people from expressing their religious faith which seemed to be a crucial element of their courage." [5] At the conclusion of the service, we quietly returned to our homes. Again, I wore my boots to bed and lay on top of the sleeping bag. Despite the silence, I did not sleep.

Although we were restricted to the space inside the trenches in the morning, some scheduled meetings did take place. A few impromptu gatherings emerged as well. Unexpectedly, the delegation had the opportunity to meet four young brigadistas, volunteers in Nicaragua's literacy campaign. Like thousands of other young people, the three men and one woman had delayed their university studies for two years in order to teach reading and writing to the campesinos. The foursome, in route to meet fellow teachers in a region that had recently suffered heavy Contra attacks, were staying at Ernesto Acuño until the military gave them the approval to continue on their journey. The enthusiastic brigadistas told us that the literacy campaign, called the Second War of Liberation, had significantly raised the literacy rate in a single year but their work in the rural areas had become significantly more difficult for them because they were Contra targets. During our question-and-answer period, they reported six hundred of their fellow teachers killed, kidnapped, or forced to leave their work assignments. Those young people were literally taking their lives into their own hands when they volunteered to teach the rural poor.

Later in the morning, we met with a group of Miskito Indians who were traveling north before the onslaught of recent Contra attacks. They had planned to pick up supplies of oil, rice, and sugar at one of the rural warehouses and then return home. The Miskito, the major indigenous tribe in Nicaragua, lived primarily in the remote East Coast region of the country. Because their John Deere tractor would be an obvious Contra target, the Indians planned to leave it at the coop for the time being. "The enemy is very aggressive, and we get way behind in our production," said one of the frustrated men in the group.

At noon, a messenger on horseback arrived with bad news. Marcos came to the schoolhouse and asked us to meet with the rest of the community in the village center to hear what the man had to say. The messenger, with his wrinkled, leathery skin, wore a ten-gallon hat and boots with spurs. He looked like a Nicaraguan cowboy. "The Contra are returning," he reported. "They are coming in greater numbers." We listened intently as he explained that they were moving through the jungle at a fast pace and could soon be on top of the hill overlooking Ernesto Acuño. The calm, created by last night's Saint Anthony Feast Day commemoration, dissipated quickly.

Once again, the coop returned to full alert. As the armed

coop members moved back to the trenches and mothers led the children to their designated shelters, a grave-looking Marcos pulled our delegation together to share additional information. "The Sandinista Army cannot get through to us." He sounded even more worried than he had two days ago. Hearing sporadic gunfire in the distance, we returned to the schoolhouse and waited. Much to everyone's surprise and relief, the Sandinista Army reinforcements did manage to get through a few hours later and move into the cooperative. Dressed in olive-colored camouflage uniforms, the soldiers carried grenade throwers, automatic rifles, and rocket launchers.

We talked with one soldier. "The Contra put a heavy burden on the revolution," said Pedro, an eighteen-year-old former university student from Managua. "They mostly attack the campesinos. They are the people with the most injuries." He added, "They don't confront the army."

A heavy rain began to fall as we moved to the community center for updates. "The army has broken into three units," reported a coop member in the late afternoon. "They're going to search for the Contra." He explained that everyone needed to stay inside the compound. Families on the edge of the cooperative moved to more secure houses, closer to the shelters, and the delegation bedded down on the bare wooden floor of the schoolhouse. Despite the soldiers' arrival, it appeared as if the community anticipated an attack, but the night remained quiet. No one went to the fields in the morning, another workday lost. The immediate crisis, however, had ended.

"The army has pushed the Contra forces back toward Honduras," Marcos reported midday. Feeling greatly relieved, we met with all the host families near the barn to celebrate with guitars and Nicaraguan folksongs. The delegation understood that we would depart the next day. When I returned to my family's house for dinner, Pablo left his mother's side and again joined me at the table. When I put my arms around him and gave him a hug, a powerful feeling welled up inside of my chest. I felt protective of Pablo, like a parent must feel toward a child. I had never experienced that sensation before.

In the morning, after breakfast, Pablo watched with curiosity as I stuffed my backpack. He showed a particular interest in my Swiss Army Knife. Together we pulled out all the attachments, from the corkscrew and the fish scale, to the screwdriver and the toothpick. He also wanted to hold the small camera in my shoulder bag. After I demonstrated how to shoot a photograph, Pablo, seemingly confident, backed up, paused a moment to position me in the tiny window, and pushed the button. I took a photograph of him, too, along with his parents, and promised to mail them a print. At the appointed departure time, the little boy grabbed my hand and led me back to where we had met five days earlier. An exhausted Maria trailed close behind. Making up for lost time, her husband and eldest son were back in the fields.

"Maria, gracias por todos," I said thank you for everything as I took her hand in mine.

Pablo's mother smiled wearily. "De nada," she replied.

When I crouched down to shake hands with Pablo and say a few words, he grabbed around my neck and pulled me into a long, emotional hug. We did not say anything, no need to. When we separated, I noticed tears running down his cheeks. I turned away, loaded my backpack on top of the bus, and hopped aboard. Tears were running down my cheeks, too.

My second evening back in Portland, I met with Camille as previously planned. To my relief, we were not pregnant. For the following few weeks, I participated in radio interviews, met with newspaper and television reporters, and visited legislator's local offices. Each member of the Oregon Witness for Peace delegation had made a commitment to share our experiences and the delegation's report with faith communities, supportive political organizations, local media, and legislators.

By the end of the summer, I had begun law school. However, after attending Portland's Lewis and Clark School of Law for one week, I withdrew from the program. Although I had enjoyed my two years as a trial assistant with the Public Defender's Office, I quickly realized that I had neither the will nor the desire to study law. Following my withdrawal, I contacted Pendle Hill, a Quaker study center near Philadelphia and requested entrance into their nine-month program scheduled to begin that October. Having demonstrated an interest in Pendle Hill in the past, they already had my file, the required number of references, and promptly accepted me into their fall term. Soon, I packed what few belongings I possessed, joined Camille for a farewell dinner, spent a few days hiking with close friends from Eugene then drove across the country and eventually landed in Pennsylvania.

CHAPTER SIXTEEN

~

Weighty Friends, Silent Meetings

Driving into Pendle Hill felt like entering an Andrew Wyeth painting, the muted colors, architecture, and landscape. Spread over two-dozen acres, the grounds were planted with natural grasses, flowering gardens, and a unique variety of trees from all over the world. Two major buildings, the spacious main house, built in the Pennsylvania Farm House style, and the barn, were already there at the school's opening in 1930.

Interior spaces in both buildings brought to mind works by twentieth-century painter and commercial photographer Charles Sheeler. He shot a series of black-and-white photographs in the interior of his two-hundred-year-old Pennsylvania farmhouse and then called them the *Doylestown Series*. "Sheeler's pictures immortalize what he considered to be the best of American Craftsmanship," explained the authors of *Charles Sheeler: Paintings and Drawings*, "embodying, as did his own art, straight-forward truthfulness-modest, functional, and unadorned."[1]

The barn, a solid stone and wood structure, and one time home to animals and farm machinery, had been remodeled to accommodate the Silent Meeting room and offices on the first floor with residential rooms and suites on the second. As time passed, the school added a two-story dormitory, a library with rooms on its second and third floors, and a small cluster of staff apartments to the complex. Other residences that had such names as Upmeads and Edgehill, in addition to Crosslands and Wakefield, honored Quakerism's English heritage.

My room, on the dormitory's second floor where we observed quiet hours, day and night, had a large picture window looking out onto a cluster of aged trees and a flower garden. Much like a monk's cell, it had a single bed, a desk with a lamp, and an easy chair but no religious symbols.

Orientation, that lasted one week, allowed time to ease into the daily schedule and become acquainted with the others in the program. "Pendle Hill has been called an adult school, a folk school, an enlarged family, a Quaker type of monastery, an ashram, an intentional community, a watch tower, a laboratory for ideas, a fellowship of cooperation," explained Howard H. Brinton. "To some extent it partakes of the characteristics of them all."[2] Brinton, a man highly respected in Quaker circles and what those of the faith called a "Weighty Friend", made it clear that the school granted no grades or examinations, offered no degrees, and disavowed competition.

A longtime Quaker academic and activist, Brinton commented on the size of Pendle Hill that would necessarily have to remain small "if it is to be an organic self-regulating type of community." He believed the ideal size "in the neighborhood of seventy," including staff and students without a "sharp distinction" between the two groups. "All take some part in teaching, in presenting papers, in the daily Meeting for Worship, and in the tasks of household, office, and garden. The essential entrance requirement is sufficient stability and maturity in life's experience, both educational and practical, to make proper use of the freedom afforded. It goes without saying that persons of all creeds, races and nationalities are included."[3]

In the beginning, Howard Brinton clarified the meaning of Silent Meeting for worship in the community. "Since the [traditional] Quaker form of worship, un-programmed and based on silence, interspersed sometimes by messages from anyone present, requires no creedal commitment it can be accepted by anyone, Quaker or non-Quaker, Christian or non-Christian.

Experience has shown that such worship becomes a powerful bond holding the group together and adding a sense of depth to all pursuits."[4]

Within the first few days, I had been assigned a daily kitchen task, weekly household job, and begun to participate in the weekly work mornings. Pendle Hill residents were responsible for the upkeep of the study center. The administration paired each student with a staff member, a sort of co-counselor, with whom to meet once a week. It was a relationship intended to benefit both individuals. The staff partnered me with the Dean of Students Dyckman Vermilye. He had recently replaced Parker Palmer, a nationally recognized educator and author, who served on the Pendle Hill staff for a decade. Dyckman, about the same age as my dad, had years of experience in higher education and administration. He had also raised four children, primarily on his own, and lived and worked in Zimbabwe with a community of Jesuits for two years. An ideal match, Dyckman and I would become lifelong friends.

Fellow students, young, middle-aged, and older, came from two dozen states and a dozen countries. Kazuko taught the tea ceremony in her home country of Japan and did so at Pendle Hill. I discovered that the Evangelical Quaker minister from Kenya, named Joseph, had attended Sunday services at the Lugari Farmer's Training Center where I had done my Peace Corps training. After his first few weeks at Pendle Hill, Joseph had to be hospitalized. The chemicals in our drinking water caused havoc with his digestive system. He would gradually adjust to our treated water. Noel, a Chinese businesswoman born and raised in Hong Kong, sold a clothing line in her native city, and Trish taught high school in her home country of Zimbabwe. An octogenarian from New Zealand, named Olwen, had led the movement to declare her country a nuclear-free zone. Ivan, a Colombian, was responsible for organizing the first Quaker Meeting in Bogota. A Roman Catholic and devoted enthusiast of poet and visionary Gerald Manley Hopkins, named Sally, had spent the Second World War years living in the closed and highly secretive community of Los Alamos, New Mexico. Her husband, a scientist, worked with the Manhattan Project developing the atomic bomb. Interestingly enough, Jorge, from Mexico City, managed the Casa De Los Amigos where my Oregon Witness for Peace delegation spent the first two days of orientation before flying to Nicaragua. We were an international community that gathered every morning and evening to sit in silence.

Teaching staff, some permanent and others visiting, were as varied as the student community. William and Eugenia Durland, founders of the National Center on Law and Pacifism based in Colorado, taught theology and peace studies. Residents of California, Joanna and Fran Macy offered broad experiences in international relations and cultural exchange; Fran had directed Peace Corps programs in a half-dozen countries, while Joanna, a noted figure in Buddhist communities throughout the US, had become a recognized authority on the psychological effects of the nuclear threat and a pioneer of despair and empowerment work. A professional weaver and potter in Philadelphia, Mimi Wright shared her years of training and craft work in clay and textiles.

The nine-month stay at Pendle Hill, divided into three terms: fall, winter, and spring, offered five classes in each. We were encouraged to participate in at least two but not more than three courses. The school designed the program to allow each of us time to immerse ourselves deeply into whatever we were reading, writing, or crafting.

My first few weeks were emotionally and physically difficult. Soon after leaving the West Coast, I began to break out in a series of painful rashes. Each day they continued to get worse. I wrote a letter explaining the situation to close friends of mine in Oregon.

October 18, 1985

I will begin by saying my first few weeks at Pendle Hill have been hard. As you know, because of my phone call on the road shortly after leaving Eugene, I developed an itching, weeping rash on my arms. Rather than clearing up, it continued to spread as I drove across the country. There was a patch on my upper chest, one on my right side, and another on my right hip. The rash became painful. By the time I reached Brattleboro, VT., I was not feeling well and began to think I was showing symptoms of HIV infection.

While in Vermont, I arranged to continue my Oregon health insurance over the phone and called Pendle Hill to say that I planned to arrive a day early. Once here, I promptly made an appointment with a local doctor.

Surprisingly, the doctor did not mention HIV or AIDS but neither did I. He said that I had a serious case of skin poisoning, gave me some cortisone cream, and sent me on my way. Maybe, I thought, I had brushed up against sumac or poison ivy when hiking in Oregon just before departure. Although relieved, I questioned his diagnosis. Yet, I wanted to believe it. I did not voice any of my concerns to the Pendle Hill staff or fellow students.

The medicinal cream didn't help. Then one night I awoke with shooting pains up my left arm and soreness and swelling in my left armpit. I was sweating profusely, too. For the next few days, I was alarmed when the pain and sensations moved into my lymph glands in my neck and over to my right arm and armpit. The night sweats continued.

So I arranged to have an HIV test at a city hospital, had my blood drawn, and was told the results would be back in a week. With swollen lymph glands and ongoing night sweats, I was convinced that I had the virus. Meanwhile, I took out additional health insurance.

I began to make plans to return to Oregon, made a list of people

I would contact to notify them of my infection, thought about where I might stay upon my return, and wondered how I could avoid telling my family until the last minute. Despite the inner turmoil, I continued to attend the orientation sessions, participated in daily and weekly work assignments, and began to swim laps every other day. I took long walks, meditated, and attended Silent Meeting every morning and night. Although comforting, sitting in those meetings felt like being alone in community.

Two days ago, after breaking out with another patch of rash, I returned to the hospital for the test results. Prepared for the worst, I was stunned when the doctor said that my results were negative. I asked if it was possible that I had a false negative. Very, very, unlikely he told me but, yes, there was a remote possibility. The doctor told me I could return in six months to be re-tested but he continued to impress upon me that I did not have the virus. Instead, I had a very nasty case of the shingles.

Because I insisted, he drew more blood and ran a series of additional tests to see if anything else showed up as a possible health problem. Before I left his office, the doctor impressed upon me to practice safe sex, gave me salve to apply on the rashes, and told me to expect ongoing pain, swelling, and sweats for at least the next month or two. A week later, his office called and assured me that all additional blood tests showed no signs of health problems.

You are the only people I have told about this. I needed to get it off my chest. With a negative HIV test, I feel as though I have been given an extension of life.

The experience has given me just a brief glimpse into what those individuals, who have been infected, must deal with day-to-day, hospitals that refuse to admit them, health professionals who refuse to provide assistance, feeling a sense of alienation, and fear as to who will be the next AID's victim in a circle of friends, lovers, and acquaintances. I remember organizations that I called for advice only to get a tape recording and think about the dozens of misinformed articles that I have read.

Anyway, I am angry, grateful, humbled, relieved, and sad. Through it all, I knew there would be two people in Eugene I could depend upon for support regardless of my condition. That was comforting and reassuring.

At morning Silent Meeting, weeks into the program, I noticed Elle sitting in the corner of a front pew, just across the room from me. With the pews arranged in a square, we all faced into the center of the room. Elle had closed her eyes. She always sat so still with hands folded in her lap. The smallish woman, with a pixie haircut, high cheekbones, and no make-up, wore a light blue turtleneck with a faded pair of jeans and Birkenstocks. For a moment, Elle opened her eyes, turned her head briefly to look in my direction, as if she knew I was watching her, then closed them. Elle did not move again until the end of Meeting. I know because I kept watching her.

A few days later, I made a point of sitting at the same dinner table with Elle, not next to her, but a few chairs over. After someone briefly reintroduced us, I slipped back into silence, and she returned to her conversation with the woman sitting across from her. I liked listening to Elle talk. She spoke in a clear, straightforward manner, and maintained eye contact. Elle did not chit chat, did not fill space with empty words and thoughts. I liked hearing her laugh, too, deep and generous. It made me want to laugh even when I did not know what was funny. She could be silly, as well, and make weird faces without being self-conscious. I had a sense that we would eventually get to know each other intimately but I knew that the process would be a gradual one.

The first term I signed up for "Quaker Life and Spirituality" taught by two Weighty Friends, Bill and Frances Tabor. Bill had a particular interest in holistic and spiritual healing while Frances, also a lifelong Quaker, helped supervise a pilot program of private retreats for Pendle Hill residents. As well,

I participated in a literature course taught by an Oxford Englishman, David Gray, who would only be there for a term. His assigned readings included a smattering of Chaucer and Milton, Blake and Wordsworth, along with Auden, Eliot, and Lawrence.

I enjoyed those classes, the readings, and the writing assignments but I became totally immersed in Mimi Wright's pottery class taught in the basement studio. "Clay is a wonderfully plastic medium offering infinite possibilities for creative expression," Mimi explained in our first session. She taught hand building and wheel techniques, glazing, and showed us how to load and fire the kiln. Mimi invited us to return to the studio day or night whenever we felt the urge

After a month of working with clay, I wrote a letter to the artist Mary Frank. When living in New York, I had seen her clay sculpture, *The Swimmer*, on exhibit at the Whitney Museum of Art and become very interested in her art. "Mary Frank's figure sculptures have been described as sensual, sublime, erotic, metaphorical, poetic and profoundly moving," noted Carlene Meeker. "Frank imparts a sense of the timeless and elemental to her work, placing her among the foremost figurative artists of our time."[5] Since leaving Manhattan, I had shared my interest in Frank's work with friends, collected articles about her that appeared in art publications, and sought updates on her exhibits in the States and abroad. In the letter, I introduced myself, described Pendle Hill, and explained how much her work meant to me. I asked if I could visit her studio and included my phone number and mailing address. Because I didn't have her home address, I sent the letter to the Zabriskie Gallery on West 57th, the gallery that represented Frank's work at the time. Weeks later, as I sat stuffing envelopes for an upcoming Pendle Hill evening lecture, an administrator tapped me on the shoulder. "You have a phone call," she said. "Take it in my office." Mary Frank, on the other end of the line, told me how much she appreciated hearing from me and inquired about Pendle Hill with interest. In the remainder of our conversation, she gave me her phone number, studio address, and we set a tentative date to meet in New York.

My visit with Mary became much more than I expected. The artist, with cool blue eyes and soft voice, invited me into her raw, loft-sized, studio on West 14th. Physically, Mary reminded me of the full-bodied female figures that she sculpted. There was an earthiness about her. Initially, she encouraged me to wander around the space at my leisure and then we would talk. Frank had filled the loft with scale models of sculptures completed, clay pieces in process, and recent screen prints on paper that I had never seen before. We discovered our mutual interest and work with Latin American Solidarity groups, love of folk music, and background in movement and dance. When younger, Mary had studied with Martha Graham and taken painting classes with my most favorite Abstract Expressionist artist, Hans Hofmann. A few months after our initial meeting, I felt privileged when Mary invited me to join her for an art opening of archaeological sculptures by Gonzalo Fonseca at the Arnold Herstand Gallery in mid-Manhattan. We would remain in contact by letter and arrange future visits.

Returning to Pendle Hill, following my New York visit, I decided to begin working on a large-scale project in Mimi's pottery studio. My time with Frank had been inspirational. I wanted to create an assemblage of various sizes of folded and fired clay pieces, partially glazed, that would fit together in an archetypal ceremonial form. The size, colors, and shapes evolved week to week with the aid of my vivid dream world, classroom readings, and meditations in Silent Meeting. I eventually exhibited the ceremonial piece, at Pendle Hill, spread out on Navajo rugs and sand.

As the term progressed, Elle and I quit circling one another and began to communicate almost daily. Sometimes we shared meals and sat next to one another in Silent Meeting. Once-in-a-while we would take a walk together but continued to remain protective of our private time. One day, she left a note in my mailbox. "I keep wondering what I am meant to learn from you. I don't want to keep asking <u>myself</u> this so I'm asking you. I like being around you. I want to know … oh a lot. I'm not gonna make a list. This is it plain. I like you. "I had longed for her message. When she opened that door, I walked right in. Soon, we began to hold hands.

I shared with her that I considered myself bisexual and talked about my family and background in politics and theater. Elle revealed that most of her previous relationships had been with other women. A longtime activist in the feminist movement, she had also participated in running marathons for years. Prior to coming to Pendle Hill, Elle lived in Minnesota and worked as a documentary filmmaker but she had grown up in a theatrical family on the East Coast. Her father, Joe Anthony, was a much-acclaimed Broadway and film director. Perry, her mother, had danced on Broadway before having children.

Just before Christmas break, Elle asked me to participate in a mutli-media piece of hers titled *Prayer Theater*. She was in the throes of creating the work and planned to perform it in a series of events during the second term. I said yes, of course.

At the end of each term, faculty encouraged individuals to share a creative project with the community. Ruth, from New Jersey, recreated a seventeenth-century traditional Quaker wedding with costumes and the appropriate order of service, including the wedding certificate signed by all witnesses. A pianist from Ohio, Thomas, played a series of improvisational numbers on the piano that reminded me of George Winston's New Age compositions. Poets, artists, and writers in our community produced projects that nurtured us all. I liked to think of Pendle Hill as a spiritual Black Mountain College.

During the holiday break, I arranged to return to the Benedictine Weston Priory where I had spent Thanksgiving five years earlier. Since my previous visit, the monks had declared their monastery a sanctuary for Central American political refugees and opened an educational center in Cuernavaca, Mexico. The monks spent six months out of every year there. From the Weston Priory, I drove to St. Joseph's Abbey, a Trappist monastery near Spencer, Massachusetts, where I stayed until my return to Pennsylvania.

Second term at Pendle Hill seemed to move along more quickly than the first. Early in the new year, I had the honor of spending an afternoon with Philip Berrigan, the former priest, antinuclear weapons activist, and older brother of Jesuit Dan Berrigan. Tall, thin, and stern-looking, Philip visited our community to share stories about his decades of activism, years spent in prison, and the Jonah House, an intentional community where his family lived in a low-income Baltimore neighborhood.

Members of the Woodcrest Bruderhof Community, from Rifton, New York, visited Pendle Hill for a week. Known for their a-cappella singing, the Bruderhof performed for us during their stay. Originating in Germany in the early 1920s, the Bruderhof were Christian pacifists who lived in intentional communities, held all material goods in common, and became engaged in local, national, and international social issues. When the Nazi movement grew in power and influence, the Bruderhof fled to other European countries as well as Canada, the United States, and South America.

One week, our community decided to integrate a foot-washing ritual at the conclusion of the evening Silent Meeting. Some residents had grown up practicing the ritual in their respective faiths. I understood that within a Christian context, the intimate and sacred act derived from Christ washing his disciple's feet at the Last Supper but in a larger spiritual and cultural context, the ceremony symbolized humility and a willingness to serve. That's how I could relate to it.

I paired off with Richard, an Episcopal priest. Twice my age but as agile and physically fit as I, we had climbed trees together on the Pendle Hill grounds. A lanky and gregarious clergyman, he sported a full-length white beard giving him the look of Father Time. Having voluntarily gone to Japan, after the US bombing of Hiroshima and Nagasaki near the end of the Second World War, Richard had spent most of his adult life in the city of Nagano. As a result, he had come to identify more as Japanese than he did American. Washing Richard's feet did become an act of humility and willing service. It felt as intimate as holding hands, perhaps even more so.

Midway through the Winter Term, I left briefly to participate in a Witness for Peace conference in Washington, DC, and lobby members of Congress to stop funding the Contra forces in Nicaragua. Upon returning to Philly, I had the opportunity to join hundreds of others in a demonstration at Independence Hall. "Chanting and waving banners, about 400 people staged a peace rally at Independence Mall yesterday afternoon, their protests at one point forcing the closing of Independence Hall and the Liberty Bell museum," reported *The Philadelphia Inquirer*. "The three-hour demonstration was organized by the Pledge of Resistance, a peace group committed to fighting–by non-violent civil disobedience, letter-writing campaigns and other protests–the buildup of U. S. military aid to Central America." [6] There were no arrests that day, too many tourists to witness the event.

That second term, I had signed up for "Genesis: The Foundation of a Faith," taught by my co-counselor and friend Dyckman, in addition to a vocation's class but Joanna Macy's course offering, "East-West Spiritual Dialogue," grabbed my attention in particular.

Although I did not realize it at the time, Macy's class would greatly influence my future interests as a writer. Her assigned

readings, lectures, and discussions explored the spiritual resources of the Hindu and Buddhist traditions in relationship
to Quaker and Judeo-Christian heritage. We dipped into *The
Bhagavad Gita*, read sections of Huston Smith's *The Religions
of Man,* and discussed Thomas Merton's familiar book *The
Asian Journal.* Joanna led me deeper into Vipassana meditation, the practice introduced to me by Buddhist master Ruth
Denison. Ruth had directed my first ten-day Vipassana retreat
at Breitenbush Hot Springs in Oregon.

Meanwhile, Elle focused on creating her *Prayer Theater* project, working with clay, and keeping up with the readings in
her chosen classes as we continued getting to know one another. Before the end of the term and spring break, I invited Elle
to join me for a retreat at Nova Nada. It was the coed monastic
community outside of Yarmouth, Nova Scotia, that I had tried
to visit the summer of 1980 when hitchhiking through eastern
Canada. Confident that she would join me, I had reserved two
retreat spaces. Along with the retreat applications, Nova Nada
had mailed me a pamphlet with a brief description about what
to expect. "Is the Nova Nada wilderness experience retreat for
you?" asked the pamphlet. "A good amount of ruggedness and
solitude await you here. Bring warm clothes in the winter.
Without central heating, you'll be more comfortable dressed
in several layers." Elle accepted my invitation.

We drove to Bar Harbor, Maine, loaded my car onto the ferry, and disembarked in Yarmouth. Parking in the YMCA lot
that I recognized from years past, we made a call to the community and then waited. Arriving in a weathered pick-up, the
no-nonsense young woman in overalls, two heavy sweaters,
and mud-caked boots, informed us that the return trip would
take more than an hour. Driving through the snow-covered
wilderness, we remained comfortably quiet as if preparing for
the retreat.

Nova Nada, a former hunting and fishing lodge built adjacent to a lake, at that time frozen, had become a settlement for solitude. Onetime hunting cabins became individual hermitages where community members and retreatants lived. Upon arrival, our driver explained the daily schedule, informed us that we had no running water, and showed us where to collect it from a nearby well. She then accompanied us to our respective hermitages and left us to settle in. My small log cabin, much like Elle's, was rustic and ideal for one person. Each had a loft bed with a built-in desk underneath and a pile of folded blankets. A comfortable, stuffed rocker, near the black, pot-bellied stove, looked out onto the wooded landscape. Having brought basic food supplies, I put them away in the partially filled food larder next to the hot plate. Outside, by the front door, I discovered a stack of firewood that would keep my hermitage toasty for several days. Prior to beginning the trip, Elle and I had agreed not to contact one another unless we had an emergency. We held to that agreement. Even when the two of us gathered with the community members for their few weekly common meals, Elle and I spoke only when addressed by a Nova Nada member. During the remainder of the week, community members prepared meals in their respective hermitages.

In Charles A. Fracchia's *Living Together Alone*, a Nova Nada contemplative named David Levin clarified their use of the word nada, what it meant to them. "The Spanish word nada, which means 'nothing,' was chosen for our communities because nothing, the abyss, the void, is the experience of the wilderness. Nothingness is also the one mystery in which all religious traditions – East and West – converge. Saint John of the Cross and others sum up the spiritual life in terms of it; unless you are detached from everything that is not God, you cannot belong to God; unless you are emptied, you cannot be filled; unless you lose your life, you cannot find it."[7]

In their recorded conversation, Levin told Fracchia that his chosen life did not reject the world. "The hermit is not a cave-man or a spook, luxuriating in isolated splendor. He does not flee from the world to be free of it, but enters into it to trans-figure it; he does not scorn the good pleasure of the world, but integrates them with the spiritual. He aims not at rejection out of fear, but consecration born of love."[8]

Each morning and evening the Nova Nada community met for worship and chanting in their recently completed wood and stone chapel, library, and community center, which they had designed and built themselves. The structure had a bell tower and two circular buildings, with high vaulted ceilings, connected by a rectangular entryway. One circular structure housed the chapel; the other provided a library with books and tapes.

Frequently, the chapel services were accompanied by sounds of ice cracking because the lake had begun to thaw. The shift-ing of ice would shake the chapel, giving the feel of a low-grade earthquake or possibly an awesome message from the beyond.

In the chapel, above the large stone altar covered with a half dozen flickering votive candles, hung a life-sized nude figure of Jesus cast in metal. Well-endowed with penis and testicles, I had never seen Jesus portrayed with genitals. His sex had always been denied him; covered over or simply non-existent. The representative figure looked so very human. Rather than splayed on a cross, their Jesus held his right arm toward the heavens with his left arm extended out to the world. He sym-bolized a spiritual vessel between heaven and earth. The figure brought to mind a Sufi Whirling Dervish who, when moving in a circular trance, always had one arm extended up to the heavens and the other arm pointing down to the earth. Like their Jesus figure, the Sufi Whirling Dervish symbolized a spir-itual vessel, too.

On either side of the altar were contemporary, eight-foot stained glass windows in strikingly rich blues and yellows, oranges and reds. Although filled with religious symbology, the dominant figures appeared strong and bold. In one window stood a female, with her hair blowing in the wind and arms extended. In the other, a steed reared up on his hind legs. They were certainly the most unique stained glass windows that I had ever seen in a monastic chapel or a Christian church.

Throughout the retreat, I continued to return to Fracchia's book to gather more insight into Nova Nada, the community and the "not" community. "We have chosen to live together alone," expounded David Levin to the author. Levin, who had grown up on the East and West Coasts, attended private boarding school in Arizona, and worked in Los Angeles for Columbia Pictures after college, helped found Nova Nada in 1972. "It is almost impossible to be a hermit on your own, for practical as well as psychological reasons. We live together to provide the mutual support needed to overcome the difficulties we would encounter without other hermits living nearby. We avoid the degree of organization needed for community, yet maintain a simple structure which enables us to help one another be hermits without hindering one another."[9]

On the return to Pendle Hill, I spent a few days with Elle and her parents on Cape Cod. Because she had arrived at Pendle Hill a term earlier than I, Elle would not be participating in the final session, spring term. She would, however, arrange for extended visits during that time.

Joe and Perry's residence, near Provincetown, Cape Cod, and a short distance from the ocean, stood out among summer homes and grassy sand dunes made famous by artist Edward Hopper's paintings. Elle and I stayed in an adjacent barn remodeled into a two-floor apartment with a light, airy, workspace and kitchen on the ground level. I enjoyed the family environment and the sense of welcome extended by her mother and father. Joe and I tended to use the kitchen as our conversation space, whereas Elle and her mother claimed the living room for their heart-to-hearts. Joe and I hit it off immediately, and we talked for hours sharing stories of the theater and our lives. We were at ease with one another; I regretted that I only had two days to spend with the man.

Shortly after returning to Pendle Hill, I received a lengthy letter from Joe. It meant a lot to me so I kept it. Joe wrote, just as he talked, with wit and humor. "Hi! This be the ninth day of April in '86. A gray day without promise. Even the dog, Marty, senses it. I can tell. He went out reluctantly, peed quickly without pleasure, and hurried back inside where everything is as it was. Ugh. That's all that I have to say about it: this day I mean, this sky, this morning, and YOU! Damn, darn, doggone you! Writing me such a generous note of gratitude for your stay here. But that's not what galls me. It's that vast amount of your presence you left behind . . ."

During my final term, I participated in William Durland's class "Living in the Kingdom". I wanted to get to know him better. His course description intrigued me: "will examine the fruits of living in the kingdom once more–community, hospitality, resistance in the specifics of sanctuary, plowshares, civil disobedience, draft resistance, war tax resistance, poverty, and prisons." That would be a lot of territory to cover. Durland's personal development and history proved to be as broad and diverse as mine. He had, however, come from a place of conventional power in American culture; Navy captain, lawyer, and Virginia legislator but by the time he reached Pendle Hill, Durland was applying his legal skills to defending peace activists and working with communities of war tax resisters. I admired the man.

Primarily because of Durland's class discussions and assigned readings, I decided to return to Latin America for a year soon after leaving Pendle Hill. I planned to begin in Guatemala, where I would study Spanish, then eventually work my way through Central America and into South America.

Elle had no interest in traveling to Latin America. Instead, her three terms in community had confirmed plans to move back to the Cape and settle down. Although we participated in a Clearness Committee, a decision-making process frequently used in Quaker circles for clarity on difficult issues, and talked at length about maintaining our relationship despite significantly differing paths, it began to unravel. By the time I left for Guatemala in late June, Elle and I were longer in contact. For the next four years, I would live, study, and work in Central and South America or be serving the Hispanic community Washington, DC.

Years later, however, in April 1993, Elle and I would meet again in Washington, DC, to participate together in a massive Lesbian, Gay, Bisexual, Trans-gender demonstration. At the time, I had one more semester to complete in my graduate journalism program at the University of Missouri/Columbia and Elle had settled into her life on the Cape. Parading down Pennsylvania Avenue I walked on one side of Elle and her wife-to-be walked on the other. "Hundreds of thousands of gay men and lesbians from across the country marched past the White House and flooded the mall yesterday in a largely peaceful procession to demand an equal place in American society," reported *The Washington Post*. "The marchers, accompanied by family, friends, and other supporters, streamed for more than six hours down Pennsylvania Avenue, NW, waving thousands of rainbow flags, a symbol of gay liberation. " [10]

CHAPTER SEVENTEEN

⁓

Three Sisters' Hotel

Since the disappearance of two of their leading members, the Group for Mutual Support or Grupo de Apoyo Mutuo, Guatemala's only functional human rights organization, had called for their first demonstration to take place in the capitol city in late August 1986. Activists, inspired by the Mothers of the Plaza de Mayo, the Madres de Plaza de Mayo in Buenos Aires, Argentina, turned out by the thousands: students and laborers, professionals and Mayan tribal representatives, international observers and news correspondents. The large turn-out of Mayans, most of whom lived in small villages scattered throughout the highlands, clearly demonstrated that they were the primary victims of the military "scorched earth" policy, a policy that entailed widespread destruction of life, property, and resources. Hundreds of demonstrators carried placards with enlarged photographs of relatives and friends that were disappeared during recent military-controlled regimes.

The march began at the Plaza Italia, in the capital city, then proceeded down a major avenue to the National Palace. From the steps of the grand and ornate building Nineth Garcia, the Group for Mutual Support's leader, spoke passionately about the organization's work. Their demand remained the same: the government must account for the tens of thousands of disappeared men, women, and children. Garcia's late husband, a university political activist, was disappeared two years earlier. At the event, volunteers from the Canadian based Peace Brigades International provided escorts for

Ms. Garcia and other organizational leaders. The escorts always accompanied them to meetings and speaking engagements during the day and provided them with protection at night.

The turnout was particularly impressive given the fact that armed police officers and paramilitary were everywhere in sight. Association with a human rights organization necessarily required a significant, and sometimes fatal, commitment. All along the parade route were grotesquely large, black, SUVs with tinted windows, parked by the side of the road. Locals called them "death mobiles". Military and paramilitary death squads used similar vehicles, perhaps the very same ones, to kidnap victims off the streets or out of their homes late at night. During political marches and demonstrations, anonymous individuals would sit behind the tinted glass shooting photographs.

Shortly after participating in the demonstration, I traveled by bus from the colonial town of Antigua, where I studied Spanish, into the northern highlands where the majority of Mayans lived. Given the condition of the roads, erratic bus schedules, and frequent checkpoints, the trip required several days. "The scenery on the way up is spectacular, as it is throughout the highlands, with cloud-lidded mountain valleys, cornfield-terraced slopes, raw green hillsides, damp evergreen forests that look black through the perpetual mist, and volcanoes–there are thirty-three volcanoes in Guatemala, and they give the landscape its bewitchingly primitive mystique," explained Guatemalan journalist Francis Goldman. "The highlands are where the Indians traditionally reside, often in tiny villages called aldeas, many accessible not even by dirt road." [1] Goldman explained that more than half of the country's population was comprised of Mayan Indians scattered among twenty-two tribes that spoke as many languages. The majority of Mayans were subsistence farmers in a country where two percent of the population owned three-quarters of the agricultural land.

I promptly sat up at attention when the bus screeched to an abrupt stop, beside a military checkpoint, just outside of my destination of Nebaj. The bald, heavyset, bus driver let out a weighted sigh as he pulled himself up and swung open the double doors. Two soldiers in dark green camouflage uniforms, with black berets angled on their shaved heads, climbed aboard, and swaggered down the aisle. Strapped automatic rifles hung menacingly from the men's shoulders. Their heavy black boots left a trail of mud down the center aisle as they began randomly searching straw baskets and cloth bound satchels stored in the racks above our heads. They looked like Mayans. I had read that indigenous recruits could be the most merciless of soldiers. In basic training, the military stripped away their tribal identity and indoctrinated them into believing that their people were backward, ignorant, and a threat to national security. To please their military superiors, indigenous recruits often became tougher and more brutal than their Ladino counterparts.

"All of the men off the bus, NOW!" commanded the shorter of the two men in Spanish. "Bring your identification. Everyone else stay in your seats." I joined the other men as we made a hasty exit off the bus and stood waiting in the muddy road. The soldiers took their time. "Line up alongside the bus!" one of them shouted. I pulled the money belt out from under my khaki pants, fumbled with the zipper then retrieved the passport and a letter from my Antigua language school. The soldiers began to move down the line, one by one, checking our papers. When they stopped in front of me, I handed over the items. "Why are you traveling to Nebaj?" asked the taller one in a stern voice. "Long trip from Antigua."

"I have a two-week vacation from language school," I replied in Spanish, "wanted to visit the highlands." I said only what I needed to say. They lingered a moment passing my two pieces of identification back and forth. The taller one wrote down my name and passport number on his clipboard, handed back my papers, and continued down the line. Thankfully, they pulled no one out. "Everyone back on the bus!" was the final command. I quickly boarded and settled back into my seat. The driver glanced over at me, shook his head, rolled his eyes, but said nothing. He closed the doors and continued to drive the old transport toward Nebaj, a mountain village in the Guatemalan state of Quiche known as the Ixil Triangle.

"The Ixil in northern Quiche have always been different from other ethnic groups. Geographically isolated from the rest of Quiche by mountains and surrounded by non-Ixil speaking neighbors, they have always been self-contained."[2]

Because of its relative isolation from the rest of the country, the area became an early base of operation for the opposition forces in Guatemala's long civil war: "the Ixil region was a special target of the military counterinsurgency campaigns of the early 1980s."[3] The army destroyed outlying settlements near Nebaj, as they did throughout the region, and slaughtered tens of thousands of Indians. Families that managed to escape the horror fled deeper into the mountains, crossed the border into Mexico's state of Chiapas, or found refuge in urban centers. Years later, the army temporarily housed returning refugees in Nebaj before transferring them into what they called model villages. "If phrases like 'beans and rifles' and 'model villages' and slogans like 'Winning Hearts and Minds' sound like they are from the Vietnam War, this is because many top level Guatemalan officers have been trained by the US Army at Fort Benning [School of the Americas], Georgia, and the Panama Canal Zone [former School of the Americas]," revealed Guatemalan American Victor Perera.[4] The army maintained strict control over the highlands through their imposed system of model villages and civil patrols. One of those villages, Acúl, was located a few-hours hike into the mountains from Nebaj.

The military required all able-bodied Indian males between the ages of fourteen and sixty to participate in civil patrols. Armed with rifles and shotguns, the local indigenous men had to facilitate army operations by monitoring the movements of their fellow citizens. The system strictly limited the travels of both villagers and outsiders throughout the rural areas.

As our bus arrived in Nebaj, the sun broke through the early morning heavy fog. Soon, the driver parked next to a handsome, whitewashed, adobe cathedral in the middle of the central plaza. My alternative guidebook noted that just inside the church doors stood a cluster of white crosses as a memorial to the locals killed in the civil war. When departing the bus, the driver gave me a warning. "Cuidado, señor," he said in a muffled voice, "aqui, la vida es muy dificil." He told me to watch out because life was very difficult there.

The Mayans, in their traditional clothing, began to retrieve belongings as one of their own handed them down from the top of the bus. If the Indians talked at all, they spoke in hushed tones and stayed to themselves.

Every Mayan tribe had unique clothing sewn and woven in myriad colors and designs. The designs identified each. That identification disadvantaged them when the military decided to victimize one particular, easily identifiable, ethnic group. Ixil women decorated their blouses, called huipiles, with intricate and symbolic birds, animals, and geometric designs in dominant colors of crimson, plum velvet, and papaya orange, mixed with cobalt blue, bright gold, and shamrock green. They embroidered them onto thick, white, cotton cloth imported from England. Their wraparound, ankle-length, skirts were a durable brilliant yellow and venetian red striped cotton cloth. The women's headdresses, made of long narrow pieces of multicolored, hand-loomed cloth with dangling pompoms, were tied intricately into their hair.

"I have always said that the weavings of Guatemala are the book, the written history of the Indian," remarked Mayan human rights leader Rigoberta Menchu, winner of the 1992 Nobel Peace Prize. Ms. Menchu spent her youth in the Ixil Triangle. "The weavings are the biggest texts that the Indian has. Above all, they are the product of a woman's thoughts and imagination."[5]

After retrieving my backpack, I entered the cathedral briefly and found the multitude of white crosses mentioned in my book. Leaving the church, I sat down in the middle of the plaza to watch the morning activities. The sun's warmth cut through the morning chill as the traditional adobe village began to wake up. On a hillside, not far off in the distance, I spotted an imposing military base painted white for everyone to see. A watchtower hovered over the complex, strategically located so army personnel could monitor civilians moving in and out of Nebaj.

Indians and Ladinos began to fill the streets as shopkeepers unlocked their doors and opened their windows. Clusters of green camouflage uniforms, with automatic rifle appendages, lingered about, their presence stifling. Occasionally, a native looked in my direction without acknowledging me. I had become invisible.

Hungry, I began to walk the cobblestone streets and discovered a tienda where I ordered eggs, beans, and tortillas. Waiting for the food, I attempted to strike up a conversation with the solemn-looking man behind the counter but he ignored me and served the food in silence. Finishing the meal, I set out in search of a particular hotel where I hoped to stay for the next few nights.

"Buenas dias, señora," I greeted the stately, older woman when she opened the door at the Hotel of the Three Sisters, the Pensión de Las Tres Hermanas. "Do you have a room for one person?" I asked in Spanish. "Si, señor," she replied and invited me into the foyer. I followed as she led me out a side door and into a tidy but undecorated courtyard. The tall, thin woman, with shiny grey hair pulled tightly into a bun, wore a navy blue dress with a narrow black leather belt and low-heeled shoes. A friend had recommended Las Tres Hermanas. He said its central location made it safe.

"The three sisters who manage the pensión are spinster daughters of Ladino parents who exude an odd blend of provincial innocence and worldliness–although we soon learn that they seldom travel outside Nebaj," pointed out journalist Victor Perera. "Their conversation, sprinkled liberally with Christian imagery and local folklore, might have leapt out of the pages of Gabriel Garcia Marquez or Frederico Garcia Lorca, save for the jarring shift in contexts."[6] In the courtyard, the proprietor led me to a single, windowless, adobe room with a concrete floor. The cold, musty-smelling, sparsely furnished cubicle contained a bed, a chair, and a small table with an oil lamp. Held up by squeaky bedsprings, the lumpy mattress had been fitted with course-feeling sheets and two heavy blankets. I had hoped for something a bit more inviting.

Leaving the room and moving across the courtyard, I noticed a cluster of rooms attached to the main house. They had windows and wooden floors. Two of them looked uninhabited. Turning around, I got the woman's attention and pointed to the seemingly empty rooms. "I would prefer one of these," I told her. "Oh, no, that is not possible," the woman responded. "Those rooms are always reserved." She offered no further explanation, but later I discovered that the local army base maintained those rooms for military officers and their "ladies of the evening."

Resigned to the windowless room, I filled out the guest book, paid for two nights, settled in, and spent the remainder of the day exploring Nebaj and writing in my journal. Armed soldiers were everywhere: at the markets, in the shops, and on the streets moving in groups of two or three. Their presence constantly reminded residents who controlled the town.

In the evening, I joined other backpackers for dinner in the hotel's simple dining room lit by a half-dozen oil lamps. Fellow backpackers, three couples and I, sat at the long decoratively carved wooden table. Collectively we were citizens of England, West Germany, Holland, and the US. The evening's company felt reassuring and protective despite the stifling presence of the army outside the hotel walls. As we carried on conversation, a Mayan woman served the simple meal that included a savory vegetable soup. Meanwhile, the proprietors floated in and out of the dining area while keeping an eye on things. They dressed alike but in different colors, wore the same hairdo, spoke in a similar tone of voice, and carried themselves in a like manner. The attractive sisters wore no make-up, and their well-scrubbed, light-skinned faces revealed few wrinkles. Occasionally, one or two of the sisters would join us at the table and make casual conversation. Most of the time, however, they stood a short distance away with clasped hands and faint smiles.

Contrary to Victor Perera's comment about the sisters leaping out of a Marquez novel or a Lorca poem, I sensed that the three women were potential characters in a book by Isabel Allende, the Chilean author. Allende would capture, in words, the mystical feel of the hotel and the charm of the unique and mysterious proprietors.

As we finished dinner, there was a light knock on the door, at one end of the dining room that opened out onto a back alley. A sister, the one wearing the navy blue dress with the black belt, walked over and opened it. "Venga, venga," she said smiling and motioning for the visitors to enter. They chatted briefly as if old friends. The guests, four Mayan women dressed in their traditional garb, were carrying native blouses, woven cloth belts, and other colorful textiles. Older pieces, the more expensive ones, were a finer weave made from cotton or wool and colored with natural dyes. "My friends are not allowed to leave the community to sell their items," explained the sister in the cranberry colored dress with the white leather belt. "So we welcome them into our home a few times each week to meet our guests." With that explanation, the three siblings quietly exited the dining room as the Indian women began moving around the table showing their wares and quoting prices.

While army officers recreated in two hotel rooms nearby, the proprietors ushered indigenous women into the dining room through the back door to sell their wares. Clearly, the sisters had discovered a way to appease both groups.

In the morning, after a breakfast, I told a sister that I planned to hike over to Acúl. I had traveled to Nebaj in order to witness and write about the model village. She appeared surprised then told me that the narrow mountainous path could take a few hours to climb depending on the weather. "It's safer to hike the path with four eyes rather than two," she warned me. I knew that.

The night before, I had tried to recruit some of the internationals to join me on the trek, but no one appeared interested. "Too dangerous," remarked one of the British backpackers. "I wouldn't suggest going it alone." The three couples planned to stay in town that day and hike along the nearby river within sight of Nebaj.

Before leaving, I made a point of telling the sister that I planned to return later in the afternoon and to eat dinner in their dining room. I gave her a Xerox copy of my passport and a copy of the introductory letter from my language school. In my shoulder bag, I packed a canteen of water, an orange, a banana, and two tortillas along with a map, a pen, my green nylon rain poncho, trusty Swiss army knife, and a blank notebook. My passport and another copy of the school letter were zipped inside my money belt but I left my camera behind–no reason to carry anything that might have created unnecessary suspicion.

On the outskirts of Nebaj, I found a narrow path that wound upward through the mountain walls. It appeared to be the right one. My guidebook explained that the trail switched back and forth up the steep mountainside then led over a narrow pass into the next valley where it would descend into the village of Acúl. "Excuse me. Is this the path to Acúl?" I asked three Mayan women in Spanish as they passed by. They neither lifted their heads nor uttered a word. Maybe their silence indicated they did not speak Spanish; many Ixil only spoke their tribal language. I suspected, however, that they felt threatened by my presence.

As the path began to climb, I passed an adobe hut covered with a thatched roof and caught sight of a man about to go inside. "Excuse me, is this the way to Acúl?" I yelled. "Si," he confirmed. As I continued to ascend the trail, I came face to face with an old man pulling his lean, swaybacked horse. The animal's ribs protruded from his undernourished body. Deep lines in the man's dark, leather-like face revealed the years he had spent working under the scorching sun. I greeted him and asked if he was well.

"Muy bien, muy bien," The man replied his voice quavering, "es muy tranquilo aqui." Without my asking, he had told me that things were good and very calm. "Es muy tranquilo, aqui" he repeated before walking away. Perhaps the soldiers told him to say that?

A short distance farther, the path snaked around a bend and began to descend. I could see Acúl at the bottom of the valley, probably another hour away.

Years before, Acúl was one of a cluster of four, small communities. In his report for the Guatemalan Human Rights Commissions, attorney Mikkel Jordahl disclosed that there were two schools and a community center, traditional huts made of bricks and adobe, a potable water project, health center, and a savings and loan cooperative in Acúl. "The Indians shared the pasture-land and the surrounding forests. Community members raised animals for meat, milk, wool, and cheese, and they grew their own food—corn, beans, tomatoes, and chilies, as well as tending beehives." In 1983, the military bombed Acúl and burned the other three villages to the ground. "Since most of the [model] villages are built on the ruins of the communities destroyed by the army between 1981 and 1983, the army has had a free hand in construction of the model villages, usually sacrificing traditional living patterns for strategic concerns. For that reason, houses in most model villages are laid out in a strict grid pattern in a central location, allowing for the most efficient use of army surveillance capabilities."[7] Jordahl reported that Acúl residents now lived in row houses with street names like Liberty Street and New Life Road.

Continuing my descent, I could clearly see the layout of the village, one central grid of wooden structures, covered with corrugated tin roofs, tightly organized in parallel rows. Although someone had cleared the land around the village, there were no crops growing within site. The scene reminded me of the clear-cuts that scarred the Oregon mountainsides I witnessed as a tree-planter. Built on a nearby hillside and overlooking the village, stood a military base that boasted strategically positioned watchtowers. I walked with caution as I moved closer.

In front of a small, wood plank, civil patrol station sat two elderly Mayan men dressed in tattered civilian clothes. Armed with rifles, they stood up as I walked toward them. Trying to project a non-threatening presence, I greeted them. They were at least a head shorter. When asked why I had come, I told them about my vacation from language school, that I wanted to travel around the country and visit different places including Nebaj. My reply satisfied them.

Holding out his hand, one of the men asked for identification papers. I gave him the school letter and showed him the photograph in my passport. The passport stayed in my hand. Speaking their native tongue, the men conversed as they passed the letter between them. Perhaps they could not read Spanish. When the other patrol member pointed to my shoulder bag, I opened it, and he searched the contents. After a few moments passed, they motioned for me to continue on my way.

Returning to the path, I heard automatic rifle fire coming from the mountains just on the other side of Acúl but echoes could be deceiving. I looked back at the men to note their reaction. They had returned to their conversation as if there was no reason to be concerned. Upon entering the village, I saw no one in the streets, but I did notice faces peering out from the windows of the row houses. Residents were watching me. Jordahl had written in his report that since the destruction of the original Acúl and the other three villages, the population had decreased by one-half. The military had forced villagers to grow asparagus, Brussels sprouts, and peas–export crops. The villagers were now dependent upon outside resources for their food staples of beans and corn, meat and milk. I proceeded deeper into the community where a large adobe brick complex sat empty. The stark, partially completed plaza looked unused.

As a hard rain began to fall and I pulled on my nylon poncho, the sounds of distant automatic rifle fire commenced once again. The ear-piercing shots bounced off the mountain walls enclosing the village. From the deserted complex, I meandered down the main road and stopped at a one-room shop where the counter faced the street. A tall, thin, sallow-looking Ladino stood inside. A woman, breastfeeding her baby, sat at a small table behind him. No other shops in the village were open. I had entered the Twilight Zone.

I purchased a warm soda, a package of crackers, and began to eat while we exchanged small talk. Soon the woman stood up, cradled the baby in her arms, and walked out the back door without acknowledging my presence. "How long have you lived here?" I asked. The shop owner told me that he and his wife had moved there a year before, but he offered no additional personal information; I chose not to probe.

The automatic rifle fire became more frequent and possibly moving closer. I asked about it. He said there were bandits in the mountains, but the army would take care of them. His long, sad face spoke volumes. "Where are the village people?" I inquired. "Working in the fields," he told me. There were no cultivated fields within eyesight. Did the military transport the laborers to distant fields?

I felt increasingly uncomfortable. Perhaps my presence at the shop would jeopardize the man's standing in the community or make the authorities suspicious. I finished my soft drink and crackers, thanked him, and continued my self-guided tour. Two armed soldiers and a humpbacked Ixil woman passed me on the street without a word–invisible again. Despite a brief search, I did not find any remnants of the previous village. Rifle fire continued steadily and the rain began to fall even harder. Time to leave.

On the outskirts of the community, I approached the civil patrol station hoping that the same men would still be on guard duty and just wave me by–no such luck. Instead, four young replacements, armed with rifles, watched as I began to pass them from a distance. I yelled "Adios" to the men, waved, and continued walking.

A civil patrol member yelled back. "Venga, venga," he said and motioned for me to go over to their one-room station. I stopped for a moment debating whether I should just ignore his request and keep on walking but decided against it. Leaving the trail, l plodded over to the foursome and immediately noticed that two of them had bloodshot eyes and smelled of alcohol.

Once again, I retrieved the school letter, gave it to one of the sober ones then pulled out my passport. Holding on to it while keeping it covered with my poncho, I flashed the photograph in front of the men. After they had passed the wet letter around, upside down, the sober guard returned the limp sheet of paper. That is when his fellow guards began to ask questions in Spanish. Why had I come to Acúl? Did I bring anything with me that I left behind? Did I have a camera? Did I know anyone in the village? They spoke over each another. I could not understand some of what they asked, but I answered what I could. Unfortunately, I had become their afternoon's entertainment. None of the men searched my bag. Perhaps they did not notice it under my poncho. As they continued to ask questions, I realized that I needed to extricate myself and walk away or continue falling victim to their game.

Slowly, I began to back away from them toward the path. "Need to go now," I said. "Have to get back to my friends in Nebaj." I paused then continued to talk loudly. "They know that I came here today." I wanted the civil patrol to realize that someone knew where I had gone. Someone expected me to return to Nebaj by the end of the day. "Friends are expecting me for dinner." I had reached the path. Surprisingly, they said nothing more. "Adios," I yelled back at them, waved one last time, turned around, and began to hike up the muddy path. The rain had not let up. If I could make it to the bend up the trail, without someone following me, I assumed I would be safe. Just before reaching it, I turned around, path clear but rifle fire unceasing. My shoulders relaxed a bit and I slowed my pace. By late afternoon, I arrived in Nebaj.

Taking a back road into the village, I came upon a Mayan funeral procession. Men and women in their native dress walked barefoot and in silence. At the front of the procession, four older males carried a simple wooden casket on their shoulders. Respectfully, I followed the group from a distance.

When an army truck roared up from behind us, without a warning, we glanced back in alarm. The large, olive green military transport with a muddy, silver-colored grill stopped abruptly. The passenger side door swung open and a soldier leaned out waving his hand. "Get out of the way!" he yelled contemptuously. "You hear me? Get out of the way!"

The solemn procession split in half as people scurried to either side of the road. One pallbearer slipped and fell onto his hands and knees, in the muck, as the other three men tried to balance the tipping coffin. Either oblivious or uncaring, the driver drove the truck down the center of the road and barreled through. The monster-sized tires splattered mud on us all. For a moment, the Mayans stood by the side of the road divided and stunned, as did I. Determined to honor their dead, however, they united once again and continued their procession down the narrow, slippery road.

CHAPTER EIGHTEEN

~

Sitting on the Fault Line

A yellowish haze hung in the air. I could feel the heat radiate from the asphalt when I stuck my arm out of the shattered bus window. It would be another steamy day in the capital city of a country in its seventh year of civil war. Good morning, San Salvador.

As the bus moved at a snail's pace, I watched ice cream vendors push their carts along the avenues where dark-haired women, in frilly colored aprons, stocked their curbside stands with everything imaginable, fruits, vegetables, and tamales, clothing, plastic toys, and greeting cards. Behind them, shop owners unlatched padlocks and opened up screeching metal gates that protected their front doors and display windows. When I stepped off the bus, pulled out the city map from my day-pack, and opened it like an accordion, my eyes began to water. The dust, grime, and exhaust fumes made it difficult to read the fine print. I wanted to nail down a specific residential street. That afternoon, the Committee of Mothers and Relatives of Political Prisoners, Disappeared, and Assassinated of El Salvador, COMADRES, were planning to meet with me in a private home near the city center.

Jennifer Casolo, a human rights activist from the United States, made the arrangements. She had been working in El Salvador for close to a year. The previous week we managed to meet in the capitol, for coffee, despite her precarious position in the country. When I first spoke to Jennifer by phone, the intrepid activist could not guarantee that our rendezvous would take place. The military had recently labeled her a subversive. She lived under constant military surveillance.

I had also received permission to visit the overcrowded and underfunded refugee camps on the outskirts of the city. The archbishop's office and the Association for Salvadoran Human Rights provided me with introductory letters. They would serve as my passports into the camps. Those visits would probably take up most of the following day. "The number of displaced persons is estimated at one million, or 20 percent of the Salvadoran population," stated a reliable source. "Of those roughly half have remained within El Salvador. They face severe overcrowding and harassment from security forces."[1]

Human rights activists in El Salvador encouraged US and European visitors to meet with COMADRES and get into the refugee camps for the same reasons that Witness for Peace sent delegations to Nicaragua. When outsiders witnessed the reality of the situation, they became potential advocates for ending the Pentagon's ongoing funding and military training that perpetuated the endless, barbarous, civil wars. The presence of international visitors communicated an unwritten message to the Salvadoran civil and military authorities. You are being watched.

Eventually, I found my way to the address and confirmed the time for that afternoon's meeting. Meandering through the neighborhood, on my way back to center city, I spotted a makeshift, four-table café in the side yard of a humble adobe house where the owner served as cook, waitress, and dishwasher. Hungry, I stopped and ordered the only items on the menu: black beans, fried eggs, and tortillas. After breakfast, I visited the Iglesia Catedral Metropolitnana, San Salvador's major Roman Catholic cathedral and burial place of Archbishop Oscar Romero assassinated six years earlier.

The late Archbishop Romero's Sunday homilies had been

broadcast, nationally, by independent radio; a practice adamantly opposed by the extreme right-wing military authorities. I read that in the villages without electricity, civilians would connect radios to car batteries in order to listen to Romero's sermons. He would name those persons most recently killed or threatened with death. In his acclaimed final homily, given on March 23, 1980, the one-time conservative church leader, who later evolved into an unyielding advocate for the poor, denounced the violence and boldly challenged the perpetrators. Author Michael J. Walsh wrote that Romero "called firmly upon the troops and the national guardsmen to obey the law of God and therefore not obey the orders of officers who might instruct them to kill their brothers and sisters. 'In the name of God, then, and in the name of this suffering people whose cries rise daily more loudly to heaven, I plead with you, I beg you, I order you in the name of God: put an end to this repression.'"[2]

Romero had challenged the authority not only of the army but also of the civilian government that provided legitimacy to the military. He had ordered recruits to disobey their commanders. A day later, as the archbishop said Mass in a hospital chapel, an unidentified armed man gunned him down. At that moment, the civil war truly began.

The cathedral's interior had the look and feel of a gigantic vault, cold, gray, and ugly but the coolness of the interior offered temporary relief from the oppressive heat in the streets. I took a seat in a pew near the front of the sanctuary and began to read my *South American Handbook*. Occasionally, I looked up to watch the Salvadorans go quietly about the business of their faith. Some visitors made their way to the Romero burial place with flowers in hand while others knelt and prayed in the pews. Many people simply sat in silence, taking a brief retreat from their daily schedule. Scores of believers lit a votive candle, or two, maybe more, before departing. "This is the cathedral that the late Archbishop Oscar Arnulfo Romero refused to finish, on the premise that the work of the Church took precedence over its display, and the high walls of raw concrete bristle with structural rods, rusting now, staining the concrete, sticking out at wrenched and violent angles," revealed writer Joan Didion. "The wiring is exposed. Fluorescent tubes hang askew. The great high altar is backed by warped plyboard. The cross on the altar is of bare incandescent bulbs"[3] Didion referred to the behemoth as political art. She accurately called the cathedral a statement about El Salvador much like Picasso's famous painting *Guernica* became a graphic political statement regarding the Spanish Civil War and fascism.

Shortly before noon, I left the church and joined the crowds on Calle Ruben Dario, a major downtown commercial avenue. Passing by the eight-story Ruben Dario Office Building, I casually strolled to the end of the block then turned off onto a side street in search of the main post office. Without warning, a forceful jolt knocked me off the sidewalk into the street, and a powerful rumble shook the earth. An earthquake, a terramoto, had just wrenched San Salvador apart. A major fault line lay directly underneath city center. "Get out! Get out!" I could hear the frantic shouts. Nearby, a screaming woman ran into the street with hands covering her head. Untold numbers of office workers poured out of buildings that had just cracked open like eggs. Then, Mother Earth delivered another deadly blow, an aftershock as powerful as the initial quake, and yet another. Salvadorans were running in every direction desperately trying to escape the falling debris.

My rubbery legs were shaking. Standing in the middle of the narrow street, I could not take the next step. I had lived through floods and tornadoes but never an earthquake. "Get to an open area!" a man yelled at me as he ran by; his pin-striped suit tattered and bloody. His command abruptly woke me out my fear, and I began to move.

I followed the surging crowd toward an unfamiliar intersection. It was chaos. People flooded into the open space from all directions and traffic came to a halt. Men and women held on to one another offering physical and emotional support. Neither police officers nor soldiers were in sight.

A fourth and then a fifth aftershock violently jarred the earth in quick succession. They were getting stronger. Will the ground split open and swallow us up? Soon groups of citizens began to mobilize. More accustomed than I to earthquakes, they attempted to get the traffic moving again and provided assistance to the injured.

Still disoriented, I stood on a curb at the edge of a city park trying to figure out my location on the map. Unexpectedly, a late model car screeched to a stop beside me. When the driver stuck his head out the window, he began to shout angrily in English. The man was drunk, "First the army then the guerillas, now an earthquake!" The young Salvadoran raged on. I knew that he knew I was an American. I backed away from the car.

The man continued to yell and glare at me in a threatening manner. A few moments passed. The other fellow, sitting in the passenger seat, continued to shout at the driver. They were talking over one another in Spanish so rapidly that I could not understand what they were saying. Finally, the man at the wheel spit on the pavement beside me, pulled away from the curb, and stepped on the accelerator. His car weaved dangerously in and out of the crowds and the debris.

I sunk down onto the grass for a moment. People were wailing in the streets. Gradually, police officers and soldiers began to filter into the intersection. Calming, I needed to find my way back to the bus depot. Bracing myself for another aftershock, I began to retrace my steps unprepared for what I witnessed along the way.

The eight-story office building on Calle Ruben Dario had

pancaked and buried untold numbers. Civilians scrambled over the top of the rubble shouting names and desperately trying to lift massive chunks of concrete and steel off their family members, friends, and strangers buried below, an impossible task. Street merchants, who had earlier been selling their wares along the curb-sides, lay dead beneath collapsed exterior walls.

"You alright?" someone behind me inquired.

I turned around to face a young couple wearing hiking boots with faded jeans and T-shirts. They looked disheveled and weary. "Fine, thanks," I replied.

"We were in our hotel room when it hit," the blond woman told me. Her tall male companion, with a severe crew cut, said they just ran out of the hotel without grabbing their backpacks. The couple had flown in from West Berlin the night before. I invited them to return with me to the village of Zaragoza where I was staying with friends, but they did not want to leave their gear in the hotel overnight.

I found the depot intact, although many of the buses were not in service. Those that were running overflowed with people anxious to get out of the city of death and destruction. I managed to squeeze onto one heading west, toward Zaragoza. Making its way around the debris in the city streets, the bus progressed slowly. We were crowded into the seats and standing shoulder to shoulder in the aisle. Some windows were sealed and the overwhelming smell of sweat filled the bus. Passengers were silent or communicating in whispers, almost apologetically, as if they thought they should be praying instead of talking.

"Thank God you're safe!" exclaimed Sister Kathy when I walked into the small parish house in Zaragoza. Approaching, she leaned into me with a hug. I welcomed the affectionate physical contact after the day's tragedies. "Everyone is accounted for," she reported with relief as the radio news blared in the background. A nun and a native Clevelander, Sister

Kathy worked at the parish alongside a priest, and two volunteers; also natives of The Rock and Roll Capital of the World. In her mid-forties, Kathy had the stamina of a woman half her age. She worked closely with local organizations in the village. Kathy provided a good balance to the reserved and somewhat distant priest whom the diocese had assigned to work with her.

"Some parish women have already started collecting clothes. They plan to take food into the capitol in the morning," Sister Kathy informed me. "You and I'll provide the transportation."

We listened to radio news late into the night. Government authorities estimated more than one thousand dead and ten times that number of injured. A newswoman reported that most people were sleeping in the streets for fear of more aftershocks or because their homes were uninhabitable. At the close of the newscast, the reporter estimated two hundred civilians buried under the Ruben Dario Office Building rubble.

Two weeks before, I had arrived in Zaragoza from Antigua, Guatemala, where I had continued to study Spanish and live with a local family. I would be living in Central America four more months and in South America for the remainder of the time. Laura, a former Antigua language school classmate and friend, invited me to visit the Zaragoza parish. She had volunteered to work for at least a year with the Cleveland Latin American Mission group. I jumped at the opportunity to visit for a short time and assist in whatever way possible. Soon after I arrived, Laura received an assignment to a work in another village, located in a conflict zone, where she remained indefinitely.

Little more than two decades before, in 1964, the Cleveland Diocese began to send priests, sisters, and lay volunteers to serve the people of El Salvador. Years later, one of their priests established a Children's Village, just outside Zaragoza, to house hundreds of youngsters whose parents were killed or up-rooted by the civil war. Staffed primarily by Salvadorans, the complex included group homes and a medical clinic in addition to agricultural projects and schools. The late Sister Dorothy Kazel and lay volunteer, Jean Donovan, both members of the Cleveland Mission, assisted the priest in the beginning months of the Children's Village. The year the complex officially opened, soldiers on the roadside abducted Dorothy and Jean, and two other women religious, Maura Clark and Ita Ford, then raped and murdered them.

Early the next morning, Sister Kathy and I loaded two boxes of clothing, donated by the villagers, into the back of the jeep. "These people don't have enough food and clothing for their own families," she remarked as we drove out into the countryside. "But they still manage to find a way to give something." We soon reached our first destination. "Buenos dias, Hermana Kathy," Claudia yelled out as we drove up to her three-room, wood and adobe house with a dirt floor and a corrugated tin roof. "Buenos dias, Guillermo," she added. Claudia's three children were playing in the hammock that hung outside on the veranda. I had met their mother the week before at a meeting in the parish church. Claudia and her husband were subsistence farmers, community activists, and leaders in the Zaragoza parish.

"Its name [El Salvador] is sometimes translated as 'Savior of the World,' but its people are among the world's five worst fed populations," revealed academic Walter LeFeber. "One reason: at least half of all Salvadorans depend on the land for their living, but fewer than two percent (the 'oligarchs' of 'Fourteen Families') control nearly all the fertile soil and 60 percent of the land."[4]

Claudia and three other women had stayed up most of the night grinding corn, kneading dough, and making tortillas. Two large cloth-covered plastic basins, already filled, sat on a wobbly side table. A third basin soon overflowed with more tortillas. I loaded all three into the very back of the jeep, next to the clothing, while the Salvadoran women squeezed into the back seat. Claudia stuck her blue bandanna-covered head out the jeep as she gave last minute instructions to her children. Her spouse stayed to watch the kids and work the field behind their house.

"Vamos," Claudia commanded good-naturedly. The Zaragoza food and clothing brigade took off for the capitol.

City streets were difficult to maneuver because debris still covered many roadways. Police officers and soldiers had re-routed traffic onto the cleared major avenues. Makeshift shelters made from blankets, large pieces of cardboard, sheets of clear plastic, and black trash bags covered the city's open spaces. "Don't have anywhere else to go," commented Claudia in Spanish, shaking her head and clicking her tongue. The other women clicked their tongues, too, nodding in agreement.

As we drove past a large, relatively undamaged, outdoor market, Claudia instructed Kathy to pull over to the side of the road and park. She must have known the place. "Just leave the jeep here," said Claudia as she climbed out. We followed her without question. Dressed in a sleeveless blouse with a mended skirt and green flip-flops, Claudia still wore her apron from the morning cooking, as did her helpers. Each of us carried something. After our leader handed me a plastic basin, I hoisted it to the top of my head and moved to the end of the line. Claudia appeared to know where she wanted to go and carried herself with confidence.

When we approached a cordoned-off area guarded by two armed soldiers, the situation did not appear to present a barrier for Claudia. She simply walked around the ropes, past the soldiers, as we followed closely behind. "Hey there," shouted one the military men. Undeterred, she kept walking. "Halt!" the other one commanded.

Without stopping, Claudia turned her head to look back at them. She refused to be intimidated. "We have food and clothes for our people," she shouted. "We know where we're going." The soldiers backed off as Claudia continued to walk at a fast pace while the rest of us tried to keep up. A few blocks farther down the road, she stopped by the curbside. "This is the spot," declared our leader. We trusted her intuition. As we opened the two boxes of clothing and uncovered the basins filled with tortillas, earthquake victims began to line up. No one pushed or shoved.

Personal Journal
November 1, 1986

In Zaragoza and other villages throughout the country, there were ongoing clothing drives and food collections. At two of the Cleveland Catholic Missions, in the villages of La Libertad and Chirilagua, staff members operated ham radios day and night. Telephone communications were non-existent throughout the country. The ham operators provided information about family members and assisted with aid operations from Nicaragua, Guatemala, Western European countries, and the US. In essence, the ham operators were crucial lines of communication to the outside world. Infrastructure recovery would take years.

A week following the earthquake, I traveled with mission members to La Libertad then on to Chirilagua. When crossing the Lampa River we had to use Bailey Bridges, one-lane portable and prefabricated truss bridges. All of the permanent bridges along the river had been blown-up. The area is a conflict zone and heavily militarized with frequent checkpoints along the roads.

El Salvador is equivalent in size to Massachusetts with a population of five million. At its widest point, it only stretches seventy miles. Our trip took about five hours.

Chirilagua, alternately controlled by both government and opposition forces since the beginning of the civil war, is normally without telephone communications. It is a village where opposi-

tion forces have spray-painted political slogans all over the walls and later covered over with black paint by the government troops. It is also a village where the mayor has been kidnapped numerous times and the telephone office, ANTEL, blown up so often that reconstruction seems futile. During my stay there, I had the opportunity to travel with the mission team, by foot, into remote mountain villages.

On my last day in Chirilagua, they gave me a ride into the city of San Miguel where I boarded a bus for the capitol. As we drove into San Miguel, there were military trucks in front of us loaded with young men many of whom were holding assignment papers. One means by which the Salvadoran Army obtain recruits is to drive through the streets picking up young men that appear eligible to serve, beginning at age fifteen. Within a matter of days, the teenagers would be in basic training.

When I arrived back in San Salvador, it was obvious that security had tightened around recovery operations. With military presence everywhere, sections of the city were closed to pedestrians.

I read in Newsweek's article, "A Quake Shakes up Duarte" (October 27, 1986), that Salvadoran President José Napoleón Duarte ordered that monies for disaster relief be distributed through private channels rather than his own governmental institutions. It was an uncomfortable admission that the money would be stolen if handled by his government. It reminded me of events that I had read about in Nicaragua back in 1972, when a devastating earthquake destroyed Managua, the capital. Nicaragua's then President Anastasio Somoza, and members of his National Guard, reportedly pocketed most of the money sent to the country for the purpose of disaster relief and reconstruction. Downtown Managua never recovered.

I took a local bus back to Zaragoza then left for Guatemala the following day.

CHAPTER NINETEEN

~

Meyers, Briggs, and Carl Jung

Surrounded by suits of all kinds. They were navy blue, gray, and a few brown, too. Some even had stripes. There were suits with white oxford cloth shirts, buttoned-down collars, ties, and wingtip shoes. A handful came with vests. A commensurate number of suits wore blouses, neatly tucked into skirts, under form-fitting suit coats, and propped up with low heels. Being the only unsuitable person in the room, I showed up wearing loose-fitting khakis, a faded blue work shirt, and desert boots. I stood out like a bald-head in a barbershop.

We had gathered in a comfortable, light-filled conference room in early September 1988. After mingling and helping ourselves to the sweet rolls, fruit cocktail, and coffee, nicely presented on a buffet table, the facilitator asked us to take our seats. I positioned myself in the middle of the layered desks facing the imposing white board hanging from the wall in front of the room. I wanted to make sure I could see and hear everyone in the room. The workshop would begin shortly.

The suits, I assumed, were straight, middle-aged, and married with children. They most probably lived in suburban New Jersey and New York, and corporate America employed them. Without question, they were a *Fortune* magazine crowd.

I, however, happened to be single, thirty-nine years old, never married, and recently come out as gay, no longer considering myself bisexual. In little more than a decade, I had evolved from one end of Dr. Alfred Kinsey's sexual orientation scale to the other. Over the previous two years, I had worked

285

with a Latin American not-for-profit organization focused on housing and immigration issues. Although my Washington, DC, office had recently relocated to the Adams Morgan neighborhood, I resided in a cooperative household on Rhode Island Avenue, NE, near Howard University. At one end of my block, a street drug business flourished. On the other end was a boarded-up crack house.

Sitting down with my fellow boomers, I felt like I might be in the wrong place at the right time but I soon realized l was exactly where I needed to be. We were all there for the same reason, to seek guidance.

"This program is positive and motivating, resulting in a specific plan of action for your new career direction," stated the workshop's promotional material. That is what I had in common with my corporate brothers and sisters. Seeking a new direction for our skills and experiences would be the glue that held us together for the following three days.

Months before, each of us had signed up for the career workshop and paid the fees, which included all tests and materials. Weeks prior to the event, we received a packet with a variety of tests, a career development questionnaire, and an accomplishment list assignment. The instructions told us to complete the tests and questionnaires promptly and return them to the career development organization for analysis. The accomplishment list, however, was to be completed then brought to the first day's session.

"Welcome to the workshop!" announced Dan, the facilitator. Tall, tan, and athletic-looking, he began promptly on time. The well-dressed, middle-aged man wore penny loafers with tassels, light brown slacks and a short-sleeved, pastel orange cotton sport shirt with a logo, the kind you would see on a golf course. In his right hand, Dan held a large green erasable marker as he launched into the first day of our program. He stood rock solid with legs slightly spread apart and feet flat on the ground. Dan reminded me of a drill sergeant at Shattuck Military Academy, in Faribault, Minnesota, where I spent an intense and disciplined stretch of time during my teen years. My parents had sent me there to head off what they had rightly perceived as my fast track to juvenile delinquency.

"Like previous participants, you are about to undertake a most stimulating learning experience," Dan announced, exuding confidence in voice and stature. I liked him immediately. "Before we begin, I want to be clear about our purpose and approach," he said snapping the marker cap on and off and swinging around to face the white board. "This career workshop is," said Dan in his clear baritone voice as he began to write big and swirly on the board, "Supportive of you just as you are in this moment." Dan turned around to face us, to make sure that his statement had landed. Convinced, he swung back around to write big and swirly again and read aloud point number two, "A self-study process." Again, he turned back around. Dan took an extended period of silence to make eye contact with each of us in the room. The brief but surprisingly intimate moment made more than a few of the suits squirm in their seats. I welcomed it. His third and final point received an extra fancy swirly. "Focused on your career," he read aloud. Tan Dan told us that in the next three days we were going to generate data about ourselves in more than two dozen areas of importance.

"Please take out your accomplishment lists," he said in his energetic tone of voice. "You were requested to complete them before coming to the workshop." The instructions had told us to list fifty or more satisfying accomplishments in our lives.

"You may view many of these incidents as insignificant, " explained the instructions. "You may even be a little embarrassed about some. Never-the-less, include them if you enjoyed them, did them well, produced a result, and felt good about them. " Chronological order was not important. We could start anywhere we wanted, covering all periods of our lives then we were to select our top ten and note the date and location where each took place.

"Who would like to read their top-ten list?" Dan asked. He continued to snap that darn cap on and off his erasable marker, a nervous tick fast becoming a distraction.

Without hesitation, my hand shot up. I had listed more than sixty personal accomplishments. Ready and determined to get my money's worth of support, self-study, and focus, I wanted to show Dan that I could benefit from his attention and expertise.

"I had a hard time selecting my top ten," I admitted. "Everything on my list seemed to be significant." The suits tittered a bit at my comment. I heard some throat clearing in the crowd. The boss man at the board gave me a nod, a strong indication to get on with it. I began to read my list:

"Completed 605 consecutive sit-ups in a junior high gym class competition and won–Newton, KS–1963."

I hesitated sharing that one. A grown man still being proud of doing hundreds of sit-ups sounded silly or immature but I still felt proud of that accomplishment.

"Learned to play the Bumble Bee Boogie on the piano, in junior high, and performed it at various venues in my hometown–Newton, KS–1964."

That one got a few chuckles. I even chuckled myself.

"Worked as a volunteer in a Quaker sponsored summer work project when in high school–Brandon, VT–1966."

"Accepted into VISTA (Volunteers in Service to America) and worked as a community organizer–Louisville, KY–1969 to 1971."

"Arrested for my first nonviolent act of civil disobedience during a sit-in at the public assistance office–Louisville, KY–1970."

I heard some mumbling from my fellow boomers. More than a few people turned around to look at me with judgmental expressions on their faces. "Please keep your opinions to yourselves," Dan said. "We're not here to judge." I continued to read from my list.

"Made my first monastic retreat at the Trappist Abbey of Gethsemani–Bardstown, KY–1973."

"Worked as a laborer on Kibbutz Maabarot–Israel–1974."

More than a few heads nodded up and down. Maybe they were volunteers themselves or had family members who had signed up.

"Hitchhiked from New York to Alaska and back–July 1976."

There were a few "Wows!" in the group. I appreciated those responses.

"Performed as the Sheriff in an Off-Off Broadway production of Stephen Black's one-act play titled The Pokey–Manhattan, NY–1979."

"Traveled to Nicaragua as a member of the Oregon Witness for Peace delegation–Summer 1985."

A few heads were shaking, perhaps with disapproval. There were, however, no verbal responses.

Having completed my list of ten, Dan asked me a few questions. Then he moved on to another workshop participant, and another, until everyone had an opportunity to share their accomplishments.

Many of the suits were reluctant to claim significant personal achievements in their lives. Obviously, they were bright, accomplished, and, I assumed successful in their work place but a significant number of men and women admitted that they were hard pressed to come up with a mere twenty-five or thirty significant accomplishments in their lives. Puzzled and surprised, I wondered if that said something about corporate America. Was honoring personal accomplishments, outside of the business, disregarded in the corporate cosmos?

I did realize, however, had the original request been to list our five-year career plans since junior high, the suits would have probably completed the task without a problem. I would have been sitting there with a blank sheet of paper.

During the next three days, each of us determined which abilities we most wanted to use on the job, identified personal strengths, and clarified our most fundamental values. The results of my tests confirmed that my strengths were in research, investigation, comparisons, and data observation. In dealing with people, I enjoyed advising, counseling, and instructing as well as motivating, inspiring, and demonstrating. When it came to work projects, I preferred to present them artistically in collections, arrangements, and displays.

An analysis of my Strong-Campbell Interest Inventory confirmed that my general occupational themes were Artistic and Social. My highest scoring in the basic interest scales included adventure, nature, and music in addition to dramatics, writing, and religious activities. I was not surprised. My highest categories in the occupational scales ranged from college professor, fine artist, and actor to musician, broadcaster, reporter, and librarian.

When I took the Myers-Briggs Type Indicator, a personality profile, I discovered that I was an INFP: an introverted, intuitive, feeling, and perceptive individual. What did those letters infer? During a break, I eagerly read over a brief explanation of an INFP in a workshop handout. "Full of enthusiasm and loyalties, but seldom talk of these until they know you well. Cares about learning, ideas, language and independent projects of their own. Tends to undertake too much, then somehow gets it done. Friendly, but often too absorbed in what they are doing to be sociable. Little concerned with possessions or physical surroundings. Live their outer life more with intuition, inner life more with feeling. An INFP enjoys people but needs space, energy drawn inward, and needs time to reflect." [1] That sounded like me, alright. In the past, I had participated in several personality profile evaluations. My experience, however, with the Myers-Briggs was the first time that a profile analysis spoke my truth. It provided a place and an identity for me that I had not known existed.

According to the workshop handout, INFPs represented about one percent of the population in the US. That alone explained volumes. Based on Dr. Carl Jung's theory of psychological types, the Myers-Briggs Type Indicator revealed to me what an astrologer's chart might provide a true believer in the stars or an Enneagram would confirm for a devotee who identified with one of its nine personality profile categories.

"The INFP questor probably has more problems in mating than any other type. Their problem lies in their primary outlook on life. 'Life,' says the INFP, 'is a very serious matter.' Now when a person makes his life a kind of crusade or a series of crusades, then there's bound to be some taxing of the spouse. If the INFP takes the other tack, the 'monastic' (and the same person can tack back and forth–now a crusader, now a monastic), the spouse will find himself again taxed, trying to draw the monastic out of his meditative cave."[2] The terms crusader and monastic were very familiar to me. I had identified with those two characters for decades.

At the conclusion of the workshop, I had narrowed down my likely career choices to visual anthropology and journalism. Before leaving, I arranged to meet with Dan in Washington, DC, for a follow-up, one-on-one session. During our consultation in the city, I made the decision to pursue a graduate journalism degree.

Soon after I returned to the nation's capital, I signed-up to participate in an upcoming nonviolent civil disobedience action billed as "Blockade the Pentagon." I notified my workplace that I expected an arrest and spoke with legal advisors about the possible ramifications of such an action. They informed me that a very steep fine and lengthy jail time were possibilities. Along with tens of thousands of other activists around the country, I had signed a Pledge of Resistance, a commitment to join with others in ongoing nonviolent opposition to the US war in Central America. "Blockade the Pentagon" focused specifically on El Salvador's civil war and the Defense Departments continued military support for that country's brutal shadow government. Our detailed plan of action included blocking entrance roads and doorways into the Pentagon to raise public awareness.

Before dawn, in mid-October, dozens of our affinity groups began to arrive by Metro and gather on the Pentagon grounds. Following a brief spiritual service and last minute instructions, we took our designated positions. Sitting in the middle of an entrance road, I locked arms with a dozen other demonstrators as Pentagon employees began to arrive at their workplace. I recall the silver grill on the first car that drove up to our line of resistance with its glaring bright lights. I can still hear it screech to a stop just a few feet in front of us. The car's inside light illuminated the two military officers sitting in the front seat with their windows rolled down.

"Run 'em over!" screamed the officer on the passenger's side. He did not mask his rage. "Run 'em over, Goddamnit! Run 'em over!" I just knew they were going to do it. Lawyers for the defense would call it a crime of passion. I had an urge to get up and walk away. Just as the driver began to inch toward us, Laura, our affinity leader, leaped out from nowhere and landed, spread-eagled, on the hood of their car. The fearless activist, a slight woman in her mid-twenties, scared the bejesus out of those officers. Straightaway, the driver threw the car into reverse and hastily backed down the entrance road.

"At least 1,000 rowdy but mostly peaceful protesters of US involvement in El Salvador blockaded the south entrances to the Pentagon early yesterday, sitting in front of moving cars and buses and creating a sea of bodies at the building's doorsteps . . ." reported *The Washington Post*. "At least 215 demonstrators were arrested, most of them charged with obstructing a passageway, a misdemeanor that carries a maximum penalty of a $1,000 fine and one year in jail . . . Pentagon employees arriving for work found themselves engulfed in swaying human waves. Some workers broke through with the help of helmeted police while others retreated to the unblocked entrances. By sunrise the protesters had managed to close the 3,700-space south parking lot, causing major commuting delays in all the roads around the complex and halting bus service to the Pentagon."[3]

What I had learned in the career workshop, observed in my workplace, and experienced at the Pentagon prompted my return to Latin America. Prior to my July 1989 departure, however, I submitted graduate journalism school applications.

Initially, I flew into Bolivia to participate in an intense, four month, Latin American orientation program sponsored by the Maryknoll Language Institute. Later, I would return to Central America. An activist Roman Catholic order, the Maryknoll were intrepid advocates of Liberation Theology, a revolutionary theology opposed by the Catholic hierarchy and the military. I had met members of their order, four years earlier, as a Witness for Peace delegate in Nicaragua.

Most students were Catholic lay volunteers. My situation, however, was unique. I no longer identified as either Catholic or Protestant but I understood the importance of a spiritual practice in my life.

"To this day, I am drawn joyfully to cathedrals in every land – mosques and temples, too," wrote Peter Matthiessen in *The Circle of Life*, "the stone, the light, the soaring naves, the murmuring and mystery and quiet. With gratitude, I kneel and lose myself amidst the bent humanity crouched in the pews. In the great hush, we breathe as one. Before the altar, I cross myself, not as a dutiful Christian or Catholic – I am neither – but because I am *healed* by the anonymity of the gesture."

Endnotes

Preface

1. Bill Peterson, "Welfare Office Occupied: 22 Arrested" (*Louisville Courier Journal*, August 11, 1970), p. 5.

2. Howard Zinn, *Declaration of Independence: Cross Examining American Ideology* (Perennial, 1991), P. 123.

Part One

Have, Have Nots, Have a Little

1. Saul Alinsky, *Rules for Radicals* (Random House, 1971), book cover.

2. "Playboy Interview: Saul Alinsky (*Playboy* magazine, March 1972).

3. Lawrence Bailis, *Bread or Justice: Grassroots Organizing in the Welfare Rights Movement* (Lexington Books, 1974), p. 11.

4. Gloria Steinem, *My Life on the Road* (Random House, 2016), pp. 64-65.

5. Richard A. Cloward and Francis Fox Piven, "The Weight of the Poor," (*The Nation*, May 2, 1966), p. 51.

6. David Zeiger, *Sir! No Sir* (Docurama 2005).

7. Ibid.

8. Richard A. Cloward and Francis Fox Piven, "Rent Strike: Disrupting the Slum System," (*The New Republic*, December 2, 1967), p. 13.

9. David H. Lawrence, *Women in Love* (Dover Edition, 2002), pp. 111-1V.

Walking Backward

1. Thomas Merton, *The Asian Journal* (New Directions, 1973), p. 305.

2. Ibid., Appendix vii.

3. Henri J. M. Nouwen, *A Genesee Diary* (Image, 1981), p. 161.

Dear John Letter

1. Leo Rosten, *Joys of Yiddish* (Pocket Books, 1970), pp. 273-74.

2. Dr. Henry Rosenfeld, Yehuda Hanegbi, and Marc Segal, *The Kibbutz* (Sadan Publishing, 1973), p. 3.

3. Leo Rosten, *Joys of Yiddish* (Pocket Books, 1970), p. 474.

4. Dan Leon, *The Kibbutz: Portrait from Within* (Israel Horizons, 1964), p. 9.

5. Dr. Henry Rosenfeld, Yehuda Hanegbi, and Marc Segal, *The Kibbutz* (Sadan Publishing, 1973), p. 1.

6. Leo Rosten, *Joys of Yiddish* (Pocket Books, 1970), pp. 184-185.

7. Ibid., p. 103.

8. Dan Leon, *The Kibbutz: Portrait from Within* (Israel Horizons, 1964), p. 98.

9. Rina Shir, *A Riddle Called Kibbutz* (Kibbutz Aliya Desk), p. 12.

10. *The Israeli Road to Socialism* (Alpha Press, 1972), p. 40.

11. Leo Rosten, *Joys of Yiddish* (Pocket Books, 1970), pp. 355-356.

Hitchhiker's Sinkhole

1. John McPhee, *Coming into the Country* (Farrar, Straus & Giroux, 1976), p. 143.

Wise Men Fish Here

1. Jerzy Grotowski, *Toward a Poor Theatre* (First Vintage, 1968), back cover.

2. Richard Schechner, "A Mentor with Wisdom and a Drive to Learn" (*The New York Times*, January 31, 1999), Section 2:10.

3. Per Ola and Emily d' Aulaire, "Now What Are They Doing at that Crazy St. John the Divine," (*Smithsonian*, December 1992), pp. 34-35.

4. William Shakespeare, *Measure for Measure* (Signet Classic, 1988), pp. 67-68.

5. Michael Herr, *Dispatches* (First Vintage, 1970), p. 14.

Swimming in Sand

1. Jane H. Furse, "A Lost Art on Broadway: Sneaking in for the Second Act" (*The New York Times*, September 25, 2016), p 33.

2. Deborah Jowitt, *Meredith Monk* (Johns Hopkins University Press, 1997), pp. 4,10.

3. Hayden Herrera, *Mary Frank* (Harry N. Abrams, 1990), p. 8.

4. Robert Frank, *The Americans* (Viking Adult, 1974), p. 5.

5. Grace Glueck, "Eleven Ways to Use the Word to See" (*New York Times*, February 25, 1977), Section C, 18.

6. Ibid.

Part Two

Call Me a Madman

1. Antoine Saint-Exupéry, *The Little Prince* (Harcourt Brace and Company, 1943), p. 70.

Bare Ass Naked

1. Tennessee Williams, *Cat on a Hot Tin Roof* (Dramatists Play Service, 1986), p. 6.

2. Jon Krampner, *Female Brando: The Legend of Kim Stanley* (Back Stage Books, 2006), p. 294.

3. Ibid., p. 288.

4. Uta Hagen, *Respect for Acting* (Wiley, 1971), p. 70.

5. Don Nelsen, "Stretching is a Disservice to 'Knitters'" (*The New York Daily News*, March 26, 1980).

Sleeping with the Dead

1. Thomas Merton, *Disputed Questions* (Harvest Books, 1985), pp. 218-219.

Rural Free Delivery

1. Adler, Stella, *The Art of Acting* (Applause Books, 2000), p. 86

2. Book of Isaiah, *Bible* (English Standard Version), 2:4.

3. Karen Malpede, "Remembering Judith Malina" (*American Theatre Magazine*, July/August 2015), p. 18.

Desert Spirit

1. Walter Claassen, *Life and Times of a Kansas Banker* (Claassen Publishing, 2002), p. 1.

2. Tom Spanbauer, *Faraway Places* (Harper Perennial, 1988), pp. 12-13.

Red Star Recruit

1. Greg Nagle, "Hoedads" (*The Next Whole Earth Catalog*, September, 1980).

2. Bob Rogers, "Cheap Thrills" (*Wyoming Outdoor Reporter*, June 20, 1980) p. 2.

3. Greg Nagle, "Hoedads" (*The Next Whole Earth Catalog*, September 1980).

4. Nina Shengold, *Clearcut* (Anchor Books, 2005), p. 62.

5. Greg Nagle, "Hoedads" (*The Next Whole Earth Catalog*, September 1980).

6. Gracie Lyons, *Constructive Criticism: A Handbook* (Inkworks Press, 1976), p. 15.

Elephants, Giraffes, Hyenas, Oh My

1. George Russell and Marsha Clark, "Kenya: Flaws in the Showcase" (*Time Magazine*, August 16, 1982), p. 39.

2. James Verini, "Trial and Error" (*The New York Times Magazine*, June 26, 2016), pp. 47-48.

3. Kamante Gatura and Peter Beard, *Longing for Darkness: Kamante's Tales of Out of Africa* (Harcourt Brace Jovanovich, 1975), pp. 4-5.

4. "Animal Appeal–Giraffe's take center stage" (*The San Francisco Chronicle*, May 27, 2004), p. 10.

5. Jon Bowmaster, *The Adventures and Misadventures of Peter Beard in Africa* (Bullfinch, 1993), p. 9.

6. Richard Critchfiled, "Women are Leading Africa in the 20th Century" (*The Record*, April 27, 1982), p. 13.

Part Three

Don't Think, Do It

1. Ruth Zaporah, *Action Theater: Improvisation of Presence* (North Atlantic Books, 1995), p. XV.

2. Ibid., *Improvisation on the Edge* (North Atlantic Books, 2014), p. 3.

3. Cheryl Pallant, *An Introduction to a Vitalizing Dance Form* (McFarland and Company, 2006), pp. 9-10.

4. Cynthia J. Novak, *Sharing the Dance: Contact Improvisation and American Culture* (University of Wisconsin Press, 1990), pp. 8,9.

5. Melinda Buckwalter, *An Improviser's Companion: composing while dancing* (University of Wisconsin Press, 2010), p. 169.

Blue Plate Special

1. Jeff Landers, "Oswegan Works for Peace in Central America" (*Lake Oswego Review*, July 5, 1985), p. A6.

2. Tom Treick, "Singing the Praises of Sanctuary" (*The Oregonian*, March 28, 1985), p. 18.

3. Walter LaFeber, *Inevitable Revolutions: The United States in Central America* (W.W. Norton & Company), 1983, p. 11.

4. Elisabeth Malkin, "Science Fuels Writing, and Faith, of a Nicaraguan Poet" (*The New York Times*, January 3, 2015), p. A8.

5. Oregon Witness for Peace Delegation, *For the Future of Our Children*, (Clergy and Laity Concerned, 1985), p. 2.

Weighty Friends, Silent Meetings

1. Carol Troyen and Erica E. Hirshler, *Charles Sheeler: Paintings and Drawings* (Little, Brown and Company), 1987, p. 25.

2. Howard H. Brinton, *Pendle Hill: A Chronological Survey*, Pendle

Hill Bulletin, (Pendle Hill, October 1964), p. 1.

3. Ibid., p. 3.

4. Ibid., p. 4.

5. Carlene Meeker, "Mary Frank," *Jewish Women: A Comprehensive Historical Encyclopedia* (Jewish Publishing Society, 2007), p. 1.

6. Amy Linn, "400 Stage Rally Against Aid to Contras" (*The Philadelphia Inquirer*, March 16, 1986), p. 22.

7. Charles A. Fracchia, *Living Together Alone* (Harper & Row, 1979), p. 63.

8. Ibid., p. 65.

9. Ibid., p. 63.

10. Ren Sanchez and Linde Wheeler, "Gays Demand Rights in 6-Hour March" (*The Washington Post*, April 26, 1993), p. A1.

Three Sisters' Hotel

1. Francis Goldman, "Guatemalan Death Masque: Pomp and Terror in a Dark Country" (*Harper's Magazine*, January 1986), p. 56.

2. Frank, Louis, and Wheaton, Philip, *Indian Guatemala: Path to Liberation*, (Epica Task Force, 1984), p. 4.

3. "The Indians of Guatemala," (*Cultural Survival*, Fall 1987), p. 24.

4. Victor Perera, "Can Guatemala Change" (*The New York Review of Books*, August 14, 1986), p. 41.

5. "Interview with Indian Leader Rigoberta Menchu" (Guatemalan News and Information Bureau, University of Texas, 1986), Volume 7-3, p. 8.

6. Victor Perera, *Unfinished Conquest: The Guatemala Tragedy* (University of California Press, 1995), p. 77.

7. Mikkel Jordahl, *Counterinsurgency and Development in the Altiplano* (Guatemalan Human Rights Commission, February 1, 1987), pp. 13, 14, 15.

Sitting on the Fault Line

1. *El Salvador: A Look at the Reality* (Quixote Center, August 1985), p. 6.

2. Archbishop Adolfo Romero and Michael J. Walsh, *Voice of the Voiceless* (Orbis Books, 1985), p. 18.

3. Joan Didion, *Salvador* (Vintage Books, 1983), p. 79.

4. Walter LaFeber, *Inevitable Revolutions: The United States in Central America* (W. W. Norton, 1983), p. 10.

Meyers, Briggs, and Carl Jung

1. Isabel Briggs Myers, *Introduction to Type* (Consulting Psychological Press, 1987), p. 8.

2. David Keirsy and Marilyn Bates, *Please Understand Me: Character & Temperament* (Prometheus Nemesis Book Company, 1984), pp. 73-74.

3. Dana Pries and Steve Bales, "Protest at Pentagon" (*The Washington Post*, October 18, 1988), p. B1.

About the Author

William Claassen is a longtime social activist, writer, traveler, photographer, and teacher. His broad range of interests, from politics and cultural diversity to comparative religions and the arts, has taken him to more than forty countries on five continents. The author's previous books include *Alone in Community: Journeys into Monastic Life around the World*, *Another World: A Retreat in the Ozarks*, and *Journey Man: A World Calling*. Claassen's three-character, one-act play, is titled *Quiet Gardens*. He lives in Columbia, Missouri.